Interrogating Imperialism

Interrogating Imperialism
Conversations on Gender, Race, and War

Edited by
Robin L. Riley and Naeem Inayatullah

INTERROGATING IMPERIALISM CONVERSATIONS ON GENDER, RACE, AND WAR
Copyright © Robin L. Riley and Naeem Inayatullah, 2006.

First published in 2006 by
PALGRAVE MACMILLAN™
175 Fifth Avenue, New York, N.Y. 10010 and
Houndmills, Basingstoke, Hampshire, England RG21 6XS.
Companies and representatives throughout the world.

PALGRAVE MACMILLAN is the global academic imprint of the Palgrave Macmillan division of St. Martin's Press, LLC and of Palgrave Macmillan Ltd. Macmillan® is a registered trademark in the United States, United Kingdom and other countries. Palgrave is a registered trademark in the European Union and other countries.

ISBN-10: 1-4039-7462-4   hardcover
ISBN-13: 978-1-4039-7462-4 hardcover

Library of Congress Cataloging-in-Publication Data

Robin L. Riley and Naeem Inayatullah.
Interrogating imperialism: edited by conversations on gender, race, and war/Robin L. Riley and Naeem Inayatullah.
     p. cm.
   Includes bibliographical references and index.
   Contents: Solidarity across movements: women at war–Shame and rage: international relations and the world school of colonialism–Patriotism in the U.S. Peace Movement: the limits of nationalist resistance to global imperialism–Deja'Vu: the fantasy of benign military rule in Pakistan–Bewildered? women's studies and the war on terror–Trading places: juxtaposing south Africa and the U.S.–Valiant, virtuous or vicious representation, and the problem of women warriors–Not just (any) body can be a patriot: on time of empire both "here" and "there".

     ISBN 1-4039-7462-4

1. United States–Foreign relations. 2. United States–Politics and government.
3. Feminism–Political aspects. I. Riley, Robin L., 1952-II. Inayatullah, Naeem.

   JZ1480.I59 2006
   327.730082–dc22   2006047627

A catalogue record for this book is available from the British Library.

Design by Macmillan India Ltd.

First edition: 2006

10 9 8 7 6 5 4 3 2 1

Printed in the United States of America.

Contents

Acknowledgments

We would like to thank Minnie Bruce Pratt for work that inspires us and for early encouragement on this project. Thanks also to Cynthia Enloe and Zillah Eisenstein for their careful attention to this collection. We are particularly grateful to each of the contributors for producing sparkling narratives, thereby turning editing into a labor of love, and for cultivating a sweet solidarity.

Naeem thanks Robin L. Riley for acting as a continuous motivating force for this project; his colleagues in the Department of Politics at Ithaca College for providing such a hospitable home; and Sorayya and the boys for their profound joyfulness.

Robin thanks Naeem Inayatullah, who listened to early unformed ideas about a book and helped make something happen; the participants on the Gender and War panels sponsored by the Women's Studies Program at Syracuse University who inspired this idea; and Hannah Britton for enduring friendship. Finally, words fail to sufficiently express my gratitude to Margaret Himley, who makes everything possible.

This book is dedicated to Kamal Naeem and Shahid Naeem.

Foreword

Cynthia Enloe

Most readers will read this book's engaging essays at a time when both the U.S. invasions and subsequent occupations of Afghanistan and Iraq have faded from the daily news. Print, radio, and television companies are in the bad habit of reducing their journalist crews—or pulling them out altogether—as soon as the "story" loses its simple plot. This encourages all of us—their audiences—to have short attention spans.

That, in turn, has the result of politically deskilling us: we find ourselves confused or impatient when new political parties start forming and vying with each other in Afghanistan or Iraq; we can't remember the difference between Sunni and Shiite Muslims or why it matters; we don't learn how to trace the important relationships between the U.S. government's agencies and its key private contractors; we don't know how to make sense of water politics or oil politics; we pay attention to Afghan or Iraqi women only when we glance at a short caption under a photograph of veiled—or unveiled—women; we don't hone the skills needed to follow foreign influence unless we see an American president or one of his cabinet secretaries landing on the overseas tarmac and donning a flack jacket.

Such deskilling is making us politically naïve. This then makes us unreliable either as citizens of the United States or as citizens of the world. We might be tempted to camouflage our lack of long-term attention and analytical subtlety with offhand cynical remarks ("Oh, it's all about oil;" or "They're just a bunch of warlords anyway"). But cynicism is no substitute for persistent curiosity and nuanced understanding.

Thankfully, the authors brought together here by Robin L. Riley and Naeem Inayatullah try to roll back our deskilled political naïvete. First, their essays are written from the vantage points of both the United States and other countries—Trinidad, Pakistan, South Africa, and so on. Most people in the world today routinely read works by commentators situated outside their own countries. Talk to someone from Singapore or Italy or Canada. Ask them whom they read or watch or listen to. Most of them think it would be foolhardy to pay attention only to observers from within their own societies. One of the major risks of living in the United States today is that it is too easy to surf the channels and imagine that one has a vast variety of news sources to choose from, whereas in reality most of those sources are either U.S. owned or, as in the case of those owned by Rupert Murdoch, are designed to appeal to a specifically U.S. audience, treating as "news" only what seems directly relevant to Americans with short attention spans.

Secondly, Riley and Inayatullah have invited to join them here a group of writers and thinkers who are historically conscious, who don't think American imperialism reached liftoff only in response to the attacks on the World Trade Center in September, 2001. Take a quick poll among your friends and classmates: How many of them (and you) spent serious time in their high school history classes digging into the commonly held American racial and economic presumptions that undergirded U.S. colonization of Hawaii? Of Puerto Rico? Of the Philippines? Recently, I watched a PBS television documentary called "The Massie Affair." The filmmakers used archival footage, trial transcripts, contemporary press coverage, and present-day interviews to tell of a sexual scandal in Hawai'i in the early 1900s—a scandal that turned out to be far less about sex and much more about racism, navy marriages, miscarriages of justice, and the ways in which local Honolulu white residents and their official supporters in Washington were governing their Hawaiian colony. This was all news to me. And while I too had had no books or class discussions on American occupation and rule of any of its colonies when I was in high school (or, unfortunately, in college either), in the past decades I had been trying to fill this gaping chasm in my understanding of America in the world, encouraged by my friends from Malaysia, the Philippines, Canada, and Mexico. Still, "The Massie Affair," which had caused a nationwide controversy a century ago, was today news to me. Thus it is never too late to acquire a historical consciousness of how and why and when Americans have launched invasions into, and occupations of, other people's countries. Reading—and now rereading—this book's historically minded authors is a good place to start. Perhaps one could now begin a list, a candid list: write down everything about U.S. past actions in the rest of the world that comes as news to you as you read these chapters. Then—and this is a political action—write next to each item on your list *why* you think you were never told about this before.

Third, these authors teach us how to become smarter about unequal global dynamics by taking *women* seriously. The authors you are about to read here do take women seriously. They have learned that if we ignore the ideas and the experiences of women, and if we overlook or treat casually how women are imagined by policy elites, media editors, and ordinary citizens, we are likely to fail to adequately and reliably make sense of how the British, French, Spanish, Russians, and Americans went about creating their international imperialist projects. We are thus also likely to remain naïve about how the current American government and its citizens are justifying their occupations of Iraq and Afghanistan. "Women" is not synonymous with "gender." Yet both terms are important for making realistic sense of how imperialism works—how it is justified, how it is imposed on others, how it is made to seem "normal" to those in the invading or controlling country, and how it has been and is being criticized and resisted. "Women" refers to those people who are of the female sex; women are amazingly diverse in their economic resources, their historical experiences, how racialized notions are used by others to relate to them, their sexual identities, and how they are located in this world. Yet most women—in all their diversity—share the experience of being treated as if they have little to teach us about how imperialism works. If women are mentioned, it is chiefly as mere symbols of the nation, as someone else's justification for "civilizing missions," or as targets of sexual violence by men of the other, allegedly less honorable, nation/society/community/state. Of course, if you are reduced to a symbol, a justification, or a target, no one bothers to take seriously your own explanations, aspirations, and strategies.

Gender, by contrast, refers to the ideas of "femininity" and "masculinity." As such, gender is a tool for making sense of how and why so many men find it reasonable and even necessary to try to turn women into symbols, justifications, and targets. The manipulations of—and confusions over and challenges to—conventional ideas about women's "naturally feminine roles," "modern femininity," and "respectable femininity" are woven tightly into invading militaries' recruitment efforts and foreign-designed modernization enterprises.

Finally, all of the authors who speak to us in these pages urge us to see politics more broadly. They are both stretching us to think in fresh ways and stretching the very idea of what "politics" is. They are showing us how understanding the causes and consequences of politics cannot be understood just by looking at people in official government positions, or just at those people's official policies. Instead, imperialist tendencies and actions in any society can be made sense of—that is, analyzed or explained—if we draw on a whole range of thinking tools, from psychology, film studies, history, anthropology, economics, even art history. So if as you read the chapters here you sometimes wonder, "Is this really the study of foreign policy?" this is a good question to pose. But now try to answer it. Here is a question I often find useful when I'm being asked to stretch my analytical muscles in new and uncomfortable ways: "What would I miss if I didn't use this new way of seeing?"

Imperialism is sometimes blatant—statues of Queen Victoria in the public gardens of Guyana and India; heavily armed American soldiers breaking down the doors of Iraqis' homes at 2 a.m. But, more often, imperialism is subtle: Who gets to assign the meanings to an Afghan woman casting a ballot? Who has sold off once-public Iraqi industries and to whom? How do Americans personally justify their own government's overseas actions? This book gives us a set of questions and a box of analytical tools to reskill ourselves so that we can delve into these subtle international dynamics and stay attentive to them long after the television cameras have been packed up and sent home.

Chapter 1

Introduction

Naeem Inayatullah and Robin L. Riley

The end of World War II left a globe in which the European powers were no longer able to defer formal independence to parts of the third world. European domination crumbled just long enough for third-world liberation struggles to forge numerous new states. Today one has to constantly keep in mind that the formal recognition of new states did not produce substantive independence—a condition that requires movement toward economic sovereignty or toward a global political economy that actively counters hundred-year-old but still living structures and systems that limit third-world peoples to the hewing of wood and the drawing of water.

At that time the United States taunted the "European empires"—the Portuguese, Spanish, Dutch, French, and British—as too old-fashioned and out of touch to do business in a world of independent third-world states. Meanwhile, the USSR vaunted itself as a champion, not merely of formal third-world independence, but of the real struggle to achieve substantive economic democracy. These two superpowers trumpeted the cause of liberation even as both hid—especially from themselves and their inhabitants—their own track record of empire building. Nor did their purported support for former colonies' independence stop them from using the new states as grounds within which to stage their proxy wars—cold wars that resulted in devastating "hot" effects for those objectified as mere props for a Western play. As the African proverb says, "The grass is trampled when elephants fight."

The end of the Cold War has been hailed, celebrated, and fully adorned with an abundance of self-nominated and self-decorating candidates who insist on proclaiming their decisive role in the demise of the Soviet Union. And yet to declare, "The Cold War is dead; long live the Cold War," is not merely to allude to a figure of speech. If on the surface some things change, other things seem to partake in longer cycles and deeper patterns.

Perhaps the concealed story of our two empire-building superpowers now, at last, becomes discernible even to the most enshrouded. Here a kind of achievement belongs to the Soviet Union. When its leaders found themselves confronted by their own hypocrisy, they succumbed, admitting an inability to hold their image as freedom's best hope while waging a brutal war in Afghanistan. Perhaps, the United States's snide mockery of the old empires now comes back to haunt it as it finds that its trust in the invisible-hand operations of neocolonialism requires the more visible footprint of military occupation. Out of the woodwork of irony appear dozens of old military and colonial historians offering their counsel on how to run empire in an unsentimentally old-fashioned way.

Perhaps the joke is on us—we contributors to this volume. Some of us kept faith with the idea that colonialism and empire were things of the past; that the abstract forces of progress combined with the more tangible counterpressure of the world's conscience would disallow what we now see as horribly manifest in Iraq and Afghanistan. We should have known that those who know how to sustain internal colonies—"Indian reservations," black and white "ghettos," and whole islands such as those of Hawaii—are unlikely to have lost their taste for subjugating others elsewhere in the name of, say, democracy, justice, and freedom. Perhaps the post–World War II era was an anomaly, a glitch, an aberration within the larger patterns demonstrating that no power can resist empire building in the name of saving the damned.

But, of course, to use and invert another aphorism, "The more things stay the same, the more they change." If the United States has displayed an old and very predictable imperial arrogance, it has done so in a new context. This arrogance creates a state of affairs where feminist principles are used to justify saving brown women from the patriarchy of brown men; where working-class women's participation in the U.S. military threatens to undermine conceptions of femininity as well as the masculinist military and security order; where U.S. support of military dictators is justified on the grounds that they are useful weapons in a new proxy war to fight Islamist foes, even when that strategy unwittingly supports the very foes the United States seeks to defeat.

It is a state of affairs where the very efforts to export democracy undermine all actual efforts to create democratic process on the ground; where the most progressive academic and political forces within the

United States unsuspectingly support the empire makers either by willfully ignoring, in the name of patriotism, U. S. participation in centuries of imperialism or by missing ample opportunities to create solidarity with third-world liberation movements. It is a state of affairs where scores of third-world scholars with newly minted first-world degrees suspend their outrage for the sake of producing objective science, and where a former apartheid state warns of how U.S. policies are producing a virtual apartheidization of the globe.

This worldwide capitalist, white supremacist, patriarchal form of imperialism requires interrogation because it combines hundreds of years of "more of the same" with new technology, new social hybridizations, and new modes of rationalization. This new oldness points to a new/old complicity as well as new/old[1] anger that the writers in this volume combine, shape, and sharpen with the hope that the reader will move toward a more critical consciousness and thereby a more liberatory practice.

Gender, Race, and the War on Terror

After September 11, 2001, news shows and panels at universities in the United States seeking analysis of that day's events and the subsequent "war on terror" trotted out the usual suspects: white male political scientists talking about U.S. foreign policy, international relations, and "the terrorist threat"; anthropologists discussing cultural differences; and white male experts on Afghanistan, the Middle East, or Islam weighing in with their opinions. Sometimes, on antiwar panels, a westernized Muslim scholar of religion (often male) was asked to comment, or the voice of a third world—often male—brown-skinned Other would provide insight into "his people's way of thinking."

The absence of women speaking in public forums prompted questions about whether their exclusion was based on old ideas about gender and war. Did gender signal something to institutions and individuals about women's roles in times of crisis and war? As citizens of empire, were white women expected to move immediately into cheerleader mode for the duration of the "war on terror," while women of color filled the military's male-depleted ranks?

Were both the Left and the Right inviting individuals to speak on the basis of their perceived subject positions? Were brown-skinned Muslim men in the United States being called upon to explain the actions of other brown-skinned Muslim men? Were men of color being invited to explain the "inscrutable Oriental" once more? And what about the Left? Was the contemporary antiwar movement guilty of the racism and the sexism that had tarnished the antiwar movements of the '60s and '70s? Did men, and then only certain men, have permission to resist the "war on terror" and the new imperialism? In the years since September 11, 2001, the relationship of gender to war and imperialism and expectations about citizens' (both within and outside the United States) reactions to these relationships, events, and processes have continued to be significant, but mostly invisible.

Because war is believed to be a male endeavor, gender, followed by race, ethnicity, and religion, was and is the primary identity category considered by policymakers deciding to wage war *and* by those who seek to support, explain, or critique war making.

Evidence that would suggest that these identity categories are not guarantees of certain support or resistance has not dissuaded U.S. policymakers or the Western media that the rhetoric about race and ideas about gender no longer make sense. Although the empire has a long history of gender and race troubles, the rhetoric of the "new war on terror," along with the complicity of U.S. citizens in the new imperialism, has served, for a time, to obscure the persistence of race and gender differences within the United States. The discourse of "United We Stand" helped obfuscate long-standing issues of racism against, in particular, African Americans. Economic opportunities offered by military service created false ideas of a new equality abroad where men and women of all races fought side by side against the newly created, albeit racially marked, male Arab or South Asian enemy. Belief in the binary nature of anatomical differences and lifelong gender training though do not guarantee acquiescence to war making and empire building, nor do they create enthusiastic participation for these ventures. Race and gender troubles have reemerged from their temporary hiding places, as it has not been possible to erase racial inequality inside the United States by a simple slogan, and because war and military service do not provide a context in which real gender equality can be achieved.

Race and class exacerbate the empire's current gender troubles because in this culture, race, class, and sexuality all influence what it means to be a man or a woman. Focusing on gender and race reveals the ways in which these categories are utilized to foment enthusiasm for war, to construct an enemy, and to exploit ideas about femininity in order to engage both men and women in the "war on terror." However, if one looks carefully at how these categories really work, one can observe the empire's weakness as within these categories are pockets of resistance. During the time that we solicited and received contributions to this volume, the United States moved from military aggression against Afghanistan and Iraq to occupation of these states. Outside the academy, gender and race still seem not to be a part of the national, much less international, conversations about war and the new imperialism. Even inside academic circles, how gender works in order to prepare for and wage war and the racism inherent in constructions of the enemy are peripheralized into subgenres within disciplines—feminist international relations, postcolonial studies, or gender studies. Nevertheless, such race-based and feminist "curiosities," as Cynthia Enloe calls them, reveal the many machinations of the new imperialism and the complexity of racial and gender formations within it.

Given all this we can ask: What about the voices represented in this volume? These are the voices of those who have been taken for granted—the immigrant, the lesbian, the new citizen, the "good" colonial subject. These voices challenge and complicate our explicit and implicit commitments to the new/old empire.

The Chapters

Focusing on women's movements in Vietnam, Iraq, and Afghanistan, Elisabeth Armstrong and Vijay Prashad's chapter illuminates the intricate, complex, and revealing history of efforts to create solidarity between various progressive movements in the United States and women's liberation movements in the third world. While not ignoring the fact that often solidarity *with* someone is also solidarity *against* others, Lisa and Vijay portray their key concept, solidarity, in poetic terms: "Solidarity . . . has a wondrous quality, one that surpasses our parochial interests and worn patterns of kinship, love, and affection." They suggest that the best kind of solidarity is built on the basis of shared needs whose mutual pursuit nevertheless nurtures the particularity of specific peoples. The problem with solidarity is that the balance, self-awareness, and nimbleness it requires are too often cramped by the assumption that one occupies a relatively higher position within a presumed hierarchy. Such vertical gestures of embrace can smother.

Returning to the period of the Vietnam War, Lisa and Vijay show the significant influence of Vietnamese women and their organizations on the peace movement, the civil rights movement, the New Left, and women's liberation movements in the United States. While these U.S. movements drew inspiration from Vietnamese women, the lessons they accrued fell short, Lisa and Vijay argue, because these organizations weren't particularly humble toward the Vietnamese.

A more self-critical approach might have detected how Vietnamese women in particular and other third-world women's movements in general self-consciously saw themselves enmeshed in national liberation movements against imperialism. The third-world feminist view of the time was that imperialism was the major enemy. But this does not mean, say Lisa and Vijay, that "patriarchy and other oppressions were sidelined from the struggle." Rather, imperialism made it impossible to create political rights, and without political rights, third world women could not imagine struggling forward.

The mostly hidden history of third-world women's inspiration and influence on U.S. organizations contains significant lessons. Lisa and Vijay demonstrate how such edification is still available for U.S. feminist antiwar activists today. They retrieve for us the meaning and practice of solidarity, uncover the significance of third-world women's liberation movements, and revalorize aspects of anticolonial resistance—all as a of way giving us tools with which to resist and struggle against the current manifestations of imperialism.

The shortest of the chapters, Himadeep Muppidi's "Shame and Rage: International Relations and the World School of Colonialism," provokes us as editors to provide the reader with a rather ornate contextual frame. Moved by the work of Minnie Bruce Pratt, both of us have been inspired to read, write, and teach within the overlap between the systematic precision of science and the intimate urgency of biography. In Himadeep Muppidi's chapter we hear the ripping (and potentially healing) screams of someone artfully shaping his anger so that his calls might sustain in us responses of lasting insight. He sets the tone of his prose by opening with a poem—words that fearlessly announce, in both form and content, his desire to place his whole being within his scholarly deliberations.

Following the poem we recognize immediately that Himadeep stresses the boundary between "I/we" and "you"—not to separate self and other, but so that he can move back and forth between the West and the Rest, the colonizer and the colonized, the teacher and the taught, the objectifier and the object. His perspectival sliding generates a subtle but deftly sculpted energy whose momentum he funnels back and forth between his feelings of rage and of shame; rage at the "brazen and easy resurgence of a discourse of empire" and shame at his all too complicit participation in various schools of world colonialism.

The chapter's material and institutional focus is King Leopold II's design to create a world school of colonialism—a complex that was to include conference and sports centers, and a museum. Leopold's death cut short his grand realization, leaving only the museum. Himadeep's travels through this museum generate in him a kind of vertigo, the effect of which is to make him stop and wonder whether he was meant less to be a tourist in its halls and more to be a specimen in its displays. He expands this disorientation so that problems about his place in the museum lead him and us into ever more troubling haunts—specters of other schools of colonialism and lingering insinuations about our participation in their design and in their effects. He has in mind, for example, degree-granting institutions of higher education. Having earned a license of his own to preach and teach, Himadeep corners himself with this: "How certain was I that my degree was not from an affiliate of the World School of Colonialism?" He wonders whether it was in such schools and with such degrees that his *anti*colonialism was declawed, tamed, and displayed as *post*colonialism. Is he teacher, tourist, or specimen?

If his essay ends not without a small sense of a desired future, still Himadeep refuses barter in easy currency. Hopes beyond both rage and shame must openly bear, he seems to suggest, the scars of complicity in colonialism's destructive wake.

In February 2003, just before the invasion of Iraq, Shampa Biswas found herself in the streets. She confesses that "the palpable frustration, rage, and energy of those days immediately preceding the war on Iraq . . . took me, like so many others, to the peace rallies, marches, vigils, to find communities of solidarity, to belong on the inside in a country in which I increasingly found myself on the outside." Even though she was grateful "to have their shelter and warmth on some cold, dark nights," Shampa discovered that her hope of creating solidarity with those in the peace movement turned instead into a further alienation: "What I found . . . was that for a 'foreigner' in the United States, most peace communities did not offer the comfort of 'home,' so thoroughly 'Americanized' had that space become." In her chapter, Shampa converts the thwarted hope of finding solidarity into a consideration of how and why the peace movement became complicit in U.S. dreams of empire.

Shampa's appraisal documents the material basis of U.S. power, the emergence of a "common sense" that legitimates empire building—including numerous advocates that highlight the benign purposes of U.S. empire—and the return of international relations theory toward an interventionary neo-idealism. Locating the U.S. peace movement inside this frame, Shampa demonstrates how it emerges within a context of hypernationalism and American exceptionalism. She reveals the inadequacy of the peace movement's response to the current global condition by showing how easily it accepts, and how deeply it subsists within, the terms set by empire promoters.

Shampa anticipates that the marshaling of detailed and rigorous documentation may strike some readers, to use her own words, as "painstaking." Assessing writing's rhythm, however, is never an innocent or casual act. Such an assessment depends on a prior judgment about whether what one is reading is deemed crucial or incidental. If the reader supposes that skewering the peace movement is rather beside the point, since the Right has so dominated politics in recent times, then Shampa's thorough critique may seem tough to internalize. If, on the other hand, one is open to the deeper danger that the Right's free hand at home and abroad pivots on liberal complicity in dreams of empire, then one can savor Shampa's systematicity. Indeed, we extol her willingness to place her professional social science skills at the service of her profound sense of incredulity that empire and colonialism, rather than being defeated and discredited, have returned not only with fuller force but, once again, veiled in responsibility, duty, and pedagogic burden.

In closing, Shampa presents another voice, one that moves beyond critique and toward a reformulation of hopefulness. She sketches what must be done so that the U.S. peace movement can begin to confront its peculiar and decisive role within a global agenda that strives for justice. Shampa's chapter vividly illustrates how the calm tools of science and a visceral commitment to justice can serve to vivify each other.

When in 1979 the United States embarked on a mission that would eventually result in the largest covert operation since the Vietnam War, its primary goal was the slow bleeding and eventual withdrawal of the Soviet military from Afghanistan. To the degree that U.S. policymakers took heed of the Afghan people, they were likely to have calculated that their training of "Jihadists" and their introduction of weapons and money into Afghanistan was all to the good. If this infusion was to have a few negative consequences for Afghans, these would be nothing compared with Afghan agony under Soviet occupation. In a January 1998 interview, Zbigniew Brzezinski, national security advisor under Jimmy Carter, was asked whether, given the near destruction of Afghanistan, he had second thoughts about setting the "Bear Trap"—the U.S. covert actions designed to make sure that Soviets did in fact invade Afghanistan. Brzezinski scoffed at the question. The damage done to an unknown people on the outskirts of civilization seemed to him a small price to pay to defeat the Soviet Empire and end the Cold War. Today, one wonders whether Brzezinski would retain his petulant tone if in his assessment of the costs of "winning" the Cold War he included the U.S. role in the cultivation of worldwide Jihadist organizations, as well as the collateral damage of 9/11—both the results of the recruiting/training of an Islamic army and the massive injections of guns and money into Afghanistan's complex social landscape.

Ayesha Khan worries whether the United States and the current military-led government of Pakistan are not now unwitting partners in a similarly catastrophic myopia. Ayesha's primary concerns are for the Pakistani people. She informs us, "The consequences of over-simplifications, characteristic of analysis of global events since 9/11, are, as usual, devastating for the people of Pakistan and their aspirations for a more prosperous and just society."

Such an assessment might come as a sobering surprise, given our usually unchallenged propensity to assume that the alliance between the United States and General Musharraf is leading to an increased democratization of Pakistan. The reality of this relationship suggests quite the opposite, since "in the face of the government's strategic alliance with the United States and its anti-terror agenda, the very political and social enfranchisement that is promised is in fact the first casualty of the new friendship."

Ayesha exposes four myths commonly held by international observers, influential actors in Pakistan, the domestic and international media, and the many wishful Pakistanis: that the United States is a friend to Pakistan, that the current government is a benign military regime, that General Musharraf will help overturn the internationally held belief that all Muslims are terrorists, and that democratic processes and institutions are gaining ground under the military regime.

At the heart of the matter is the false impression that there is a fight for control over Pakistan between extremist Islam and Musharraf's moderate military regime. Closer to the truth is that "the army and the religious right wing are actually on the same far-right of the spectrum, both ultimately authoritarian." The U.S. patronage of Musharraf works against the needs of the Pakistani people, not least because their mutual security agendas defer, yet again, a necessary national debate on the democratic forms and processes Pakistan requires.

For Ayesha, having witnessed firsthand the misery inflicted upon the women and children of Afghanistan in refugee camps, how Afghans came to be assessed as mere collateral damage in superpower machinations is no abstraction. The restrained punch line of her chapter is that having seen all this before, we seem set to see it again.

In his "Sense Outa Nansense," the poet and singer Linton Kwesi Johnson declares that the "innocent" and the "fool" can pass for twins. What separates the two, however, is "di innocent wi habah dout/ check things out/ an maybe fine out." While Johnson endorses the "innocent's" curiosity, he expresses clipped annoyance toward the fool. Similarly, Monisha Das Gupta compares these two modalities, but articulates the fool as a "complacent." The complacent, she writes, "falter toward an awakening" because they "conflate innocence with complacence." Monisha offers a systematic analysis of how such complacency is structured.

Like many of us, Monisha's reaction to the bewilderment that produced the post-9/11 question, "Why did this happen?" (a liberal variation of the insufferable "Why do they hate us?"), is a mixture of anger and incredulity at the false pretense of those asking the question. Why is it, she asks, that taxi drivers in New York City could correctly predict how they would soon be treated by the city's white population, while even academics on the other side of the divide confessed an inability to locate Afghanistan on a map or to specify any particular characteristic of the Taliban?

For Monisha, the inability of her students to intuit an answer, or of scholars to explicitly provide responses to "Why did this happen?", represents a failure of academia, of the social sciences, and of Women's Studies. Monisha states that in the United States, "Women's Studies continues to be an imperial site implicated in the American State's long history of empire building." She demonstrates that while Women's Studies' strategy of exposing the intersectionality and simultaneity of race, class, and gender has led to great insights, this paradigm has primarily performed its work by abstracting attention away from the capitalist state's imperialist history within a global division of labor. The result is that the domestic "inside" gets separated from the international "outside," creating a blindness to the

many ways those in the "economic North and South" are intercon-
nected via grids of unequal power. This blindness continues to deepen
even though black and third world feminists have long theorized the
intersection of imperialism, race, class, and gender. Monisha indicts
the academic community and most of the U.S. populace, therefore, of
"willful ignorance."

She calls on U.S. scholars to employ a framework that exposes their
daily reliance on the third world as a means not only of knowing the
other but also of coming to know themselves. An agenda of securing
justice depends, for Monisha, on a willingness to shed the illusion of
an inside separated from an outside and an acceptance of how forces
of imperialism, race, class, and gender simultaneously construct both
inside and outside, self and other.

Hannah Britton's chapter relies on a strategy of spatial juxtaposition in which she has us moving back and forth with her from the
United States to South Africa. Her eyes, ears, and words serve as windows that allow us to witness, for example, the streets of Soweto, township meetings, riots perpetrated by South African police, and the living
rooms of the various families with whom she lives. There is the
encounter with a white woman in a Laundromat who claims George W.
Bush as "her general," and another one with black students whose
familiarity with U.S. domestic politics produce astute and pointed questions aimed at her. We enter her U.S. classroom on a day when she
presents video clips from South Africa's Truth and Reconciliation
Commission for her students. They are deeply moved by the depiction
of the traumatic engagements between the tortured and the torturers;
some are at a loss as to why retribution is not a major part of the
Commission's mandate. Returning to their dorm rooms that same
evening her students are faced with CBS's *60 Minutes II*'s revelations
about their own nation's torturers and the tortured in Iraq.

Often told in the first person, Hannah's narrative nevertheless flat-
tens the urgency of her own voice. Her tone bespeaks sensitivity to the
problematic political role of U.S. academics reporting on third-world
others as well as to the complex problems posed by a desire to convey
the voices of everyday South Africans. If these difficulties temper her
delivery, they do not altogether outweigh her responsibility to report on
her travels. Hannah warns of the potential crisis the world faces as the
United States comes to assume the posture that South Africa once occupied under apartheid, namely, the status of pariah state. Rather than
demonstrating principles of democratic process that others might emu-
late, the United States is instead internationalizing an apartheidization

of the world by pressuring African states to prioritize concerns of security over those of social and economic justice.

Hannah presents her journey as a movement from her own relative naiveté to greater awareness. With this quasi-confessional tone Hannah not only hints at the perspectival origins of all knowledge, she also formulates how to generate a politicized empathy with others. Refusing to minimize the structural problems faced by South Africans, now or in the past, Hannah conveys how South Africans struggle to overcome the deep legacy of apartheid. In this struggle, she claims, is a lesson available for the United States and for anyone willing to learn.

Assessing the experiences of Jessica Lynch, Shoshana Johnson, and Lori Piestewa in the war on Iraq, Robin L. Riley compares the media coverage dedicated to these three women: massive for Jessica; scant for Shoshana who was shot and captured; and scarce for Lori, who was the first U.S. woman killed in this war. Robin's analysis of the media coverage shows how Jessica's white body is deemed more valuable than that of the other two women, how the suffering of women of color is deemed less newsworthy because they are thought to be stronger than white women, and how Jessica serves to expose barely subconscious fears in white society when white women are thought to fall prey to black or brown foreign men.

The disparity in attention toward Jessica is not determined by racism alone. Part of the explanation concerns the military's dire need to fulfill its recruitment needs. Further, Robin reminds us that wars are often fought on the pretext of protecting women; she shows how the "ideology of 'national security' relies on a narrative of femininity" in which women are limited to playing the role of a helpless object of protection. However, the complex stories of Jessica, Shoshana, and Lori cannot begin to be contained by even the broadest understanding of "helpless object of protection." Their experience forces us to question the received narrative of femininity and thereby moves toward undermining both the gender and military order.

In "Not Just (Any) *body* Can Be a Patriot," Jacqui Alexander demonstrates that while the ideology of contemporary empire relies upon a clearly indicated inside that needs to be protected from a sharply marked and dangerous outside, this same ideology directs our attention to the simultaneity and overlap between inside and outside. Her claim that "empire building *is* nation(al) security" indicates the totalizing reach within which "internal and external correlates . . . racialize and sexualize both the internal patriot and the external enemy while at the same time linking the war at home with the war abroad."

Similarly and crucially, capitalism and democracy trumpet the complete transition from the ascribed status of the traditional life to modern life; that is, from a condition where life opportunities follow from natal status to one in which status results from individual action. Despite such triumphal pronouncements, imperial capitalism and democracy retain the tradition in which the assessment of threat follows not from action but from status; risk follows from the presumed nature of actors, not from their performance. Some people—heterosexual white males operating on behalf of the policing state—are given permission to act upon others whose actions may be preemptively read from their status as dark, immigrant, or queer. Thus, "in this move from 'act' to 'risk,' the distinction between terrorist and nonterrorist turns and the demarcation between citizen and immigrant is made, a gross alignment between immigrant and terrorist drawn." Specifically, as she notes:

> The judgment of a reasonable heterosexual unit Commander can identify the propensity of the lesbian soldier; legalized citizen patriots, "Americans," the Attorney General and the President can make judgments about immigrant propensity for terrorism; reasonable tax-paying, consuming citizens can make judgments about the propensity for laziness of recipients of public assistance. The point here is that propensities work to marginalize, that is, they exact different forms of terror and violence on the bodies of different groups of people.

So permissive has the writ of the state become, and so pervasive and ever present its tools for surveillance and violence, that it raises a set of prior questions for everyone, even perhaps for those trying to create transformative politics: How can we become aware of the work we are unwittingly doing on behalf of the state? How can we divest ourselves of such labor? By exposing the kind and quantity of work the U.S. state perpetrates domestically and globally in order to secure its version of the political economy, Jacqui's chapter takes the first step toward arresting the state's use of our actions. It performs this necessary critical task while also suggesting how we can simultaneously build "strategic solidarities."

Note

1. The language of "old/new" is borrowed from Zillah Eisenstein's "epilogue" in this volume.

method makes sense to puncture the arrogance of masculine protectionism? In this essay, we follow two divergent, but related, tracks. First, we provide a historically informed analysis of the political alliances forged between women in times of war. Our example here is from the U.S. war on Vietnam, when women created international and transnational linkages to protest imperialism and patriarchy. Our analysis of the underlying ideological assumptions in these linkages assumes that most readers will be familiar with the women and their organizations that emanate from within the United States. Lineages of first-wave and the emerging second-wave movements of women are usually known through the central framework of "feminism" or the idea that women have individual rights. However, numerous historians of the U.S. women's movement, including Dorothy Sue Cobble (2004), Kimberly Springer (2005), and Kate Weigand (2000), amply demonstrate that traces of other individualisms as well as other principles of women's activism cannot be ignored simply because they did not prevail. Since this individual rights notion of feminism enjoys a global hegemony, it is imperative that we offer an analysis of the idea of "women's rights" that operated in the world of national liberation movements — the other half of the international and transnational linkages of the 1960s. For this reason, our second track offers a history of the emergence of "women's rights" within the ambit of the anti-imperialist nationalist movements of the 1950s, whose formative meeting was held at Bandung in 1955, and whose main meeting for "women's rights" took place in Cairo in 1961. The constitution of the category "Bandung women" allows us to situate an alternative to masculine protectionism.

The appearance of "women's rights" during a time of war is not new. It figured in nascent and hidden ways during the Vietnam War, both as a tenacious deterrent to U.S. aggression and as an unexpected reward for U.S. antiwar activists. Unlike women's rights in Afghanistan and Iraq, the story of women's rights during the Vietnam War is often told as one that heralded a recovered feminist consciousness and new organizational horizons for women's activism in the United States. Scholars such as Sara Evans (1979), Amy Swerdlow (1993), and Nina Adams (1992) give ample credit for the foment of women's liberation in the United States to the influence of Vietnamese National Liberation Front delegates in meetings with U.S. antiwar contingents, particularly when the latter met with the women from the Women's Union of North Vietnam and the Union of

Women for the Liberation of South Vietnam. More recent research has begun to unearth how Vietnamese women's armed struggle for national liberation from French, and later U.S., aggression became enmeshed with their support for women's rights (Ninh 2002; Tai 1992; Taylor 1999; Turner and Hao 1998; and Tetreault 2000).[1] What that research does not do is to center the history of women's liberation in Vietnam in the discourse not so much of individual rights, but of national liberation.

The tradition of national liberation bore within it a lively strain of feminism — one not reducible to individual rights alone—that was the resource for Vietnamese women among the partisans of Vietnamese liberation. Our essay will document this strain as a caution not to suborn any "feminism" into the history of Euro-American feminism or claim that it is derivative. The celebratory narrative of the cross-fertilization of movements and activists in Vietnam contains possibilities for feminist antiwar activists today. But the lopsided misunderstanding of the history of national liberation struggles, and of the place of women's rights in those movements, heralds more sinister developments, such as the cynical use of masculinist protectionism to co-opt feminist support for U.S. military invasions.

To untangle women's rights from war, our discussion abandons the fiction of embodied innocence in the rhetoric of "women and children first" as well as the ahistorical and parochial use of "women's rights." This bundling of biology with enlightenment humanism erases how the rights of women are negotiated and re-etched even as they seem to be won. "Women's rights" in war illuminate with heartbreaking clarity the battles still to be lost and fought again.

Fair Equality

Born on U.S. soil, during the upheavals of the early twentieth century, International Women's Day is now a major event in the former third world. The day marks the valuable risks of international solidarity, a connection veined with utopian dreams and forged between women across national borders and even across nationalisms. Today in a time of triumphant neoliberal transnationalism and supranationalism, this solidarity ventures through the minefield of the undead nation-state. International Women's Day may solicit a weary nostalgia in its country of origin, but elsewhere the day still gives life to other futures and new terms for present certainties.

Despite the U.S. bombardment of her country, Nguyen Thi Binh sent her own International Women's Day greetings to U.S. women on March 8, 1972:

> All of us, women of Viet Nam and America alike, long for a rapid end to the war . . . We all want to establish between us, between our children, between the people of the two countries, new friendly relations based on fair equality . . . We hope that, given our common ardent aspirations for peace, the American women and people will enhance solidarity with the Vietnamese women and people, make strenuous efforts to press the Nixon administration to listen to the voices of reason—the voices of peace. Peace and justice will triumph!
>
> (Bergman 1975, 162)

Binh revives those familiar distinctions between the lands of citizenship and the nation that fails to fully imagine its people. The sinews of humanism create bonds between women, between children, and between people that can loosen the ties of abstract patriotism. The imagined nation can reflect anew its people through international solidarity, and women can make that future history. In Binh's words, the solidarity between the women of Vietnam and the United States can produce international relations that reflect their "fair equality" over dominance and submission. The nation-state is her target, since women's voices organized across continents demand a citizenry willing to express internationalist views for peace and justice in a nationalist frame. But international women's solidarity operating within the confines of the Nixon administration, in this case, also has strategic implications for solidarity between movements and between the activists in those movements. Binh's description of "fair equality" as the measure of connections between women's movements in Vietnam and the United States raises a number of concerns. On the surface the term appears to be tautological: what is equality if not fair, or what is fairness without equality? But perhaps Binh suggests something that is more ambiguous. If "equality" indicates the abstract sameness of individuals in bourgeois law, "fair" is far less specific. Two people can be equal, but must they be equal in the same way? Must they be identical? Can two movements see each other as equal, but respect each other for their separate, although intertwined, traditions?

The history of U.S. feminism has more stakes in individual civil rights, while Vietnamese feminism emerges from national liberation— both these traditions are related to each other even as they are legitimately different. This is not to say that there is a radical difference between the "East" and the "West," between the advanced industrial states of the first world and the political space called the third world. Nor do we intend to advance an argument for cultural relativism, or cultural diversity. What we are arguing is that there are divergent, but related political traditions that motivate the broad expanse of U.S. feminists and of feminists in the context of places such as Vietnam or Iraq. Binh's phrase allows us to imagine solidarity based on equality between and among women—not on the assumption of our own superiority of rights, but on a fair assessment of our mutual interdependence. What follows is a more detailed evaluation, not just of movements' reliance on one another during the Vietnam War, but also of hybridized inspiration, creative mistranslation, and the ghosts left behind that still haunt present solidarities between women from imperial and postcolonial nations. The words of activists in the U.S. antiwar movement, in the student Left, and in the disparate women's liberation movements contain traces rather than proof of the threads that sustained and sometimes frayed the solidarities Binh called upon so confidently in the early months of 1972.

Between 1968 and 1973, Binh held the position of chief negotiator for the Provisional Revolutionary Government of Vietnam at the Paris peace talks. If the U.S. women saw Binh only in Paris, her own people had known of her for decades already, as a leader of the Long Haired Army (the political section of the Vietnamese national liberation movement), and as a well-regarded leader in the women's union movement. But where did Binh come from? The U.S. women's movement had only just begun to broach that question.

1. Women's Liberation in Translation

Solidarity by its very function is freighted with symbolism. People and organizations express their solidarity against a common foe across oceans, cultures, histories, and knowledge. We often know more about our enemies than we do about our friends. Solidarity, given these built-in constraints, has a wondrous quality, one that surpasses our parochial interests and worn patterns of kinship, love, and affection. To give solidarities history, contradictions, and affect may rob them of their more supernatural qualities, but may also allow for more durable bonds between our unknown cohorts in struggle. Women in the Vietnamese national liberation struggle occupy a prominent position on the roll call of influences for the U.S. women's liberation movement. The existence of Vietnamese women in active and leading positions in their national fight for freedom shocked many women in various justice struggles in the United States, and spurred their demands for more movement space.

The Vietnamese example played an important role, but it was not the only one. Women who felt compelled by the Vietnamese example had also been frustrated by the rampant sexism in the New Left, by the increasing exclusion of women in the antiwar movement after 1966, and by the limitations of the issue-based women's organizations such as Women Strike for Peace (WSP) as well as of women's legal rights mobilization groups such as the National Organization for Women (NOW).[2] In addition, movement separatism rose alongside and in contradistinction to solidarity between movements. While separatism forged the possibility of "women's liberation movements" in the United States, separatism also justified the exclusion and marginalization of women in antiwar and nationalist movements, even those they had founded and led.

The very name, "the women's liberation movement," imagined women's politics in the United States through the vocabulary of the revolutionary women's groups in Vietnam (Du Plessis and Snitow 1998, 43). The activist Vivian Rothstein traveled to Vietnam in 1967 to meet with delegates from the National Liberation Front (NLF) and the Women's Union of North Vietnam. In her memoir of the trip, Rothstein describes how the Vietnamese delegates insisted that U.S. women form an integral part of their delegation. "That's how I came to visit Vietnam," she reported many years afterward, "where I was introduced to the Women's Union. This was, then and now, the largest membership organization in Vietnam, running its own women's institutions including schools, clinics, museums and economic enterprises. That's where I first understood the importance of independent women's organizations" (Du Plessis and Snitow 1998, 39).

During a meeting between the NLF and the U.S. New Left in Vladislove, Czechoslovakia, the Vietnamese requested, as they usually did, a meeting between women delegates only. They proposed to discuss the conditions of war, whose social costs, such as rape and prostitution, were borne by women. The NLF cadres suggested a separate meeting to facilitate open communication on political analysis by women on both sides of the war. This request of separate meetings between women, alongside the compulsory space for women to speak first at any political negotiations or gathering, had become part of NLF protocol. Begun as demands from the women's union, these practices were formalized by the NLF in 1966 as part of their commitment to recognize and sustain women's value to revolutionary struggle. In the words of one early document, "To pay utmost attention to raising the political, cultural and vocational standard of women in view of their merits in the struggle against US aggression, for national salvation. To develop the Vietnamese women's tradition of heroism, dauntlessness, fidelity and ability to shoulder responsibilities" (Taylor 1999, 16).

Unlike older peace groups such as WSP, the young women of the student delegation at first refused the Vietnamese women's invitation to meet apart from the larger delegations (Evans 1979, 188). The younger U.S. women took umbrage at the suggestion that women had a special perspective on the war, or had specific interests regarding war. Nevertheless, the U.S. women delegates listened attentively to Vietnamese women's accounts of rape and prostitution caused by the devastation of the war and gendered methods of torture. While the U.S. women may have recognized the special interests of the Vietnamese women, this did not immediately lead to a recognition that they might as well (despite their own legitimate grouse against the sexism of their male comrades). U.S. women's arrogance that their own rights were superior to those of other women from the third world was not necessarily unsettled just by listening to the Vietnamese women delegates' reports.[3] The Vietnamese women's groups did not see their separate meetings as a sign of inferiority, but as the creation of a necessary space to challenge the persistence of sexism within their own struggles as well as to underscore the misogyny of war in very specific terms.

The experiences in Czechoslovakia and Vietnam pushed Rothstein, among others, to imagine meetings between women, and to reconfigure women's equality within political movements. The year after her return from Vietnam, Rothstein helped found the Chicago Women's Liberation Union, a title that echoed as it significantly reinterpreted the Women's Union for the Liberation of South Vietnam. The difference is significant, for whereas in the U.S. group the goal of liberation for women created the union, in Vietnam, the women's union fought in unity with other groups toward the liberation of Vietnam from imperialism. "Women's liberation" gave name to a distinct shift in U.S. women's political organization that did not mirror its ally in Vietnam even while it borrowed some of its ideas. "In order to be politically potent," Rothstein was quoted from an organizational planning meeting in the mid-1960s, "women must have opportunities to develop skills and leadership. This development was unlikely to happen in mixed organizations because of competition from men and the distance women had to first travel in building confidence and abilities" (Du Plessis and Snitow 1998, 43). Rothstein's explanation also echoes an antiracist nationalism closer to home, that of the emerging black nationalist movement led by Stokley Carmichael and others. Notably, she emphasizes women's separatism over movements' solidarity when she imagines groups for women's liberation.

The inspiration of women in Vietnam spanned across women in the peace movement, the civil rights movement, as well as the student Left movement. Pamela Allen emerged from the civil rights movement to become an early organizer for women's liberation in New York and then in the Bay Area in California. Allen also wrote "Small Groups," the first publication about how to run consciousness-raising groups as a means to organize women. In 1968, Allen (1968, 9) provided an example of one of the least reductive commentaries when she described the inspiration of Vietnamese women for all dimensions of the U.S. women's movement:

> The example of the success of the Vietnamese women, who combined the fight for their rights with the fight against imperialism, and the failure of an earlier bourgeois Vietnamese women's movement which refused to deal with the nature of oppression, should show the weakness of a movement which does not deal with the oppressive nature of capitalism . . . Middle class white women must realize that their liberation can only be won in the course of a struggle to liberate all oppressed women.

Both Rothstein and Allen illustrate the powerfully instructive role of Vietnamese women and NLF gender politics. They and other activists learned how women's independent organization from men could strengthen women's political participation. Rothstein and Allen understood how organizational methods and goals for liberation intertwined in a substantive commitment to fight all women's oppression, not just middle-class women's oppression, in the fight for women's rights. Despite their efforts, neither the organizational form of women's separatism within radical movements nor the ideological lesson of women's cross-class fight for liberation had significant bases of support within the political field of U.S. Cold War politics of the early and mid-1960s (Rupp and Taylor 1987).[4] What Allen's article lacks is an explanation of what those broad-based rights were in the context of the movement for Vietnam's national liberation. Importantly, she points to the important class distinctions among that easy conglomeration called "women's rights," but she, like the majority of other commentators from this period, does not substantiate how Vietnamese women framed these rights.

These narratives ask how Vietnamese women or the gender politics of Vietnam's national liberation struggle inspired U.S. women activists as leaders in the larger movement and as leaders of women. Possibly the issues of rape and war-fueled sex work that they raised in Vladislove germinated into some of the first U.S. campaigns against sex and oppression in the late 1960s' women's liberation movement. Like their counterparts in the United States, women in Vietnam also faced sexism within their national liberation movement, a fact they sometimes challenged openly in speeches and documents as well as in meeting protocols. The women's unions fought for national liberation alongside men, but refused to delink this goal from the goal of women's substantive equality. They also sought a women's movement in the United States to build its own goals for international solidarity against occupation and war. Solidarity, then, is not an easy bond made by natural predilections of gendered experience or national pride, but a difficult process that is constantly made and unmade. Yet U.S. activists rarely articulated these more risky ventures of solidarity: specifically how their solidarity with Vietnamese women might allow them to reconceptualize "women's rights," or how to organize their own struggle to gain that fair equality. And in this regard, the example of U.S. activists in this time period shows the limited horizon of inspiration for women in the United States.

2. U.S. Transnational Models of Sisterhood

Writings by activists in the United States illustrate a range of cross-national solidarities forged during the Vietnam War. At their most objectified, women in Vietnam were rendered as symbols—of revolutionary resistance, of the third world, and perhaps most commonly, of a separatist force within the larger struggle against U.S. occupation. But alongside this simplification, even erasure, of women as active participants in the Vietnam War, there is another side that bears notice. Activists in the United States who fought both the domestic hierarchies and the imperialist wars crafted an internationalist solidarity that gave life to those in the struggle here and there, inside the United States and inside the lands being bombed by American planes. Written invocations of solidarity reveal potential avenues for solidarity actions, though not necessarily the actions ultimately chosen. These invocations provide a window onto how international solidarities between women create new political landscapes, as well as suggest the possibilities left unexplored.

When the Students for a Democratic Society (SDS) held its 1967 convention, activists drew upon one image of the Vietnamese woman in their debates over the role of women in their own organization. The Vietnamese woman that they invoked was an archetype of the revolutionary woman, though one that they wrenched from the context of the Vietnam War and the struggle around it. There was little discussion of Vietnamese women and their demands, or even of the connections between women across the waters. Rather, the organizational form of the Vietnamese women became the focus of attention, as the activists felt that they could import it to their own ends. The women's liberation caucus of SDS drafted an analysis that would not be accepted by the general body, but which offers an example of the way in which SDS activists thought of the Vietnamese women:

> As we analyze the position of women in capitalist society and especially in the United States we find that women are in a colonial relationship to men and we recognize ourselves as part of the Third World . . . Women, because of their colonial relationship to men, have to fight for their own independence. This fight for our own independence will lead to the growth and development of the revolutionary movement in this country. Only the independent woman can be truly effective in the larger revolutionary struggle.[5]

The reduction of Vietnamese women to "women," and their struggles against an imperialist war to "oppression" gravely damaged the capacity of U.S. women activists to have genuine solidarity for the Vietnamese fighters. To see oneself in another without a scrupulous account of how the one is so unlike the other, especially in this case, obliterates the differences between the two situations. First, the correspondence between "women" in Vietnam and the United States occluded the U.S. women's well-documented complicity with imperialist wars: that U.S. women do support such wars is something that needs to be discussed and combated, not overshadowed by the claim to mutual oppression. Second, if U.S. women began to see "men" as the enemy, this was not the case in the Vietnamese struggle, where the analysis of gender struggle came within the national liberation model: no social revolution would be possible, the partisans felt, without a frontal assault on feudal social relations, among which they listed patriarchy.

If the concerns and demands of Vietnamese women did not show up at the convention, their form of autonomous, but related, organization did make its appearance. The SDS's women's caucus explained the political muscle wielded by South and North Vietnamese women as being a function of their women's unions. To gain influence in a like manner, radical U.S. women needed to pay attention to how women organized in Vietnam, not to their aspirations in struggle or to the people and structures against whom they fought. The Vietnamese women, in this incarnation, became a model for U.S. women's politics rather than a "sister" to whom concrete solidarity should be demonstrated in action. Drawing from this limited interaction with the Vietnamese women's movement, women in SDS created a women's caucus that nonetheless became an important incubator for many women's liberation organizations.[6]

If the SDS had a relatively parasitic relationship with the Vietnamese women's struggle, the black women's liberation movement tried to be more organic. In 1966, a year before SDS created its women's caucus, the Student Non-Violent Coordinating Committee (SNCC) formed a black women's liberation committee to promote attention to issues of gender inequity within and beyond the movement.[7] In 1968, the committee expanded its purview in its work and in its name, which became the Black and Third World Women's Liberation Alliance.[8] The inclusion of the term "Third World" in their name was not intended to suggest the formerly colonized spaces around the planet that had begun ten years before to fashion a political unity on the basis of their place outside the bifurcated Cold War (fought between the first and the second worlds). For these activists, the adjective "Third World" allowed them to demonstrate their solidarity with that formation at the same time as they wanted to indicate that they too, as people of color within the first world, had to engage with colonial- and postcolonial-type situations.[9]

The "Third World" of the first world recognized that solidarity meant more than a gesture to people outside oneself. The Alliance's statement, "An Argument for Black Women's Liberation as a Revolutionary Force" illustrates a growing internationalist solidarity with Vietnamese women in the civil rights movement.[10] The Alliance evinced a much deeper solidarity than the SDS women's caucus, but it too did not consider the richness of women's political organization in Vietnam. When the Alliance delved into the concerns of the "Third World" itself, the issues on the table had more to do with their own lives in the United States than with the concerns of the Vietnamese women in the war. Like SDS, the Alliance also learned from the Vietnamese women on the question of autonomy. The Vietnamese women's unions showed the women in SNCC that an organization such as the Alliance was necessary for them to build power within the larger struggle. What the Alliance, like the SDS, did not do was to articulate their own struggle in relation to the character or quality of women's rights in Vietnam.

Unlike SDS, some among the Alliance did come to terms with the full implications of what it meant to identify with the Vietnamese women's liberation movement. Maryanne Weathers of the Alliance wrote in 1968:

> Women's Liberation should be considered as a strategy for an eventual tie-up with the entire revolutionary movement consisting of women, men and children. We are now speaking of real revolution (armed). If you cannot accept this fact purely and without problems, examine your reactions closely. We are playing to win and so are they. Viet Nam is simply a matter of time and geography.
>
> (Weathers 1968)

In Weathers's analysis, if the Vietnamese women found themselves in an armed struggle against the U.S. government, and if the "Third World" women within the United States found themselves structurally in the same position as the Vietnamese women, then it meant that the "Third World" women within the United States, also had to be prepared to move to the armed struggle. "Women have fought with men and we have died with men in every revolution," Weathers noted, more recently "in Cuba, Algeria, China, and now in Viet Nam." Her specificity about recent national liberation movements and the kind of leadership taken by women in those movements gave a more grounded appreciation for women in Vietnam. Her statement represents the internationalism of women's liberation movements, as it recognizes the fractured interconnections between women's struggles in Vietnam and black women's struggles in the United States. If the logic of the identification extends further without any mediation between the two different movements, the women's liberation movement in the United States would not be distinguishable from Vietnam or women fighting for Vietnamese liberation. Such an analysis, although filled with a very warm solidarity toward the Vietnamese, collapses its solidarity for the Vietnamese into an undifferentiated identification with them.

Weathers writes of the armed struggle that unites them, without any reference to its relationship with the women's unions or with Vietnamese women. Women's liberation, in such a statement, is less a movement or a political horizon for action; it becomes a precondition for revolutionary armed struggle. As a precondition, then, women's liberation recruits and organizes women for revolutionary work, but does not have discrete goals, relative autonomy, or a specific character in its struggle. This is far from the analysis of the Vietnamese women activists, who saw women's unions as playing a very specific role both as an integral part of the (armed) fight to liberate Vietnam and as a force to fight for women's full equality in the very goals and methods of the national liberation struggle.

U.S. women recognized that Vietnamese women had attained positions of power within their movements, and this perplexed them. In Weathers's (1968) words, "If you notice, it is a woman heading the 'Peace Talks' in Paris for the NLF. What is wrong with Black women? We are clearly the most oppressed and degraded minority in the world, let alone the country. Why can't we rightfully claim our place in the world?" Weathers palpably links oppressed black women in the United States to women in national liberation movements around the world, through their comparable oppression, not their comparable prominence in their struggles. Weathers cites a Vietnamese example of women's rights, in this case, to equal leadership positions, to advance the political organization of women in revolutionary movements. The role of the woman in Paris, Nguyen Thi Binh, acted as a spur for the Alliance: her place at the table pushed black women in the United States to demand more leadership roles for themselves in a movement that they had shaped and built.

Binh figured in several of the speeches, letters, and articles by the U.S. women active in the movement. Each of them wondered how a sister from the darker nations had made it to the green table. But when they did write about her, they rendered her into an icon, a figure of a woman in power, and they did not pay attention to what she was saying or how she came to be in that position.

Why did U.S. women, who organized women's liberation groups in their earliest forms, as well as those in the SDS women's caucus and in the Alliance, fail to carefully analyze the demands and views alongside the strategies of the Vietnamese women's movement? Inescapably, the resources for this depth of understanding were profoundly limited. Personal interactions, such as the meeting in Vladislove, speaking tours and writings by returnees from North and South Vietnam, and those rare Vietnamese documents translated and disseminated among them were their primary sources. Yet rights are the nation-state's unit of justice and could have translated across such different contexts as a colonized state and its current imperial occupier. Women's rights, as they constitute specific visions of equality, could provide a powerful bridge for solidarity, but not necessarily solidarity through similarity. Another explanation for this gap could be unspoken assumptions that U.S. women enjoyed more advanced and more complete rights than their Vietnamese counterparts. Neither iteration of solidarity, nor reification of or identification with Vietnamese women gave weight to the ideology of Vietnamese women or the place of their struggle in the fight for national liberation. Instead, invocations of solidarity by U.S. activists usually abstracted tactical "lessons, " such as how they could gain positions of influence within the wider U.S. movement. Liberation and women's rights, during the early days of the U.S. women's liberation movement, were most commonly rendered antithetical to one another, as revolution over reform.

Lineages

Women make a history that is never just their own. They reinterpret traditions and innovations. They take on the weight of a patriarchal and a liberatory history. The nightmare of the present is not always representative of the past; those hopes and struggles are often smothered by the counterrevolutions of the contemporary period. In this section we will trace the memories of another future and will look at the lineaments of possible futures that were squelched in the past (Sangari 1999).

Afghan and Iraqi women today appear to require the ideological and military assistance of imperial forces. Indeed, it appears that their liberation is premised upon the actions of a humanitarian imperialism (or masculine protectionism). This means that the guns of today appear as the only possible means of strengthening women's ability to seek freedom within what appears to be an intractable patriarchy. History shows us two things. First, imperialism claims to invade countries to liberate women. The best-documented use of this conceit is in the French invasion of Algeria. Second, anticolonial movements of all kinds that do not have a programmatic position on freedom for women frequently take refuge in the cover provided by this imperialist assault. They then say that women's liberation is a "Western" infringement on their culture, and discount the dreams and struggles of the women who stand beside them. When imperialism makes its gesture of support for women, it undermines the separate history of struggle by women, often within anti-imperialist movements, for their own liberation. The Fifth Afghan War (2001 onward) and the U.S. occupation of Iraq (2003 onward) replicate these two moments.

The introduction to this essay already dismissed the conceit of humanitarian imperialism—that bombs drop to liberate women. The previous section assesses the risks of international solidarity between women at war, in their exchange of strategies, forms, and the content of their struggles. This section confronts the next point: is there a history of anti-imperialist women's liberation that is anterior to that of humanitarian imperialism?

1. The Awakening in Iraq

Unlike elsewhere in the Arab world, the demand in Iraq for women's rights initially came from learned Arab men (Qasim Amin, Ma'ruf al-Rusafi, and Jamil Sidqi al-Zahawi) and from reform-minded Ottoman governors (Midhat Pasha). As these men spoke out against veiling and in favor of women's education, many women joined them (such as Na'ima Sultan Hamuda or Umm Salman). Umm Salman's daughter, Sabiha al-Shaykh Da'ud, was not only one of the first women to benefit from public education (she entered school in 1920 and entered the Iraqi school of law in 1936), but she was also a leading member of the women's branches of the Red Crescent Society and the Child Protection (or Welfare) Society, in addition to being a leading light of the Iraqi Women's Union (al-Ittihad al-Nisa'I al'-'Iraqi). She also organized the first women's conference in Baghdad (1932), and represented Iraq in a number of Arab women's conferences held during that period (such as the 1938 conference of all Arab women held in Cairo).[11]

Led by Umm Salman, women fought in the Iraqi Revolt of 1920, some even with arms. The victories won by the popular uprising, including the partial independence in 1932, did not translate into one major demand of the women: the vote. Nevertheless, women's organizations flourished in the 1930s and the 1940s. Early organizations, such as the Women's Temperance and Social Welfare Society and the women's branch of the Red Crescent Society, advocated social reform and charity. As women benefited from educational and social welfare opportunities, and as the communist movement grew within the country, a categorical shift occurred in the world of women's organizations. According to the historian Noga Efrati (2004, 168), the antifascist groups formed in the 1940s, in particular, had "a more political and feminist flavor."[12] The Women's League Against Nazism and Fascism and the Iraqi Women's Union ran campaigns to combat women's illiteracy and to challenge norms defended by the family structure (such as divorce and inheritance). In the 1948 popular uprising against British rule, 'Adawiyya al-Falaki led the march across the al-Ma'mun Bridge despite police gunfire, and her great courage earned her the title "Heroine of the Bridge." Along with this woman, we should recognize that Amina al-Rahhal was a member of the Central Committee of the Iraqi Communist Party (ICP) from 1941 to 1943 (Efrati 2004, 170–171; Batatu 1978, 403). Communist women fought to create a special women's committee in 1946; they also fought on the streets, suffered in jails, and pushed for the reformation of Iraqi social life along more equitable gender lines.

When the Nasserite Free Officers, with the help of the ICP, overthrew the British-placed monarchy in 1958, they felt the full force of popular pressure. The League for the Defense of Women's Rights (al-Rabita), with assistance from the ICP, pushed the government to codify a rational and humane legal framework, notably in what is called "personal status" (ahwal shakhsiyya). The following year, the Free Officers, led by Abdul Karim Qasim, did two monumental things: first, they passed the Iraqi Code of Personal Status, and second, they appointed the ICP's Naziha al-Dulaimi to be the minister of municipalities. It bears mention that the al-Dulaimi tribe of central Iraq had immense social power, and that it therefore came as no surprise for one of their own to be placed in a position of authority (whether Qasim appointed her to this post because she was a communist or an al-Dulaimi need not detain us here). Al-Dulaimi became the first woman to hold such a senior position within the Iraqi government; indeed, she may well be the first Arab woman to hold such a post in the entire Arab world. The Code of Personal Status created a progressive horizon for the continued struggle of Iraqi women for liberation: it laid down a minimum age for marriage (18 years), restricted polygamy and divorce, and offered a substantial reform to the inheritance laws existing since the Ottoman and British period.[13] These actions did not come from the magnanimousness of the Qasim government. Instead, Iraqi women prepared the terrain for the passage of these laws. The changed material conditions of women's lives, as a result of the generation-old fight to win them rights to education, also played an important role. Qasim's regime had little stake in women's emancipation as such, and it is highly conceivable that these reforms were intended to break the hold of Muslim clerics on the social world of the Iraqis.

2. Afghan Women's Liberation from Above

From early gestures in the 1880s to the violent conflicts over social reform in the 1920s to the early 1960s, Afghan women fought to alter the domination of tribal custom over all social relations. Chieftains of various communities rebelled violently against the nominal moves made by the monarchy to reform misogynist customs. Between 1911 and 1918, the reformer Mahmud Beg Tarzi published *Seraj ol-Akhbar-e-Afghaniye* (Torch of Afghan news), in whose pages his wife Asma Rasmiya edited "Celebrating Women of the World." Tarzi and Rasmiya drew from the social reform ideas prevalent in the rest of South Asia, and it was their periodical that introduced ideas of liberty and secularism to Afghanistan (Schinasi 1979, 3). Amanullah succeeded his assassinated father, Habibullah, in 1919 and ruled for a decade. He married Tarzi and Rasmiya's daughter, Queen Sorayya, who, along with Rasmiya, founded *Irshad-i-Niswan* (Guide for women), a women's weekly magazine. Amanullah's sister, Kubrah, led the Anjuman-i-Himayat-i-Niswan (Women's Protective Association) that placed a broad range of issues on the reform agenda (Schinasi 1998). In 1921, Amanullah promulgated a new Family Code that forbade child marriage, freed widows from the tyranny of the in-laws, set control on dowries, and gave wives some power over the rights of their husbands to take additional wives. In 1924, the king gave women the right to choose their husbands, a move that drew the ire of conservative Muslim clerics (Tapper 1984, 291–305).[14] The effects of the changes came first in urban areas, and in the main to families of means. The conservative clergy and the tribal leaders challenged the reforms by refusing to follow them, and by the creation of an alternative political bloc that would be devoted to a misogynistic paternalism (this is the core element that would later form the anti-Soviet jihadis) (Nawid 1999).

Pushed by rifts within the aristocracy and by organized social forces in the country, King Zahir Shah appointed his liberal brother-in-law Mohammed Daoud to the post of prime minister. In 1959, in honor of the fortieth anniversary of the regime, Daoud's government invited wives of his ministers to appear unveiled at a gathering. This inaugurated the end to enforced purdah in urban, aristocratic circles. The regime opened schools and the university to women, and also encouraged government ministries to accept women employees. Zahir Shah showed Daoud the door in 1964 when his courtiers convened an assembly (loya jirga) to write a constitution. This document's Article 64 declared that no law could be passed in the country that was "repugnant to the basic principles of Islam" Zahir Shah turned to the clergy to help define the "basic principles." Yet, even this counter-reform could not hold back the tide. The 1964 Constitution secured the vote for women. A few women won election to parliament, and one of them, Kubrah Nourzai, took office as the Minister of Health. If Zahir Shah and the orthodox clergy had a social problem with women's liberation, procapitalist sections of the ruling class wanted to liberate women into the workforce. For the capitalists, the veiled woman proved an irrational waste of labor.

The year after the Constitution, in 1965, six Afghan women founded the Democratic Organization of Afghan Women (DOAW), alongside the newly created People's Democratic Party of Afghanistan (PDPA). Emboldened intellectuals, unionists, and members of the armed forces created the PDPA as a platform to create a national democratic government on the road to socialism. The short-term agenda of the PDPA included universal primary education, right to employment, rationalization of labor laws, social welfare benefits for the entire population, respect for the national heritages of the various constituencies of Afghanistan, and equal rights for men and women. The DOAW, as a part of the PDPA, emphasized the latter demand, but also fought to eliminate forced marriages, bride-price (dowry), illiteracy among women.[15]

The platform of the DOAW replicated much of the history of reform in Afghanistan, and when the Marxists took power in 1978 through a coup, they attempted a "revolution from above" with their agenda (Halliday and Tanin 1998). Before the completion of ten years of the formation of the PDPA, despite its radical program, four DOAW activists took their seats in parliament. DOAW's struggle won Afghan women the right to study abroad (admittedly a narrow right enjoyed by dominant social classes) and to work outside the home (again a right that was welcomed by dominant economic classes who needed to expand the labor base). There is a temptation among many to dismiss the Afghan experiment that began in 1978 as simply the fantasy of a small Marxist leadership buttressed by the armies of the Soviet Union. Despite the fact that the Marxists had little social base outside Kabul, they did conceptualize and implement a program that had genuine effects in the countryside (Christensen 1990). President Nur Mohammed Taraki passed Decree no. 6 (against land mortgage and indebtedness) and Decree no. 7 (against dowry and for regulation of *mahr,* payment from groom to bride as part of the Islamic marriage ceremony). As Taraki noted on November 4, 1978, through "the issuance of Decree no. 6 and 7, the hard-working peasants were freed from the bonds of oppressors and money-lenders, ending the sale of girls for good as hereafter nobody would be entitled to sell any girl or woman in this country" (Moghadam 1989, 47). "Girls began to be educated in the villages and some co-educational institutions were also established," notes Tariq Ali. "In 1978, male illiteracy was 90 per cent, while female illiteracy stood at 98 per cent. Ten years later it had been substantially reduced" (2002, 206).

Among the DOAW activists was Dr. Anahita Ratebzad, who would become a crucial figure in the PDPA (she joined the Central Committee of the Party in 1976) and in the Marxist government that took power in 1978 (she was minister of social welfare).[16] Ratebzad played a central role in the formulation of the policies to reconstruct patriarchy and to embolden women. On May 28, 1978, she wrote an editorial in *Kabul Times* that defended the program of the new government. "Privileges which women, by right, must have are equal education, job security, health services, and free time to rear a healthy generation for building the future of the country. Educating and enlightening women is now the subject of close government attention" (Dupree 1984, 316).

The aspirations of the Iraqi League for the Defense of Women's Rights and of the Democratic Organization of Afghan Women faced obstacles not only in the conservative social forces within Iraq and Afghanistan, but also in the "assistance" provided to them by U.S. imperialism. The mullahs and generals wanted to annihilate national liberation women's rights, and although they might not have needed encouragement or matériel assistance, they were egged on and armed by the U.S. government and the Pentagon. Whether it was Saddam Hussein or Gulbuddin Hekmatyar in power, the U.S. government bolstered their strategic and military positions in the 1970s as a "factor of stability" against the growth of the Left that included the women's liberation agenda.

Between the 1920s and the 1970s, however, the woman's question in the third world rested squarely on the platform of national liberation (Jayawardena 1986). There is nothing that stops the latter, national liberation, from reproducing a number of patriarchal ideas and privileges. However, most of the anticolonial movements relied upon women, and several of them put women's concerns on their freedom agenda. During the major mass protests in India in 1905, 1909, 1919, 1920–1921, and 1930–1931, women held the streets (Thapar 1994). Iran's constitutional movement saw women in public protest from 1907 to 1911, and again in 1919 (Afary 1996). Much the same has been documented for women in China, Indochina, Indonesia, Ghana, and South Africa.[17] These protests, and their contacts with women from other parts of the world, emboldened the bourgeois women to form organizations and to exert themselves within the framework of national liberation.[18] Many of the pioneers of the organized women's movement came from the old social classes that had either retained their aristocratic positions despite the pressure from imperialism. A few of the leaders came from the new social classes that had been created by imperialism (military and civilian bureaucrats and merchants). From the contradictions of their privileged locations, elite women such as Sabina al-Sheikh Daub and Kiblah Norway not only put the demand for the franchise on the table, they also created organizations whose subsequent history would move far from the salons and into the byways of small villages and towns.

As Sabina al-Sheikh Daub and Kiblah Norway fought to win the franchise for Iraqi and Afghan women within their confines, in distant Latin America three women mirrored their work. Amelia Caballero de Castillo Eldon worked in the Alana de Majors de México, Minerva Bernardino worked in the Action Feminist Dominica, and Bertha Lutz worked for the Brazilian Federation for Feminine Progress. All of them came from the old social classes, and each one of them pushed a fairly conservative agenda for women's emancipation. While they fought to get women the vote, these organizations and leaders settled for fairly patriarchal social definitions of family and marriage. The Alana de Majors de México followed after the 1931 National Women's Congress of Workers and Peasants that had demanded land rights, adult education, and equality for the sexes in unions. Nothing of the sort entered the Alana, nor did it cross the minds of Action Feminist or Feminine Progress (Escandón 1998; and Besse 1996). Nonetheless, it was these three women who insisted that the phrase "the equal rights of men and women" be inserted into the Charter of the United Nations based on the discussions at Conference of Latin American states held in Chapultepec in 1945 and in Lima in 1938 (Miller 1991). Furthermore, these South American delegates pushed the UN to form the Commission on the Status of Women (CSW) as part of the UN's Economic and Social Commission.

In 1947, the CSW adopted its guidelines to "raise the status of women irrespective of nationality, race, language, or religion to equality of men in all fields of human enterprise; and to eliminate all discrimination against women in statutory law, legal maxims or rules, or in interpretations of customary law" (Galey 1979, 276). The guidelines meant nothing because they could not go into force (Galey 1979, 276–279). It was not until 1967 that the UN's Economic and Social Council put forward a Declaration on the Elimination of Discrimination Against Women for a vote to the UN General Assembly. All of this led to 1975 becoming the International Women's Year when Mexico City hosted the first UN conference on women (Fraser 1995). Bourgeois feminism of the Alana and Feminine Progress variety created a set of important international institutions and platforms that would be used later by women's rights activists aware of the deep inequality within the third world. Such activists, who would populate the third-world women's international meetings, did not emphasize gender struggles outside the broader struggle to create sovereign nations.

The agenda developed on the ground in places such as Iraq and Afghanistan would be given an international shape at the 1961 First Afro-Asian Women's Conference, held in Cairo, Egypt. Delegates to this conference crafted a coherent agenda for the struggles of women within the platform of the third world. Few of the movements' delegates who gathered in Cairo in January 1961 saw themselves as Europe's misbegotten sisters, and fewer still felt that they had no title to the concept of the third world. They came to insist that their female forebearers had fought in the national liberation movements and so, earned the right to craft the future. Karima El Said, deputy minister of education in the United Arab Republic, welcomed the delegates from thirty-seven states with this reminder: "The woman was a strong prop in these liberation movements, she struggled with the strugglers and she died with the martyrs."[19]

In the longer general report to the conference, the writers detailed the efforts of women within national liberation movements, from Vietnam to India, from Algeria to South Africa. "In Afro-Asian countries where people are still suffering under the yoke of colonialism, women are actively participating in the struggle for complete national liberation and independence of their countries. They are convinced that this is the first step for their emancipation and will equip them to occupy their real place in society" (*TFAACW*, 1961, 42). That is, participation in the anticolonial struggles would not only attack one of the impediments to the women's liberation agenda, but the contribution itself would transform the relations between men and women in the movement, and in society.[20] Not only did women join the guerrilla wars in Algeria, Cuba, Guinea, Indonesia, Kenya, Korea, Oman, Venezuela, Vietnam, and elsewhere, but they also helped supply the fighters, aided the injured, and in Egypt, India, Zanzibar, and elsewhere, dominated the street protests.

Imperialism made progress for women impossible.[21] Therefore, if women's movements did concentrate on various aspects of oppression, no women's organization could afford to ignore the anti-imperialist fight. The sisterhood of those who came to Cairo had been formed in struggle against imperialism, and with the expectation that political rights within the independent nation would allow them to take the struggle further. Without political rights, all the other reforms would be meaningless. The state could promise equal education and equal wages, but if women had no political rights, how would they make sure these reforms would be enacted and maintained? (*TFAACW* 1961, 25).

Even the brief history of independence had shown these women's rights activists that the national liberation state should not be left alone to make noble gestures.[22] The new states had not been nirvana for women. Not only did the Cairo conference offer a list of prescriptions, a vision of equal rights for men and women, but within that list was also an implicit critique of the new states for their failure to promulgate many of these policies. The list demanded not only that the new states adopt the new international standards for which they themselves had fought, such as in the International Labour Organization and in other UN bodies, but that they actually implement them.

Every right that women won was not itself the end of the struggle, but it helped build the power to further their demands. Each right built more might for an endless movement. High on the third-world women's agenda was the stipulation that women should enter into marriage not to be bound to a man and his family, but to be in partnership with him. Women should not be married before they turned eighteen, which means they must have rights to education (which is also to be compulsory) before then. If men and women have any problems in their relationship, the state should provide them with "marriage counseling and planned parenthood." To fight against the idea that marriage is simply about property or progeny, the conference demanded, "Drastic measures should be taken to abolish polygamy." To offer women some freedom from the domestic sphere, it was proposed that "working women should be entitled to free medical care during pregnancy and childbirth, and to a suitable holiday with full pay during childbirth." Finally, it was argued, "The right of married women to work must be recognized and guaranteed." Most of the policy demands are not simply for the betterment of everyday life; their purpose is to ensure creation of an engaged civil society that includes women.

Of the rights demanded by women to increase their political capacity, many of them are already familiar from the 1920s onward[23]: cultural rights (right to equal and free education being the principal one) and social rights (as listed in the previous paragraph). A long section of the 1961 Cairo Recommendations on "Equality in the Economic Field" took the point further to argue that if women did not fight for and gain economic rights, they would not be able to be full political citizens. Modern citizenship meant that women should not have to rely upon the family unit for their economic well-being, but they should be full economic partners within the family. The 1961 conference offered a detailed vision for feminist struggle in the economic arena—for the right of women to hold any job, to gain promotion commensurate to their talents and not gender, to have the right to their jobs regardless of pregnancy or convalescence, to have vocational and technical training for all types of jobs, and to have the right to join and lead trade unions. It demanded that contract work be abolished since such work is frequently done by women, without benefits and out of the clear light of legal regulation. For women agricultural workers, the Recommendations called for "Equal distribution of land for those who till it and the guarantee of means of agricultural production" (*TFAACW* 1961, 26–28).[24] Finally, the Recommendations included women who did not work for a wage. For them, the conference had two recommendations: that the state try to reduce indirect (sales) taxes on consumer goods and so lighten the burden on the household finances, and that the state find ways to give women income support without making them perform meaningless jobs.

Anticolonial nationalism, even in its reformist incarnations, has always worried about the woman question. An end to social oppression almost always found its way onto the agenda of national liberation. At its most traditional, such an end looked like the modernization of patriarchy, with the new woman relegated to the domain of the home.[25] On the more progressive side of national liberation, there were many who argued that cultural traditions had ossified under the impact of patriarchy and feudal relations, and any opportunity to redress this had been suffocated by imperialism's alliance with the old social classes, who benefited from misogyny and status. Women and men, in this model, had to struggle against conservative domesticity and reconfigure what is to be the public space of the nation and what is to be the private domain of the family. As the report on social issues puts it, women "participate in the struggle for independence of their countries and its maintenance so that they may be able to abolish all customs and traditions which are degradatory to the status of women" (*TFAACW* 1961, 29). Third-world women's rights activists sought to reconfigure the public realm in their interest; to them, in the struggle for justice, the nation was more inclusive than the family, and therefore it was within the horizon of anticolonial nationalism that they dreamed and acted.

Advances for women in the national liberation regimes, writes the political scientist Mervat Hatam, came in the guise of a "state feminism." The Nasserite regime, in her example, "produced women who were economically independent of their families, but dependent on the state for employment, important social services such as education, health and day care, and political representation" (Hatem 1992, 233). The national liberation state remained constrained by social conservatism and traditionalism. It provided some reforms, but it refused, in the main, to challenge the domain of "personal status laws." The jurisdiction over the family and the arena of family law remained in the hands of religious leaders, many of whom then provided legitimacy to a state that needed as much support from plebeian leaders. A major consequence of the lack of an emphasis on social revolution was the inculcation of patriarchal norms within the new nations. The example of Iraq is apposite. When the Ba'ath Party took power in 1968, it quickly passed laws to enhance the role of women in the workplace and within the political apparatus of the Ba'ath Party itself. Compulsory education and better workplace protections combined with the creation of an omnibus, Ba'ath-controlled women's organization (the General Federation of Iraqi Women), underscore the arrival of "state feminism" in Iraq's history.[26] The Palestinian political theorist Hisham Sharabi calls this structure the "neo-patriarchy," where the third-world project, despite its commitment to modernity and modern state formation, "is in many ways no more than a modernized version of the traditional patriarchal sultanate" (Sharabi 1988, 7). In other words, even as national liberation enabled the creation of traditions of women's rights activism in the third world, the national liberation regimes seemed incapable of a programmatic commitment to women's liberation.

Solidarity Stories

A century ago, the Marxist theoretician Rosa Luxemburg argued that the needs of capitalist accumulation in the advanced industrial states engendered a necessary colonialism of other parts of the world not under the laws of capitalism. The anticolonial movements recognized that the misery of the colonized world came hand in hand with the pleasures of the colonizer. Elements of the Left within the advanced industrial states recognized this, and it is this recognition that drove the classic Marxist alliance between socialist groups in Europe and North America and national liberation groups in Africa, Asia, and Latin America. Nevertheless, this tradition of metropolitan radicalism did not always admit to its paternalist relationship with the national liberation struggle. Often these Left-solidarity movements denied that their own "advances" were a product of the expropriated labor of the vast mass of humanity. The solidarities forged were more integrally and differentially connected than was often recognized, since the bill for the social "advances" of Europe and North America was sent to the darker world, where it was paid off by the inhuman social relations produced and reproduced by the colonial regime.

The new anticolonial states that emerged in the Bandung epoch incubated the growth of a national bourgeoisie whose own social development came at the cost of that of the bulk of their fellow citizens. Because of the role of the state in the creation of national markets and a national imaginary, the elites emerged as a parasitical bourgeoisie. They relied for their own accumulation strategies on their intimate relationship with the state. The neopatriarchy of the postcolonial state has to be seen in terms of the dominance of this class, this parasitical bourgeoisie, in these postcolonial societies. Nevertheless, within these social formations, the histories of anticolonialism and of socialist struggles, as well as the contradictions maintained by the accumulation strategies, kept alive resilient critical movements, often of the Left. Bandung women inhabited both spaces, those of "state feminism" and of its critique. The broad ideology of Bandung women in the era from the 1940s to the 1970s was to fight for women's rights within the national formation, as well as to create internationalist links among one another to further their understanding of these rights and to promote their implementation.

With the demise of the anticolonial states from the 1970s onward, we see the growth of another tendency whose role in fashioning the idea of solidarity in our contemporary world is very great indeed. As the third-world state came under assault from neoliberal policies and institutions, its dissolution led to the growth of a parasitical civil society. In other words, as the state withdrew from its role in the creation of national markets and a national imaginary, that role began to be filled by NGOs and other nonstate actors whose own visions for civil society came not only from their own histories, but significantly from their donors (who are often in the advanced industrial states). The accumulation of wealth and the social development of capitalist states continue to suppress the will of the third world. The Luxemburgian insight of hierarchical interdependence, of the development of some states through the underdevelopment and labor of others, has been lost in our current era, even as it needs to be revised. Capitalist forms have indeed emerged in the former third world, and the duality between first and third worlds requires reassessment as a result of the gains of the postcolonial era. Yet the accumulation strategies of financial capitalism are still irrevocably centered in the advanced industrial states, and continue to require that the development of certain regions of the world, notably, Africa, large parts of Asia, and Latin America, be suppressed.

Within the parasitical civil society, specific ideas of what constitutes feminism and "women's rights" develop from within host countries and with significant guidance as well as pressure from outside. These connections could be and are often celebrated as a new generation of feminist transnationalism, one that sidesteps the patriarchal values of the state. Shorthanded here as NGO feminism, this current political trajectory remains cognizant of, even as it combines, the multiplicity of strategies, goals, or ideologies for social change within these civil sphere groups. NGO feminism at its most general promotes the view that certain issues and frameworks matter, despite the fact that these are developed by nonstate, unaccountable organizations that are often dominated by experiences and histories in the advanced financial-industrial states. The difference of experience in these networks does not unravel the conceit of sameness, or of a homogenous universality. A better form of solidarity would recognize the insight of Luxemburg and Binh, that there are material constraints to "equality." Any political equality across these divides needs to be a dialectical unity of universal categories (freedom and equality) and of institutional forms capable of being true to both these categories and to the concrete differences in the social world. NGO feminism is incapable of independence from the powers that make it possible, mainly because it fails on the second part of the dialectic. It remains susceptible to ideas of "humanitarian intervention" (masculine protectionism) and of the importation, both wholesale and piecemeal, of agendas from one social world to another.

Notes

Much thanks to Naeem Inayatullah and Robin L. Riley for asking us to participate in this project, and for bearing with us as we got the essay done. An earlier version appeared thanks to Salah D. Hassan in *CR: The Centennial Review* 5, no. 1 (2005), Special issue on "Terror Wars". We have since modified many of the theses, thanks to interventions from Adriane Lentz-Smith, Alia Arasoughly, Andy Hsiao, Daphne Lamothe, Ginetta Candelario, and Jen Guglielmo. The following archives provided access to materials: University of California, Berkeley's Bancroft Library (Social Protest Collection), Wisconsin State Historical Society Archives, and the Hoover Institution Library and Archives.
  1. More recent work relies on early books and memoirs like Dinh (1976), Bergman (1975), and Weigersma (1988).
  2. Two central histories of the women's movement in Cold War United States that sketch out these originary trajectories are Evans (1979) and Echols (1989).
  3. The U.S. women's delegates did not want to meet away from the men, perhaps, because it would have threatened the guise of egalitarianism, or unmasked the power imbalances within the antiwar coalitions. For women to meet away from men might suggest that women are solely responsible for women's issues, a legitimate worry among movement women who wanted everyone to actively fight sexism.
  4. Left parties in the United States had not abandoned questions of women's leadership and women's equality, but anticommunism severely weakened their outreach and influence on activism in the 1960s.
  5. "The Liberation of Women," *New Left Notes*, July 10, 1967, 4. The text of this statement was printed alongside the now-infamous cartoon of a

Twiggy-like woman in a child's dress with bloomers holding a sign that reads, "We want our Rights & We want them NOW!"

6. The following year, no serious mention of women's third-world status entered the SDS statement on women, but the ideas continued to percolate throughout the movement. See Sutheim (1969, 7–8).

7. Perhaps the best-known written document from this group was written by the committee's founder, Frances Beal (1995). Beal's "Double Jeopardy: To Be Black and Female" was first published in the March–April 1969 issue of *Motive*.

8. Another group, the Third World Women's Alliance, later emerged from this formation. While the "Third World" formations maintained some links to SNCC, the women's caucus within SNCC also remained. See Third World Women's Alliance (1971, 8).

9. The theory is not entirely novel to U.S. radical politics. One can see shades of it in the "Black Belt" thesis of the Communist Party in the 1920s. Within the academy the theory of the internal "Third World" or of "internal colonialism" and the struggles against it had their most effective champion in the sociologist Robert Blauner (1972, 72), who argued: "Communities of color in America share essential conditions with third world nations abroad: economic underdevelopment, a heritage of colonialism and neocolonialism, and a lack of real political economy and power." An article from Blauner (1969) is very close to the Alliance use of "Third World."

10. The article was written by Maryanne Weathers (1968) and circulated in mimeographed form within the civil rights and emerging women's liberation movement. The article is also in Guy-Shefthall (1995). For more on the Alliance, see Armstrong (2002, 103–106).

11. Most of the details for this paragraph are in Efrati (2004) and Farouk-Sluglett (1993). The canonical work in English used to be Ingrams (1983); for an early, partly stereotypical, ethnographic look at rural Iraq and of women therein, see Fernea (1965).

12. For context, see Batatu (1978).

13. When the Ba'ath Party took control of the government in 1963, one of its earliest acts was to amend portions of the law to nominally weaken the polygamy law. All was not to be bemoaned, however, because in terms of inheritance laws, it judged that children (either daughters or sons) would have the first right to their parents' property, as against the larger extended family. The right of the daughter would take precedence over that of distant male cousins. For a very brief analysis of the limitations of the 1959 law, see Coulson and Hinchcliffe (1978, 44) and Anderson (1963, 1026–1031).

14. For ethnographic background, see Tapper (1991). We have benefited greatly from the analysis in Val Moghadam (1989).

15. Nancy Hatch Dupree (1984) and two essays by Fred Halliday (1978, 1980) assess the limited social base of the PDPA.

16. For details on Ratebzad, see Danesch (1981, 1496–1503), Dupree (1984), and Moghadam (1989).

17. For example, Siu (1982).

18. One good example of the conversation across regions is the influence of the Indian feminist Pandita Ramabai on the Indonesian feminist Raden Adjeng Kartini, as noted by Toer (1962).

19. *The First Afro-Asian Women's Conference, Cairo, 14–23 January 1961,* 1961, 10. Hereafter *TFAAWC.*

20. Two classic analyses of the role of women in a revolutionary situation are Fanon (1967) and Guevara (1967). Surrounded by the experience of Vilma Espín, Celia Sanchez, and Haydée Santamaria in the hills of the Sierra Maestra, Che Guevara (1967, 86) wrote, "The part that the woman can play in the development of a revolutionary process is of extraordinary importance. It is well to emphasize this, since in all our countries, with their colonial mentality, there is a certain underestimation of the woman which becomes a real discrimination against her." Following this enlightened statement, Guevara resorts to descriptions of women's work in the most stereotypical way, characterizing the woman as auxiliary, as comfort, as cook, and as nurse. The actual experiences of women in the Cuban, Algerian, and Guinea-Bissauan revolutions are far more complex, as women entered combat and took on leadership roles, even as these were challenged by men who, despite their Left analysis, did not want to relieve themselves of patriarchal privileges. See Espín (1981), Urdang (1979), and Amrane-Minne (1994).

21. As the political document puts it, "Acquisition of national independence is an essential prerequisite to women's rights. Democracy and justice can become mere words without meaning if women, who comprise more than half the population in any Asian and African state, remain isolated from political life. Nor can the Eastern world be established if the sexes do not cooperate on an equal footing. They must enjoy the rights of equality with men in their political domain in such a way that the laws arranging them may reflect the re-vindication of the rights of women, their children and the rights of their people." (*TFAACW* 1961, 25).

22. "Rights should not be only stipulated in law, they must be implemented. To turn laws into reality depends on the unity and organization of women. It involves patient and painstaking work. It requires aid and abetment of all people of good will. But it is the only way which can lead to the real equality of men and women, the fullest emancipation of womanhood and the greatest development of the nation" (*TFAACW* 1961, 52). In 1928, Jawaharlal Nehru offered a vision for the necessity of the autonomous organization of women and other oppressed groups within the nationalist framework, because justice is not a product of benevolence. He said:

> I should like to remind the women present here that no group, no community, no country, has ever got rid of its disabilities by the generosity of the oppressor. India will not be free until we are strong enough to force our will on England and the women of India will not attain their full rights by the mere generosity of the men of India. They will have to fight for them and force their will on the menfolk before they can succeed. (Jayawardena 1986, 73)

23. In 1920, Najiye Hanum of the Communist Party of Turkey laid out a similar agenda at the Baku Conference of the Toilers of the East:

> I will briefly set forth the women's demands. If you want to bring about your own emancipation, listen to our demands and render us real help and cooperation. 1. Complete equality of rights. 2. Ensuring to women unconditional access to educational and vocational institutions established for men. 3. Equality of rights of both parties to marriage and unconditional abolition of polygamy. 4. Unconditional admission of women to employment in legislative and administrative institutions. 5. Establishment of committees for the rights and protection of women everywhere, in cities, towns, and villages.
>
> There is no doubt that we are entitled to raise these demands. In recognizing that we have equal rights, the Communists have reached out their hand to us, and we women will prove their most loyal comrades. True, we may stumble in pathless darkness, we may stand on the brink of yawning chasms, but we are not afraid, because we know that in order to see the dawn one has to pass through the dark night. (Riddell 1993, 206–207)

24. The final point is poorly phrased, because in many parts of the world tilling is monopolized by men, so by this standard, men would get land rights, not women. A better phrase, for universal applicability, would have been "land to those who work it" (the phrase that emerged in the Mexican revolution of 1911, and has since become a slogan across the Spanish speaking world of the Americas).

25. This is what Partha Chatterjee (1989) analyzes, although from his essay one does not get the sense that nationalism itself remained a wide ideological arena, within which many continued to struggle despite these resolutions on a broader feminist agenda. For a critique of his views, see Himani Bannerji (2000) and Uma Chakravarti (1996).

26. See Al-Sharqi (1982, 74–87) and Amal Rassam's two essays (1982, 1992).

Bibliography

Adams, Nina. 1992. The women who left them behind. In *Give peace a chance, exploring the Vietnam antiwar movement*. Edited by Melvin Small and William Hoover. Syracuse: Syracuse University Press.

Afary, Janet. 1996. *The Iranian constitutional revolution, 1906–1911: grassroots democracy and the origins of feminism*. New York: Columbia University Press.

Ali, Tariq. 2002. *The clash of fundamentalisms: crusades, jihads and modernity*. London: Verso.

Allen, Pamela. 1968. What strategy for movement women? *Guardian*, October 5.

Al-Sharqi, Amal. 1982. The emancipation of Iraqi women. In *Iraq: the contemporary state*. Edited by Tim Niblock. London: Croom Helm.

Amrane-Minne, Danièle-Djamila. 1994. *Les femmes dan la guerre d'Algerie: entretiens,* Paris: Karthala.

Anderson, J. N. D. 1963. Changes in the law in personal status in Iraq. *International and Comparative Law Quarterly* 12 (3).

Armstrong, Elisabeth. 2002. *The retreat from organization: US feminism reconceptualized.* Albany: SUNY Press.

Bannerji, Himani. 2000. Resolution of the women's question. *Economic and Political Weekly,* March 11–17.

Batatu, Hanna. 1978. *The old social classes and the revolutionary movement of Iraq.* Princeton, NJ: Princeton University Press.

Beal, Frances. 1995. Double jeopardy: to be black and female. In *Words of fire: an anthology of African-American feminist thought.* Edited by Beverly Guy-Shefthall. New York: New Press. Originally published in *Motive* (March–April, 1969).

Bergman, Arlene Eisen. 1975. *Women of Vietnam.* San Francisco: People's Press.

Besse, Susan K. 1996. *Restructuring patriarchy: the modernization of gender in Brazil, 1914–1940.* Chapel Hill: University of North Carolina Press.

Blauner, Robert. 1969. Internal colonialism and ghetto revolt. *Social Problems* 12.

———. 1972. *Radical oppression in America.* New York: Harper and Row.

Chakravarti, Uma. 1996. The myth of "patriots" and "traitors": Pandita Ramabai, brahmanical patriarchy and militant Hindu nationalism. In *Embodied violence: communalising women's sexuality in South Asia.* Edited by Kumari Jayawardena and Malathi De Alwis. London: Zed.

Chatterjee, Partha. 1989. Nationalist resolution of the woman question. *Recasting women: essays in colonial history.* New Delhi: Kali for Women.

Christensen, Hanne. 1990. *The reconstruction of Afghanistan: a chance for rural Afghan women.* Geneva: United Nations Research Institute for Social Development.

Cobble, Dorothy Sue. 2004. *The other women's movement: workplace justice and social rights in modern America.* Princeton, NJ: Princeton University Press.

Coulson, Noel, and Doreen Hinchcliffe. 1978. Women and law reform in contemporary Islam. In *Women in the Muslim world.* Edited by Lois Beck and Nikki Keddie. Cambridge: Harvard University Press.

Danesch, Mostafa. 1981. Islam, revolution und frauenbewegung: Afghanische erfahrungen: Anahita Ratebzad im gespräch. *Blätter für Deutsche und Internationale Politik* 26.

Dinh, Nguyen Thi. trans. 1976. No other road to take: memoir of Mrs. Nguyen Thi Dinh. Ithaca: Data Paper 102, Southeast Asia Program, Cornell University.

Du Plessis, Rachel Blau, and Ann Snitow. 1998. *The feminist memoir project.* New York: Three Rivers Press.

Dupree, Nancy Hatch. 1984. Revolutionary rhetoric and Afghan women. In *Revolutions and rebellions in Afghanistan: anthropological perspectives.* Edited by M. Nazir Shahrani and Robert L. Canfield. University of California: Institute of International Studies, Research Series No. 57.

Echols, Alice. 1989. *Daring to be bad: radical feminism in America, 1967–1975.* Minneapolis: University of Minnesota Press.

Efrati, Noga. 2004. The other "awakening" in Iraq: the women's movement in the first half of the twentieth century. *British Journal of Middle East Studies* 31(2).

Escandón, Carmen Ramos. 1998. Women and power in Mexico: the forgotten heritage, 1880–1954. In *Women's participation in Mexican political life*. Edited by Victoria E. Rodríguez. Boulder, CO: Westview Press.

Espín, Vilma. 1981. The early years. In *Women and the Cuban revolution*. Edited by Elizabeth Stone. New York: Pathfinder Press.

Evans, Sara. 1979. *Personal politics: the roots of women's liberation in the civil rights movement and the new left*. New York: Alfred A. Knopf.

Fanon, Franz. 1967. Algeria unveiled. In *A dying colonialism*. New York: Grove Press.

Farouk-Sluglett, Marion. 1993. Liberation or repression? pan-Arab nationalism and the women's movement in Iraq. In *Iraq: power and society*. Edited by Derek Hopwood, Habib Ishow, and Thomas Koszinowski. Reading: Ithaca Press.

Fernea, Elizabeth Warnock. 1965. *Guests of the sheikh: an ethnography of an Iraqi village*. Garden City: Doubleday.

Fraser, Arvonne S. 1995. The convention on the elimination of all forms of discrimination against women (the Women's Convention). In *Women, politics and the United Nations*. Edited by Anne Winslow. Westport, CT: Greenwood Press.

Galey, Margaret E. 1979. Promoting nondiscrimination against women. The UN commission on the status of women. *International Studies Quarterly* 23 (2).

Guevara, Che. 1967. *Guerrilla warfare*. New York: Vintage.

Guy-Shefthall, Berverly. 1995. *Words of fire: an anthology of African-American feminist thought*. New York: The New Press.

Halliday, Fred, and Zahir Tanin. 1998. The communist regime in Afghanistan 1978–1992: Institutions and Conflicts. *Europe-Asia Studies* 50 (8).

Halliday, Fred. 1978. Revolution in Afghanistan. *New Left Review* 112, November–December 1978.

———. 1980. The war and revolution in Afghanistan. *New Left Review* 119, January–February 1980.

Hatem, Mervat. 1992. Economic and political liberation in Egypt and the demise of state feminism. *International Journal of Middle East Studies* 24.

Ingrams, Doreen. 1983. *The awakened: women in Iraq*. London: Third World Centre.

Jayawardena, Kumari. 1986. *Feminism and nationalism in the third world*. London: Zed.

Miller, Francesca. 1991. *Latin American women and the quest for justice*. Hanover: University of New England Press.

Moghadam, Val. 1989. Revolution, the state, Islam and women: gender politics in Iran and Afghanistan. *Social Text* 22 (Spring).

Nawid, Senzil. 1999. *Religious response to social change in Afghanistan, 1919–29: King Amanullah and the Afghan ulama*. Costa Mesa: Mazda Publishers.

New Left Notes. 1967. The liberation of women. July 10.

Ninh, Kim N. B. 2002. *World transformed: the politics of culture in revolutionary Vietnam, 1945–1965*. Ann Arbor: University of Michigan Press.

Rassam, Amal. 1982. Revolution within revolution? Women and state in Iraq. In *Iraq: the contemporary state*. Edited by Tim Niblock. London: Croom Helm.
———. 1992. Political ideology and women in Iraq: legislation and cultural constraints. *Journal of Developing Societies* 8.
Riddell, John. 1993. *To see the dawn: Baku, 1920-first congress of the peoples of the east*. New York: Pathfinder.
Rupp, Leila, and Verta Taylor. 1987. *Survival in the doldrums*. New York: Oxford University Press.
Sangari, Kumkum. 1999. *Politics of the possible*. New Delhi: Tulika Press.
Schinasi, May. 1979. *Afghanistan at the beginning of the twentieth century: nationalism and journalism in Afghanistan: a study of Seraj ul-akhbar (1911–1918)*. Naples: Istituto Universitario Orientale.
———. 1998. *Femme Afghanes: instruction et activités publiques pendant le règne Amaniya, 1919-1929*. Limoges: Association de la culture afghane.
Sharabi, Hisham. 1988. *Neopatriarchy: a theory of distorted change in the Arab world*. New York: Oxford University Press.
Siu, Bobby. 1982. *Women of China: imperialism and women's resistance, 1900–1949*. London: Zed, 1982.
Springer, Kimberly. 2005. *Living for the revolution: black feminist organizations, 1968–1980*. Durham, NC: Duke University Press.
Sutheim, Susan. 1969. Women shake up SDS session. *Guardian*, January 18.
Swerdlow, Amy. 1993. *Women strike for peace*. Chicago: University of Chicago Press.
Tai, Hue-Tam Ho. 1992. *Radicalism and the origins of the Vietnamese revolution*. Cambridge, MA: Harvard University Press.
Tapper, Nancy. 1984. Causes and consequences of the abolition of bride-price in Afghanistan. In *Revolutions and rebellions in Afghanistan*. Edited by M. Nazif Shahrani and Robert Canfield. UC Berkeley: Institute for International Studies.
———. 1991. *Bartered brides: politics, gender and marriage in an Afghan tribal society*. Cambridge: Cambridge University Press.
Taylor, Sandra. 1999. *Vietnamese women at war: Fighting for Ho Chi Minh and the revolution*. Lawrence: University of Kansas Press.
Tetreault, Mary Ann. 2000. Women and revolution in Vietnam. In *Global feminisms since 1945*. Edited by Bonnie G. Smith. New York: Routledge.
Thapar, Suruchi. 1994. Women as activists, women as symbols: a study of the Indian nationalist movement. *Feminist Review* 44.
The First Afro-Asian Women's Conference, Cairo, 14-23 January 1961. 1961. Proceedings. Cairo: Amalgamated Press of Egypt.
Third world women's alliance. 1971. Women in the struggle. *National SNCC Monthly* 1.6.
Toer, Pramoedya Ananta. 1962. Jang Harus Dibabat dan harus Dibangun. *Bintang Timur*, September 7.
Turner, Karen Gottschang and Phan Thanh Hao. 1998. *Even the women must fight: memories of war from North Vietnam*. New York: Wiley.
Urdang, Stephanie. 1979. *Fighting two colonialisms: women in Guinea-Bissau*. New York: Monthly Review.

Weathers, Maryanne, and the Black and Third World Women's Liberation Alliance. 1968. An argument for black women's liberation as a revolutionary force. October. Wisconsin State Historical Society. Social Action Vertical File, Box 6. Also in Guy-Shefthall (1995). Originally published by Maryanne Weathers.

Weigand, Kate. 2000. *Red feminism: American communism and the making of women's liberation.* Baltimore: Johns Hopkins University Press.

Weigersma, Nancy. 1988. *Vietnam: peasant land, peasant revolution: patriarchy and collectivity in the rural economy.* New York: St. Martin's Press.

Young, Iris. 2003. The logic of masculinist protection: reflections on the current security state. *Signs* 29.

Chapter 3

Shame and Rage: International Relations and the World School of Colonialism[1]

Himadeep Muppidi

I

Splayed objects of your worldly gaze
Captive loves of your studies abroad
Slaves, sepoys, spices
Animal specimens, software-species
Unequally sold
Civilly exchanged
Off-shored, shackled, tortured
Out-sourced
In otherwise humane designs
Are we burning, freezing, coding, bleeding
Disappearing in History
As you hum-vee and bull-doze
The *Wadi al-Uyouns* [2] of our Life.

II

Bodies, Brown and Naked

A friend emails me photographs from Abu Ghraib. I had already seen some of them. These I hadn't. The brief glimpse of the new ones roils my stomach. Disturbed, I shut down the computer. I want to erase those images from my computer; unpool their film from my eyes. I feel debased and complicit merely by looking. I want to retreat, run, from the implication in those pictures. I am possessed, simultaneously, by a desire to prove them false. They must have been staged, must be untrue, I think. I consider scanning the images closely to comfort myself in that confirmation. But I don't find the courage to look again. Then I wonder if the "truth" of these images was really the issue here. These photographs were alive and moving. They had already traveled from the Middle East to the Northeast. And it was the Bush administration that had charged these pictures with plausibility even as it had electrocuted the lives of many others.

Colleagues I respect are puzzled by my response to the photographs: "What," they inquire politely but with just that correct touch of annoyed incredulity, "did you imagine happens in war?" I don't begrudge them that annoyance: What *did* I imagine happened in war? Why was I, who so routinely preach the power of language, finding it so difficult to grasp what a language of power and war necessarily entailed? Deep down, did I continue to think that war was only "politics by other means"? Did the qualifier "only" allow me to hide from myself what the otherness of the means implied? Did I think of war as primarily a technical relationship that, addressed properly, could be clean, cleansing, and cultured? Was it then only the nakedness of the Other in Abu Ghraib that was bothering me? Was their difficult-to-hide-brownness cutting too close to my bone?

In the first Gulf War, the United States bulldozed Iraqi soldiers into the sand in order to bury the ghosts of Vietnam. In the second Gulf War, it wants to awe the world by tearing apart and suturing 25 million people. But each encounter in the invasion/occupation/liberation of Iraq by the United States only serves to galvanize the scarcely rested specters of colonialism. Every uncounted corpse, every unaccounted death, and every blasted body revivifies memories and energizes the images of those slashed, burned, buried, bombed, and napalmed in Vietnam, in the Philippines, in Iran, in Iraq, in Cuba, in the Americas . . . If this is what the United States can do in the face of global disapproval and in the name of good intentions, then what has it done when neither the mask of humanity nor the avowal of a good intention was a necessary feature of world politics? What other ghosts wait to be resurrected here?

I am reminded of Belgium's invasion/occupation/liberation of the Congo in order, ostensibly, to save it from Arab slavers. That liberation, that missionary politics by means of the other, crucified millions of Africans and had its own Abu Ghraibs: photographs of shackled, naked African women held in chains to coerce their husbands to gather rubber for the Belgians; pictures of the limbs of children and men—hands and feet chopped off by the militia of the Anglo-Belgian

India Rubber Company; photo-portraits of Belgian officers posing nobly—the archives bristle with these images (Hochschild 1998). Moonlighting as authors, artists, painters, and collectors, even as they were looting and killing, officers such as Léon Rom gaze into the future as if convinced of the grandness of their enterprise, the pedagogical necessity of their violence, and the nobility of their civilization. There is little in Mr. Rom's photo-portrait to signal to us that this member of the Entomological Society of Belgium—every time he returned to Europe he brought back many specimens of butterflies—was also renowned for collecting and displaying, in his Congolese garden, rows of severed African heads (Hochschild 1998). An officer, an entomologist, and a headhunter—cultured to the core.

But that, you might say, as the Belgians now do, was another time.

Now, some decades later, we see photo- or video-graphic beheadings as signs of the backward, brutal Other. Those uncool bastards! Made over by modernity, we talk tastefully of bombing human communities in and out of time ("into the stone age"), savor festive spectacles of mass killing ("shock and awe"), and marvel at the radiant and precise aesthetics of Predators, depleted uranium shells, and 500-pound bombs dropped on unsuspecting families suspected of harboring terrorists. So if Abu Ghraib is disquieting, is it only because it hurts my culturally honed preference for dispensing with the Other coolly and cleanly? Do I prefer my killers to be like my TV anchors: well-dressed, well-spoken, and light of color?

III

The Remains/Returns of the Colonized

The Royal Museum of Central Africa in Tervuren, Belgium, is proud of its collection of objects and animals. That collection includes, on its own authority, 350 archives, 8,000 musical instruments, 20,000 maps, 56,000 wood samples, 180,000 ethnographic objects, 250,000 rock samples, and 10,000,000 animals (Royal Museum of Central Africa 2003, 81). Notwithstanding a passion for enumeration, the Royal Museum has trouble remembering the number of human beings intimately implicated in this collection. If we distributed the animal collection alone, going by the current population of Belgium, that is nearly an animal specimen each for every living Belgian citizen. But if we counted only those who died to make this rich collection possible—5 to 8 million

Congolese—even a very conservative estimate would mean placing the remains of a murdered African in the hands of every Belgian couple.

I went to Brussels in the summer of 2004 after finding out that, nearly a hundred years ago, King Leopold II of Belgium wanted to start a World School of Colonialism (Hochschild 1998, 276). The World School of Colonialism was expected to be part of a larger architectural complex that would include a museum, a conference center, and a sports complex. Leopold's death in 1909 resulted in only the Royal Museum part of the project being realized. Trained to think of colonialism as an ideology that dissimulates even as it dismembers, I was startled by the nakedness of the king's proposal.

The Royal Museum is designed to impress. Gilded bronze sculptures welcome you into its marble-floored rotunda. You look up to see tall Belgian citizens bestowing gifts—the "values" of "civilization," "well-being," "support," and freedom from "slavery"—on Congolese children, women, and men. The prophetlike demeanor of these benevolent citizens brooks no rude question on the source of the virtues flowing from their hands. A path leads from the rotunda to sections showcasing displays marked as anthropology, history, zoology, agricultural and forest economy, geology, prehistory, and archeology, before arriving back at the entrance.

As I began my tour in the anthropology section, my eyes started, in a most unscholarly fashion, to glaze over the neatly labeled drums and masks and the many, many figurines. Something seemed amiss, something was out of focus in the long-cultivated relationship between the eye and the eyed. Try as I might, I couldn't summon the proper academic disposition that this institutional space seemed, quite silently, to demand. The pressure intensified as I became doubly aware of those around me in that section. I realized that I was reflecting on their likely reflections of me walking these corridors—brown imagining white imagining brown eyes seeking traction on black masks.

My unease kept mounting until I strolled into the zoology section. Seeing some children clustered around a teacher, I paused hesitantly, wondering whether they might have as many questions of me as of the okapi. I was not sure I was ready to hear those questions, yet. But in zoology I grasped, suddenly and sharply, that my unease was emerging from the underlying design of the museum. Understood as a manifestation of the European order of things, the museum made brilliant sense. Here was the trophy room, laboratory, library, school, hospital, and asylum of the colonizer. This was where they—the colonizer's citizen-heirs—repaired to be educated, trained, cultured, and restored to/into their patrimony. But what was my place and position in such an institution? Where did I fit in an institution displaying the colonizer's collections? In the European order of things, was I, could I be, only another animal-object?

As long as I was gazing from and moving on the observer-academic side of the glass border, I was a peculiarity in the museum, an anomaly inviting comment, not least from my own self. This museum was not built for the likes of me to gaze and move. Just as we don't design zoos to help the animals examine the displays, this museum was not designed on the premise that the colonized would, one day, be walking through its corridors. Not that there was not a place for those of my tribe. Our assigned place in the museum's archeology of knowledge was in natural history, on the observed-other side of the glass with the dead, if absent and unacknowledged Africans and the equally dead but publicly presented and proudly displayed animals. Wedged into natural history, suturing nature and history, wouldn't my normalized identity preclude any straying from the familial intimacy of traditional villages and stuffed elephants?

But crossing these borders, straying beyond my assigned positions, was also the necessary condition of my education here. To walk through the museum—anomalous as that might have been in terms of its founding principles—was to discover, as intended by King Leopold II, what a colonial education/responsibility was all about.[3] Having grasped colonization from a diligent reading of the archives of the Spanish conquistadors, Leopold II was no doubt a masterly teacher of the craft (Hochschild 1998, 37). Mobile within Europe, moving among the colonizers, at least partly because of a degree in international relations, I couldn't help wondering if and how my education differed from the one that the king wanted to offer. How certain was I that my degree was not already from an affiliate of the World School of Colonialism?

Trading places, switching gazes, looking in from the observed-other, eyed side of the glass, I understood now that I was the turbaned slaver, the rag-head, on display, whose "Arabness" was deployed as the motive for Belgium's soul-cleansing antislavery campaigns. But I was also the shackled Congolese, the coolie, animal-slave to Belgium's hunger for rubber and ivory. And universality and humanity, colonial education as well as "real and responsible" international relations were about ceaselessly rescuing one from the other, the coolie from the rag-head, the animal-slave from the slaver-object, the African from the Arab, the good Muslim from the bad one, the academic-observer from the observed-academic object, me from myself, but without ever setting any of us free.

IV

Interrogating In-betweenity

If Belgium sees itself as the "heart of Europe," then Grand-Place in Brussels presents itself and is generally regarded as one of Europe's most beautiful public squares—a market and a meeting place for citizens. Belgium claimed a place for it on the World Heritage List by asserting that it was "a masterpiece of human creative genius, with a special quality of coherency . . . " An expert mission from the World Heritage Commission evaluated Belgium's claims and agreed that it deserved a place on the List for, among other things, the ways in which "the nature . . . of its architecture" and its "outstanding quality as a public open space" illustrated "in an exceptional way" "the evolution and achievements of a highly successful mercantile city of northern Europe at the height of its prosperity."[4]

An integral part of this most beautiful of European squares, this "masterpiece of human creative genius," this "outstanding public open space," is a building called "Le Roi de l'Espagne." Built by a bakers' guild in 1696–1697, it is a "large dignified structure with a balustrade decorated with allegorical statues and surmounted by a graceful dome Ibid, p. 68."

Gracing the façade of the "Le Roi de l'Espagne," dignifying it quite prominently, are two captives: a turbaned Moor and a Native American. On their knees, hands bound behind their backs, they are towered over by the crowned head of Charles II gazing into the market cum meeting place for European citizenry.

Diagonally across "Le Roi de l'Espagne" is the bar where Karl Marx and Friedrich Engels are reported to have spent hours polishing the Communist Manifesto. Captivated by this material testimonial to "human creative genius," to the evolution and achievements of Europe, to dignity and grace, I cannot help wondering if Europe's best and brightest citizens, Marx and Engels, gave the captive Moor and the Native American some sustained and serious thought. If they had, would they have polished the Manifesto a little further, maybe until it read: "A spectre is ravaging Europe—the spectre of colonialism"? I imagine, uncharitably no doubt, the impatient response of my radical colleagues: "But that's already covered in the section on primitive accumulation. You should read your Marx more carefully."

And maybe I should. But I am straying again, wandering, thinking now of another Charles, a Charles Graner, smiling, posing, thumbs up, behind a pyramid of naked, hooded Iraqi captives in Abu Ghraib. Leaning over this, his primitive accumulation of brown bodies, smiling again, is another soldier, Megan Ambuhl. The glee in her eyes, as also the joyful participation in similar rituals of another soldier, Pfc. Lynndie England, has been the source of anxious commentary among some feminists: How can historically oppressed subjects participate so pleasurably in the torture and degradation of others?

I understand the participation, maybe not the glee.

I detect no glee in the archival pictures of Belgian colonization of the Congo (Hochschild 1998). The African soldier guarding two naked, shackled African women is fully clothed, has a gun, and is looking at the camera from in between the two hostages. But there is no smile on his face. In another picture, a *chicotte* (a whip made out of raw, sun-dried hippopotamus hide) hovers above a naked African spread-eagled on the ground, face turned away from the camera. The wielder of the *chicotte,* another African, is looking at us, his hand half-raised as if about to strike, but there's little gaiety on his face or in his demeanor. Do these overseers find it difficult to enjoy their violent power because they sense how easily their roles can be reversed with those held hostage or being whipped? Is there no glee in their faces because they know that neither the gun nor the *chicotte* have as much power as pigmentation?

But, crossing borders again, is it precisely a faith in the irreversibility of roles with the darker Others, a magical blindness induced by the color of the ostensibly foreign, that allows Marine Sergeant Robert Sarra, a veteran of the Iraq war and a peace activist, to shout, in "drunken rage," at a "foreign cabdriver": "I wiped out your entire family over there, and I'll get you, too"?[5] As I think of this outburst, I imagine neither terror nor anxiety on the face of the "foreign cabdriver" as he/she hears this. I am sure he/she knows, by now, that in the colonial order of things, they are both substitutable for varied Others—"your entire family over there"—and dispensable—"I wiped out your entire family . . . and I'll get you, too." The cabdriver is calm, but shame and rage inundate me as Robert Sarra's drunken words set off a slideshow of my "entire family over there."

Mine is the turbaned head trampled in the Royal Chapel of your Capilla Real de Granada. We circle around the tombs of the Catholic kings, Ferdinand and Isabella. You talk of canonizing Isabella as a saint. And when I remind you that the conquest of the Americas obliterated much of the Other, you hit reset by declaring that Isabella, in her will, liberated her Indian slaves.

Mine is the body you cremated twice, thoughtfully: once in Hiroshima and again in Nagasaki. Come anniversary time in August, you are suddenly silent, uncertain about whether to celebrate your technology or atone for the mass vaporizations? But, all year round, you are outraged or terrified that darker rogues might access your destructive wisdom.

Mine is the childishly thin back peeling out from your napalm; mine are the guts spilled out in your million My Lais and squashed in the rubble of bombed Afghan and Iraqi weddings. I lie among the 600 who were sniper-slaughtered to avenge the 4 dead in Fallujah. I waste away as one of the 208 who are dying every week in Iraq because you wanted "freedom to march" in my home. I perish among the hundred thousands more dead that will trail your murderous and illiterate needs. But even as the rage in me rises, I cannot escape my sense of shame. Shame and rage. Shame and rage.

You ask me if I want to interrogate imperialism. Yes, I do. But how can I interrogate it without interrogating myself, the postcolonial in between? If shame and rage are what you-I feel, why do I talk and teach about the indispensability of your thought to my being in the world? Why does the farthest reach of my pedagogy imagine only the possibility of "provincializing" you? Is it because I cannot imagine being Other than what you-I am now: the African with the *chicotte*, the Indian with the gun, the postcolonial with the keyboard? Have I, in the process of postcolonization, forgotten what it means to be anticolonial? Or, was anticolonialism never really the aim of my being?

V

A Subaltern West

While teaching Amitav Ghosh's *In an Antique Land*, this semester, I was drawn, once again, to that angry shouting match that Ghosh finally has with the Imam of the village. Needled by the Imam about the "primitive and backward" practices of cow worship and cremation, Ghosh finds it difficult to restrain himself and lashes out, furiously, about the ways in which India, his country, notwithstanding these practices, outranked the Imam's on the scale of advancement. Since advancement was measured by access to weapons, machines, and the means of violence, Ghosh claims superiority on the basis of his country's ability to test nuclear weapons. Even as the exchange winds down, a weary Ghosh is "crushed" further by the thought that this exchange itself—an effort by the representatives of two "superseded civilizations . . . to establish a prior claim to the technology of modern violence"—was proof of their "final defeat." It was indicative of a world in which the languages of mutual accommodation had been erased by the languages of "guns and tanks and bombs" (Ghosh 1992, 234–237).

Through this distressing conclusion, Ghosh draws a similarity and a difference between himself and the Imam. He points out that this moment of anger and hostility between them was also a moment of perfect understanding, since they both realized that they were travelling in the only space that each considered worth travelling—the West. But Ghosh also shadows this moment of identification with the Imam with an apparent difference in their mutual engagement with the West: "The only difference was that I had actually been there, in person: I could have told him a great deal about it, seen at first hand, its libraries, its museums, its theatres (Ghosh 1992, 236)."

Ghosh's assertion of his "first hand" experience of the West's "libraries . . . museums . . . theatres" presents the promise, however briefly, of an Other West, a different West, a West that was more than, other than, the possessor of the technologies of modern violence. I say briefly primarily because Ghosh goes on to say that this difference would not have mattered because, for millions of people around the world, this Other West was "mere fluff" (Ghosh 1992, 236). I also flag the briefness because much of this book is about the intimate connection between Western/colonial processes of knowledge acquisition and the disappearance of a global, cosmopolitan "world of accommodations." But, despite the brevity of its appearance, the promise of an Other West that Ghosh holds out may be worth revisiting. What is intriguing is that he holds out the promise of a subaltern West available for "first hand" experience in its libraries, museums, and theatres.

Contrary to Ghosh's claim, the West's subalternity, if it is to be found, is not necessarily in "its libraries, its museums, its theatres." Accumulators of knowledge, memory and art, these monopolizing institutions are but sophisticated extensions of the technologies of modern violence. They stand as visible monuments to the West's historical capacity and willingness to freeze, shock, recollect, and suture Others. The brazen and easy resurgence of a discourse of empire in the West is evidence that the educational and cultural machinery of the West offers, primarily, degrees in colonial responsibility. World Schools of Colonialism morph into World Schools, Schools of the Americas, Schools of International Relations, Schools of Global Studies . . . In that sense, King Leopold's spirit continues to animate the dominant West.

But there is a subaltern West, and I see that subalternity flourishing and perishing all around me. Its presence is calligraphed, sometimes, on those bodies that have been inadequately educated in their colonial responsibilities. Jeffrey Lucey, 23, was one such colonial—but not human—failure.[6] A lance corporal in the Marine Reserves who served six months in Iraq as a truck driver, he was ordered to shoot two unarmed Iraqi soldiers. He did. But, try as he might, he could not come to terms with his killings or the emotional agony that it brought him. Neither the flag nor the therapist could get him to relocate responsibility for his ordered murders onto some other body. He insisted on defining himself as a murderer. He sought some refuge from that honesty in a touching, childlike humanity, occasionally asking his father if he could sit in his lap. Finally, unable to cope with the grievous burden that a brutal and insensitive-to-its-own colonial state had privatized onto his body, he hanged himself in his parents' home. The doctors now present the many traces of his attempt to recover his humanity, as manifest in his seeking of a refuge in his father's lap, as "signs of regression, symptoms shown by suicidal people trying to cling to an emotionally safe memory." Ibid. If this is regression, don't we need more of it? I mourn the two unarmed Iraqi soldiers that Jeffrey Lucey killed on orders. I also mourn Lucey's subsequent killing of himself. To his credit, he could not get himself to treat only the Other as dispensable. Tragic as it is, it is bodies such as these that hold the impossible and incredible possibility of a provincialized West. The urgent project might be to reach out to them before the colonial institutions do. It is in these preemptive efforts or more successful redemptive strategies that the promise of a more provincial and hence more humane West, one that would affirm and make Life rather than History, appears to be manifest.

I feel no glee as I await the development of this Other West.

Notes

1. I am grateful to Christopher Chekuri, Andrew Davison, Katherine Hite, and members of the Delmas Seminar at Vassar College for the many wonderful conversations that have led to this paper. Naeem Inayatullah and Robin L. Riley have been excellent editors. It was truly a pleasure to be at the receiving end of their editorial comments. I am particularly indebted to Naeem for the luminosity and perceptiveness that he brought to his readings of different versions of this chapter and for constantly pressing me to revise just one more time. Thank you all.

2. The name of the oasis from which many of the characters in Munif's novel *Cities of Salt* originate.

3. "In this park we are building a museum that will be worthy of containing all these fine collections, and that will, I hope, effectively contribute to the colonial education of my countrymen." King Leopold II in conversation with the French architect Charles Girault, 1903. Quoted in Royal Museum for Central Africa (2003: 78).

4. See UNESCO's World Heritage List, Grand Place, Brussels (Belgium), No. 857, Advisory Body Evaluation, pp. 67–70. Document available online at http://whc.unesco.org/pg.cfm?cid=31&id_site=857

5. Marcella Bombardieri, "Veterans of Iraq war join forces to protest US invasion," *Boston Globe,* September 2, 2004. Available online at http://www.boston.com/news/nation/articles/2004/09/02/veterans_o

6. Adam Gorlick, Associated Press, "Marine returns from Iraq to emotional ruin, suicide," *Boston Herald,* October 16, 2004. Available online at http://news.bostonherald.com/localRegional/view.bg?articleid=49

Bibliography

Ghosh, Amitav. 1992. *In an antique land: history in the guise of a traveler's tale.* New York: Vintage.

Hochschild, Adam. 1998. *King Leopold's ghost.* New York: Mariner Books.

Munif, AbdelRahman. 1989. *Cities of salt.* New York: Vintage International.

Royal Museum for Central Africa. 2003. *The museum key: a visitor's guide to the RMCA.* Tervuren, Belgium: RMCA.

Chapter 4

Patriotism in the U.S. Peace Movement: The Limits of Nationalist Resistance to Global Imperialism

Shampa Biswas

In the historic moment of February 2003, I found myself caught in an uneasy confluence of social and political forces. Some were shrill and strident, others more reasoned and thoughtful, but the unmistakable vocabulary of old-fashioned colonialism had once again found a voice in the respectable corridors of the Anglo-American academy and in policymaking circles—goading, egging, nagging the U.S. government to take on the onerous, but necessary, task of empire building. For those of us who had built our careers inscribing difference and marginality into the heart of international relations, deeply aware of the history of colonial encounters so thoroughly embedded into every sinew of the discipline we had inherited, this resurgence of empire was a frightening prospect. However, in that same moment, there were also other diverse and resistant voices, some appropriately sharp and shrill, others more creative and nuanced, which constituted a global swell of opposition attempting to speak many different "truths" to U.S. power. The palpable frustration, rage, and energy of the days immediately preceding the war on Iraq, days that were defining the contours of empire most sharply, took me, like so many others, to the peace rallies, marches, and vigils to find communities of solidarity, to belong on the inside in a country in which I increasingly found myself on the outside. What I found, however, was that for a "foreigner" in the United States, most peace communities were not to offer the comfort of "home," so thoroughly "Americanized" had that space become; they called out to a family of which I was not a member, even though I was thankful to have their shelter and warmth on some cold, dark nights.

This chapter emerged out of my attempt to deal with the confusion of forces that left me homeless among friends and compatriots in the historic moment when the calls for empire intersected with the calls against U.S. aggression. It is possible to read this chapter as a critique of the circles of friendship from which I felt myself alienated, and there is a sense in which I lodge my complaints about the peace movement as an "outsider" speaking to the inside. But let me insist that the argument of this chapter is, much more importantly, an indictment of the "intimate enemy" that colonialism becomes, so thoroughly investing all social relations that even opposition to it remains framed by it.[1] Examining the rhetoric and tactics of the peace movement that emerged in the context of the war on Iraq, I argue that the terms on which the opposition to the war was waged were not simply inadequate to the necessary task of confronting empire, but unwittingly complicit in reproducing the colonialist imaginary that undergirds calls for empire. In advocating that the U.S. peace movement, perhaps much more so than any of the similar movements emergent in other national contexts, needs to articulate, urgently and strongly, a global ethic and idiom to relay its message, my critique is also a sympathetic and "insider" challenge to and from a community that is one of my political homes at this historical juncture. I write this chapter then quite self-consciously, straddling the insider/outsider location that marks the boundaries of many of my current habitations—as a critical, postcolonial scholar in the discipline of international relations, as a South Asian in America, as a critic of both empire and the opposition that has emerged to it in the U.S. peace movement.

I begin with an extensive discussion of the rhetorical exercises that accompanied the justifications for a preemptive war against Iraq and an examination of the material edifice of contemporary U.S. power. In somewhat painstaking detail, I document the emergence of a certain kind of common sense about the legitimacy of American "empire," with the apologists for empire springing from all over the political spectrum and from all kinds of institutional locations, urging the United States to take on the role of a "benign imperialist." I suggest here that the revival of a seemingly defunct international relations debate between "idealists" and "realists," albeit taking on new and interesting political hues, has led to the emergence of a whole army of "neoidealists." These new idealists have changed the discursive and material terrain that the "idealism" of the peace movement needs to contend with. Later, I argue that, at this particular historical-political juncture, any peace movement that does not reckon in a serious and sustained fashion with these forces of empire remains ill-equipped to the task of envisioning peace.

The second section begins with a focus on the patriotic context within which the U.S. peace movement has emerged. I describe the hypernationalistic context that emerged in the post–September 11 United States, documenting the varieties of patriotism ranging from its glamorous, commodified forms to the more mundane kinds of political vigilantism permeating U.S. society. Here I examine the emergence of another kind of common sense about what it means to be "American" that has both enabled and circumscribed political discourse in the contemporary United States, and also defined the terrain from which the U.S. peace movement responded to the war on Iraq. By critically examining each of the rhetorical strategies used by the peace movement to appropriate patriotism from the political Right, I argue that the terms on which the peace movement has waged its opposition to the war on Iraq, even if strategically sensible within the U.S. political context, remain woefully inadequate to the task of confronting the calls for empire that underlie the case for the war on Iraq.

The War on Terror and the Building of Empire

"The United States is now, as the defunct Soviet Union was decades ago, the subversive agent of a world revolution"
(Zizek 2004).

"What other country divides the world up into five military commands with four-star generals to match, keeps several hundred thousand of its legionaries on active duty in 137 countries – and is now unafraid to use them?"
(*Economist* 2003, 19)

We now know that the case for the war against Iraq had begun to be enunciated long before September 11 2001. It is now common knowledge that a 1992 Pentagon paper—authored by Paul Wolfowitz and then leaked—had been the basis for unsuccessfully urging two previous U.S. presidents to launch a military strike against Iraq. The "war on terror," however, inaugurated a whole new industry of treatises making the case for a preemptive strike against Iraq. On the one hand was the increased use of "native" voices that helped make the case for war. This included the carefully crafted analysis of the perversions of the Ba'ath regime in the Baghdad-born scholar Kanan Makiya's

Republic of Fear: the Politics of Modern Iraq[2] as well as the Orientalist scholarship of the Palestinian scholar Fouad Ajami that analyzes the Arab world's "hostility" to modernity[3]. On the other hand were the stridently polemical presentations of those with a clear policy agenda: For example, there was the former CIA analyst and member of the National Security Council Kenneth Pollack's 2002 book *The Threatening Storm: The Case for Invading Iraq*, which documents the widespread atrocities of Saddam Hussein's regime and responds extensively to criticisms of those opposed to war; and there is the well-known political philosopher Jean Bethke Elshtain's 1999 book that eagerly demonstrates how a war against Iraq would be "just." Shortly, the case for war against Iraq came to be couched in terms of the U.S. role in the Middle East and the world. In *The War over Iraq*, neoconservative thinkers William Kristol and Lawrence F. Kaplan are quite clear that "the mission begins in Baghdad, but it does not end there" (Kaplan and Kristol 2003, 124), boldly stating: "We stand at the cusp of a new historical era . . . For the United States, then, this is a decisive moment . . . it is so clearly about more than Iraq. It is about more even than the future of the Middle East . . . It is about what sort of role the United States intends to play in the twenty-first century" (Kaplan and Kristol 2003, vii–viii).[4] Indeed, long before the war on Iraq, this neoconservative position imagining a globally dominant United States had been hatched and defined in the pages of the popular conservative journal *Weekly Standard* and at well-financed conservative think tanks such as the American Enterprise Institute and Heritage Foundation. It then began its slow incursion into more mainstream publications—such as *Foreign Affairs, Foreign Policy,* and the *New York Times*—publications with wide currencies in both scholarly and policymaking circles.

1. The Empire-Mongers

Neoconservative calls for U.S. dominance need not be particularly surprising, since as Richard Falk points out, calls for U.S. hegemony had been fairly persistent since the fall of the Soviet Union, including from those such as Charles Krauthammer, celebrating the "unipolar moment," as well as from those asserting U.S. leadership capabilities during the presidencies of Bush senior and Clinton—for example, Madeleine Albright (Falk 2003). Indeed, even enthusiastic proponents of globalization such as the *New York Times* columnist Thomas Friedman had called for the necessity of a strong U.S. military presence to keep world markets "free."[5] On the heels of these open calls for U.S.

hegemony, the previously impolite colonialist arguments have been revived. As U.S. intellectuals and foreign-policy makers openly embrace an "imperialist" or "neoimperialist" mission for the United States, it has even become fashionable to articulate such positions in prestigious periodicals such as the *New York Times* and *Foreign Affairs*. Commonly invoked in these justifications for "American Empire" is the nineteenth-century theme of a "grand civilizing mission," as are comparisons to Imperial Rome and particularly Imperial Britain.[6] Indeed, advocacy for empire has occurred in conjunction with favorable reassessments of the British empire – such as the one offered in a book and television series by historian Niall Ferguson, who claims, "What the British empire proved . . . is that empire is a form of international government that can work and not just for the benefit of the ruling power . . . The British empire . . . though not without blemish . . . may have been the least bloody path to modernity for its subjects" (*Economist* 2003, 19–20). Similarly, the political analyst Dimitri Simes understands "why supporters of the Bush administration's foreign policy balk at any mention of the 'e' word" because of the bad name of many past empires, but then goes on to argue that

> despite the unpleasant present-day connotations, the imperial experience has not been uniformly negative. Some former empires were agents of change and progress and had generally good intentions vis-à-vis their subjects. The United Kingdom was a prime example of this type, approaching its empire not only with a desire to promote development, but with a self-sacrificing willingness to spend its resources toward that end.
>
> (Simes 2003)

The resuscitation of "Empire" and "Imperialism" as acceptable terms with a wide political currency has emerged from all sorts of "reputable" outlets, and empire-mongers have spanned the political spectrum. Acknowledging that the United States has had a long imperial history, Max Boot, fellow at the Council on Foreign Relations in New York and *Wall Street Journal* columnist, celebrates America's "liberal imperialism" and "progressive imperialism" for its lofty ideals and ambitions, among which was to carry the weight of the "the white man's burden" in places such as the Philippines. He documents a benign U.S. imperial history, far superior to its European counterparts, that produced "a set of colonial administrators and soldiers who would not have been out of place on a veranda in New Delhi or Nairobi" (Boot 2003, 362).[7] "America's destiny is to police the world," he asserts and, in tones that wax nostalgic of colonialism, reminds us:

> America now faces the prospect of military action in many of the same lands where generations of British colonial soldiers went on campaigns. These are all places where Western armies had to quell disorder. Afghanistan and other troubled foreign lands cry out for the sort of enlightened foreign administration once provided by self-confident Englishmen in jodhpurs and pith helmets.
>
> (Foster 2002)

More "liberal" political commentators, such as Michael Ignatieff, professor of human rights policy at the Kennedy School of Government at Harvard University, are also not shy about drawing lessons from British colonial strategy to instruct American policy makers on how to build empire (Ignatieff 2002). Writing about the U.S. presence in Afghanistan, Ignatieff argues that "imperialism used to be the white man's burden. This gave it a bad reputation. But imperialism doesn't stop being necessary just because it is politically incorrect" (Ignatieff 2002). Understanding the U.S. imperial role as "a burden" that is a product of U.S. preeminence in the world, Ignatieff argues that "the case for empire is that it has become, in a place like Iraq, the last hope of democracy and stability alike," and he calls for overcoming the American inhibition on using the "E-word" (Ignatieff 2003). It is this legitimizing of colonialist language that makes it possible for the *Economist,* using terms coined by a Brookings Institution fellow, to note without any sense of irony, George W. Bush's transformation after September 11 from an "assertive nationalist" to a "democratic imperialist," more in tune with the "neoconservatives" (*Economist* 2003).

Like Boot and Ignatieff, most commentators who urge empire also call for an honest acknowledgment of the reality of empire. Andrew Bacevich ends his long analysis of recent U.S. foreign policy by clarifying that "the question that urgently demands attention—the question that Americans can no longer afford to dodge—is not whether the United States has become an imperial power. The question is what sort of empire they intend theirs to be" (Bacevich 2002, 244). In general, the question of what sort of empire the United States is (and has been) is presumed rather than debated—the "benevolence" of a "reluctant" U.S. imperialism is taken for granted. G. John Ikenberry, professor of geopolitics and global justice at Georgetown University and a regular contributor to *Foreign Affairs*, describing the fashioning of a unipolar world out of the Bush administration's National Security Strategy (NSS), clarifies that "America's imperial goals and modus operandi are much more limited and benign than were those of age-old emperors" (Ikenberry 2002, 59). In a section titled "Manifest Destiny," Sebastian Mallaby finds empire to be accidental, thrust upon benign but "reluctant imperialists":

> Empires are not always planned. The original American colonies began as the unintended byproduct of British religious strife. The British political class was not so sure it wanted to rule India, but commercial interests dragged it in there anyway. The United States today will be an even more reluctant imperialist. But a new imperial moment has arrived, and by virtue of its power America is bound to play the leading role. The question is not whether the United States will seek to fill the void created by the demise of European empires but whether it will acknowledge that this is what it is doing. Only if Washington acknowledges this task, will its response be coherent.
>
> (Mallaby 2002) [8]

The extent to which the imperialist project is setting the terms of debate is apparent in the writings of even those who caution against imperialist overreach. While some empire-mongers such as Niall Fergusson are clearly strident and hawkish, others might be called more "pragmatic imperialists." Justifying the U.S. war against Iraq, but critiquing the financially and diplomatically expensive U.S. efforts at nation building in Iraq, Dimitri Simes argues that a justifiably expansionist U.S. foreign policy that had in fact been inaugurated with Clinton's administration has since September 11 been put onto the track of "dangerous imperial overreach." Making a case for empire by more pragmatic means, Simes argues:

> A new approach is badly needed, one that exercises power in a determined yet realistic and responsible way—keeping a close eye on American interests and values—but is not bashful about U.S. global supremacy. Only then will the United States be able to take maximum advantage of its power, without being bogged down in expensive and dangerous secondary pursuits that diminish its ability to lead.
>
> (Simes 2003)

Similar caution is advised by John Ikenberry, who also warns of "imperial overstretch" with a "hard-line imperial grand strategy" (Ikenberry 2002, 57–59). More "centrist figures" such as Joseph Nye and John Ikenberry, clearly uncomfortable with the unfashionable designations of "empire" and "imperial," advocate the United States' use of "soft power" and "multilateralism" to establish a more benevolent and legitimate world order (Falk 2003, 24). Indeed, Joseph Nye, professor of international relations and dean of the Kennedy School of Government at Harvard University, in his apology for U.S. imperialism recommends the cunning use of "soft power" and multilateral institutions such as the United Nations (UN) in order to secure legitimacy for U.S. hegemony, so that "others see the American preponderance the [National Security] strategy proclaims as benign" and to "reduce the prominence of the United States as a target for anti-imperialists" (Nye 2003, 69–72; see also Ikenberry 2002). In a similar vein, recognizing that building empire will be "expensive, difficult and potentially dangerous," Sebastian Mallaby argues on pragmatic grounds that a multilateral approach to empire building undertaken through international institutions would be more "legitimate" and hence more successful, and suggests actual mechanisms for "institutionalizing this mix of U.S. leadership and international legitimacy," which include bodies that "would assemble nation-building muscle and expertise and could be deployed wherever its American-led board decided" (Mallaby 2002). Discussing the NSS of the Bush administration in approving terms, the international relations theorist John Lewis Gaddis points to the many "cracks" that need attending to if the United States is to impose its vision upon the world (Gaddis 2002). All of these pragmatic imperialists, many of whom, such as Nye, Ikenberry, and Gaddis, are self-identified "liberal" international relations theorists, endorse U.S. hegemony while eschewing the terms "empire" and "imperialism." They take U.S. imperialism's benevolence for granted and provide recipes to make it more effective. The consensus on what role the United States should play in the world is indeed quite wide. What does this U.S. imperial vision and reality look like?

2.   The Instantiation of an Imperial Project

"We don't seek an empire," says President Bush, "We're not imperialistic," says Donald Rumsfeld (*Economist* 2003, 20), yet the foreign policy of the administration reveals in no uncertain terms the instantiation of an imperial project.[9] First, it is important to remember the material edifice of U.S. imperial power. The United States devotes more resources to its military budget than the next fifteen countries combined and possesses a huge nuclear arsenal that includes more than 8,000 strategic nuclear weapons and 22,000 tactical ones even as this administration inaugurates the development of new lines of more usable nuclear weapons. There are over 500,000 U.S. troops stationed at over 395 major bases and hundreds of minor installations in thirty-five foreign countries, and the United States has been expanding its ring of military bases (to central Asia most recently). The United States is the only country in the world to have what might be called a "global navy," with a naval strike force greater in total tonnage and firepower than that of all the other navies of the world combined, consisting of missile cruisers, nuclear submarines, nuclear aircraft carriers, and destroyers that sail every ocean and make port in every continent (Falk 2003; Parenti 2003).

Second, and more important, is the vision of the U.S. role in the world encapsulated in this administration's foreign policy practices and posture. Along with the appointment to positions of power in the Bush White House of some of the most hawkish Cold War voices, this administration's pre-9/11 approach to foreign policy reflected a strong unilateralist thrust that commenced with the cancellation of the ABM treaty and continued with the repudiation of the Kyoto Protocol on the emission of greenhouse gases, the renouncement of the treaty setting up the International Criminal Court, the rejection of the proposed enforcement and verification mechanism for the Biological and Toxin Weapons Convention, and so forth. That this unilateralist trend was going to involve a much more interventionist foreign policy was already apparent when after 9/11 the United States changed its focus from the al-Qaeda presence in Afghanistan to the "axis of evil" countries in George Bush's State of the Union address, even as the unilateralism itself was further reinforced in the negotiations leading up to the war on Iraq.

The most authoritative statement of the administration's strategic position was made in a June 2002 presidential address at West Point military academy, which portended the much more comprehensive NSS, released by the White House in September 2002. These documents lay out, in no uncertain terms, the imperial project that underlies the foreign policy posture of the Bush administration—yet drawing practically no coverage in the media and hardly any critical discussion[10]. It is clear, as John Lewis Gaddis points out, that the NSS outlines a "grand strategy"—one comparable with George Kennan's infamous Mr. X argument for the containment of the Soviet Union (published in *Foreign Affairs* in 1947) that had inaugurated another era. As Gaddis points out,

> What appears at first glance to be a lack of clarity about who's deterrable and who's not turns out, upon closer examination, to be a plan for transforming the entire Muslim Middle East: for bringing it, once and for all, into the modern world. There's been nothing like this in boldness, sweep, and vision since Americans took it upon themselves, more than half a century ago, to democratize Germany and Japan, thus setting in motion processes that stopped short of only a few places on earth, one of which was the Muslim Middle East.
>
> (Gaddis 2002, 55)[11]

What is new about the NSS is not that it commits the United States to global intervention or that it targets terrorists and rogue states, but "that it makes a long-building imperial tendency explicit and permanent" (Gitlin 2003).

Both the West Point speech and the NSS boldly and unambiguously identify the universality of liberal values ("people everywhere" want freedom and liberty, and "free markets and free trade" are the hallmarks of a free society) and chart out America's role in aggressively ("the best defense is a good offense" and this offense can be delivered with the help of America's enormous military power) bringing into being a liberal world order. The vision is ambitiously global, because the absence of freedom in even remote places such as Afghanistan threatens the United States and the rest of the world. The documents recognize a different post–September 11 world in which the Cold War strategies of deterrence and containment no longer work, and "preemptive war" to counter national-security threats is justified. While the NSS states a preference for acting multilaterally (with NATO as the prime example of multilateral cooperation), it makes clear that the United States will "not hesitate to act alone," even though it tempers such aggression with a moralistic tone that speaks of America's "responsibility," "obligation," and "duty." The NSS envisions an American global military hegemony and makes it clear that "our forces will be strong enough to dissuade potential adversaries from pursuing a military build-up in hopes of surpassing, or equaling, the power of the United States." Lacking subtlety or humility, the NSS envisions a "utopia" in which the United States is the unrivaled and unquestioned global hegemon, but preferably with international legitimacy.

3. Empire-mongers as the "Neoidealists"

The entry of empire and imperialism into the ambit of the acceptable, even fashionable, vocabulary of political commentary has revived an old, defunct international relations debate, albeit in a somewhat new manner. The dominance of political realists within the Anglo-European disciplinary boundaries of post–World War II International Relations had seemingly brought closure on the "Idealism vs. Realism" tension—previously identified as the first great International Relations debate—with the idealism of the League of Nations and global bazaar enthusiasts yielding to the cold, hard, all-too-realist(ic) strategic calculations of the bipolar Cold War. But the neoconservative zeal, expressed in the rhetoric of the writers identified above and embodied in the NSS, has now been widely termed as a kind of Wilsonian "revolutionary idealism"—almost "utopian" in its vision (Packer 2003). Gaddis spells it out in no uncertain terms: "There is compellingly realistic reason now to complete the idealistic task Woodrow Wilson began more than eight decades ago: the world must be made safe for democracy, because otherwise democracy will not be safe in the world" (Gaddis 2002, 56). Indeed, Falk argues, the "idealism" of the "benevolent empire" school (among whom he includes the "benign imperialists" of the "democratic peace theory" school) that surfaced in the 1990s, which claimed American "moral exceptionalism" and projected the United States as the best vehicle for the spread of democracy and humanitarian interventions, has been incorporated into "the refashioning of the imperial project by the Bush leadership," thus making it possible for the United States to disavow any self-aggrandizing goals (such as oil acquisition) and project humanitarian ends (freedom and democracy) even as it pursues an aggressive military strategy in Afghanistan and Iraq (Falk 2003, 28–29).[12] If the peace movement offers us a different kind of idealism, it is important to remember that it is these "neoidealists" that the movement needs to contend with.

That the "benevolent imperialists," a.k.a. "neoidealists," span the political spectrum has created some of the most interesting bedfellows in the current political landscape. Packer points to a provocative article by David Brooks, senior editor of the conservative journal the *Weekly Standard,* that divides up the post–Cold War political landscape into "progressives," who view foreign policy in moralistic terms and advocate U.S. interventionism, and "conservatives," who are more skeptical about such an American role—thus scrambling accepted understandings of those categories (Packer 2003). That Michael

Ignatieff, Joseph Nye, and William Kristol stand united in their for-eign-policy prescriptions for the United States indicates how much the "liberal imperialist" consensus has narrowed the field of political debate. Packer is correct to point out that "the temperamental differ-ence between idealists and realists is more significant for the moment than the ideological difference between left and right" (Packer 2003). As scholars and commentators from both the Right and the Left urge U.S. imperialism, even if for different reasons, the "new realists" are those who urge caution and restraint and warn of imperial overreach. As Nye points out, while agreed on the larger goals, the tug of war now is between the neoconservative "Wilsonians of the right" and the "Jacksonian unilateralists" (the former with more appetite for long-term nation building than the latter) on the one hand and the more multilateral and cautious "traditional realists" on the other (Nye 2003, 63–64).

That many of the latter are "pragmatic imperialists" (as indicated above) rather than "anti-imperialists" would seem to indicate that the mainstream political field has been considerably narrowed. Yet what it suggests, I believe, is that the parameters of the idealism versus realism debate in international relations were always narrower than what was generally appreciated by international relations schol-ars and rested on unexamined problematic presumptions, a theme to which I will return when discussing the idealistic terms on which the current peace movement is positioning its opposition to the occupa-tion of Iraq. The general framing of the "Idealism vs. Realism" debate as one between "principles" and "power" missed how much questions of "order" were privileged over questions of "justice" in that debate. However, Gaddis, who is approving of this idealistic neoimperialist U.S. role, understands clearly (but not critically) that what makes the Bush administration's foreign policy so thoroughly Wilsonian is that it finds no contradiction between power and principles (Gaddis 2002, 54). Indeed, the extent to which the visions of "liberal idealists" have been thoroughly invested in power (and premised on certain ontological divisions, such as that between a "liberal West" and a "backward East") is evidenced in the emer-gence, with vengeance, of this new school of "liberal imperialists." The rhetorical force of empire is carried by this new idealism; it imbues empire with an ethical promise and makes it a moral project, an ethic and morality that I argue the contemporary peace movement is ill-equipped to confront with its own impoverished kind of idealism.

Patriotism and the Peace Movement

From the despair and frustrations of many with the U.S. preparations for a military strike against Iraq arose a great hope in the form of a peace movement with a truly global outreach. Saturday, February 15, 2003, was arguably the largest single day of protest in world history with events ranging from rallies drawing a few hundred protesters to mass demonstrations by more than a million people staged in over 300 cities around the globe, all voicing their opposition to the impending war in Iraq. There were some estimates of 10–13 million people marching all over the world. In many places, the protests matched or surpassed the scope of the antiglobalization demonstrations in recent years, and in other places, they rivaled or exceeded the antinuclear protests of the early 1980s and the Vietnam War protests of the 1960s and '70s. It is difficult not to see this as a historic, global uprising for peace.

Western European governments that supported the war saw the biggest turnouts. In London, crowds estimated at 1 million or more turned out to protest Tony Blair's enthusiastic support of war. Crowds estimated at more than a million gathered in Rome to oppose Silvio Berlusconi's government's support of the war despite polls showing Italian opposition at nearly 70 percent, and over a million marched in Barcelona and Madrid to oppose Jose Aznar's support of the war. European states that had been highly critical of the Bush administration and firmly opposed war (such as France) saw relatively smaller demonstrations, although an estimated 600,000 people, including half a million in Berlin, still marched in Germany. In addition to other European cities such as Amsterdam and Copenhagen, large groups of protesters also came out in Hong Kong, Bangkok, Canberra, Havana, Buenos Aires, Johannesburg, Cairo, Damascus, Beirut, Algiers, and so forth.

In some of these protests, U.S. flags were burned, while in others, such as those in Ramallah, in the West Bank, protesters chanted anti-U.S. and anti-Israeli slogans and also showed solidarity with the Iraqi people. Many of the protests outside the United States had an anti-American flavor. But many displayed flags that pledged allegiance to a more global idea— the flag of Palestine, the UN banner, Italy's rainbow peace flag. In an effort to demonstrate its global character, Schell points out that on the brink of war, no public except the Israeli one (and one might add the U.S. one) supported war without a UN mandate, and that public opinion polls showed that in most countries opposition to war was closer to unanimity than simple majority. In a rare show of functioning representative democracy, most governments expressed their public's sentiments in opposing the war. Newspapers around the world opposed the war and condemned U.S. actions (Schell 2003). Indeed, governments of many poorer states dependent on U.S. investment, such as Vietnam and Nigeria, were unafraid to unequivocally condemn the war.

Although on a scale much smaller than the large European demonstrations, February 15 also saw the largest display of U.S. public opposition to the war. In New York, many more than the estimated 100,000 people turned out to fill the streets, and other large cities like San Francisco also drew large crowds.[13] In addition, rallies were scheduled in about 150 cities in the United States. American protesters also conducted a "virtual march" by swamping Senate and White House telephones, switchboards, fax machines, and e-mail inboxes with thousands of messages.[14]

On March 16, the eve of the invasion of Iraq, candlelight vigils were held all over the United States as well as in many cities and towns in other parts of the world.[15] Large demonstrations occurred in many European cities and some U.S. cities on the first few days of American and British strikes on Iraq, and violent protests occurred throughout the Middle East at around the same time. But after the war started, the protests gradually tapered off, although the first anniversary of the U.S.-led invasion of Iraq saw a new spate of demonstrations around the world, including an estimated 30,000–40,000 people who turned up in New York and an estimated 50,000 in San Francisco. After the war, antiwar protesters in the United States were often confronted by "support the troops" groups. Indeed, there were many large prowar rallies after the start of the war.[16]

Like the spectacle of the military attack against Iraq, which made full use of technology, the peace movement had also become fairly adept at the cunning use of media technology, particularly the Internet. Demonstrating the grassroots and global organizing power of the Internet, groups like United for Peace and Justice (UFPJ) and MoveOn.org were able to bring together both well-funded advocacy groups and resource-poor grassroots groups under one umbrella, bypass corporate-controlled media, and reach certain portions of the disaffected American public. Andrew Boyd notes the "sign of activists' growing confidence, post–February 15, in the potentially explosive convergence of common global concerns and the wide reach of the Net" (Boyd 2003, 13).

It is this peace movement that, in the heady days immediately before and after the war, the New York Times called "the other superpower" and Jonathan Schell calls a "world in resistance" (Schell 2003, 11). Yet while modern communications technology made possible the synchronization of simultaneous protests around the world, particular movements in particular places emerged out of very specific national conditions. Examining the very different motivations against the war in Turkey, Palestine, and Greece, Barbara Misztal argues that the perception of "global consensus" was largely a "mirage," the different protests being motivated by different national problems, attitudes, and conditions (Misztal 2003). In the United States, the conditions in which the peace movement arose were a context of hyperpatriotism.

1. The Emergence of Hyperpatriotism

> Observers of American life have seen a silver lining in the dark clouds that billowed from the Twin Towers and the Pentagon on September 11, 2001. Along with the horror wrought by the terrorist attacks came an outpouring of solidarity and patriotism—a sudden change of heart for many Americans who, prior to that fateful day, had seemed to be drifting inexorably toward individualism, self-absorption, and cynical disinterest in public affairs . . . People reached out to family members, neighbors, and friends, while proudly declaring their membership in the American national community.
>
> (Skocpol 2002, 537)

In the words of Benedict Anderson, the nation has to be "imagined." Nations are imagined "because the members of even the smallest nation will never know most of their fellow-members, meet them, or even hear of them, yet in the minds of each lives the image of their communion" (Anderson 1983, 13). Anderson traces the development of nationalism to the development of print-capitalism, which helped to produce and disseminate a common culture to ground the national imagination. But as many scholars have pointed out, the production of the nation is always an ongoing, unfinished, and contested task. Roberta Coles regards the rhetoric of the administration and that of the peace movement during the Persian Gulf crisis of 1990–91 as contestations of "what America is and what it means to be an American" (Coles 2002, 587). Pointing to the taken-for-granted character of national identity, she identifies times of international conflict or war as moments when the banality of national identity is disturbed, calling forth different nationalist discourses. One of the most salient effects of the nationalist discourses emanating after the "national tragedy" of September 11, 2001, was the production of a certain kind of "America."

The U.S. flag became a particularly powerful symbol of allegiance to the nation. In the aftermath of September 11, more than four-fifths of Americans displayed the U.S. flag on homes, cars and trucks, and clothing (Skocpol 2002). By late September, there was a run on flags at Wal-Marts across the country.[17] Indeed, one of the most interesting aspects of the production of America in this moment was its imbrication with the project of advanced capitalism, giving rise to what former labor secretary Robert Reich termed "market patriotism." The September 11 attacks gave rise to "a new and rarely seen type of political advertising, the attempt by corporations to take advantage of the patriotic mood of the country to associate their own corporate interests with the United States government and its people" (Connolly-Ahern and Kaid 2002, 96). This kind of "corporate advocacy advertising" was engaged in by both corporations directly affected by the attacks, such as United Airlines and the United States Postal Service[18], as well as corporations that had not witnessed any direct impacts, such as Anheuser-Busch and General Motors. These ads, adorned in the colors of the U.S. flag, used the opportunity to push their products by exhorting consumers to "preserve the American way of life" in light of attempts to destroy it (Connolly-Ahern and Kaid 2002)[19]. In a similar vein, the National Restaurant Association was exhorting Americans "to turn the tables by eating out," since "restaurants are a part of who we are as Americans" (Piore 2001, 59), and the Travel Industry Association of America estimated that two-thirds of Americans saw the president in a television advertisement calling on people to express their "courage" by traveling (Skocpol 2002). Indeed, the president repeatedly called on Americans to do their patriotic duty by shopping. When domestic wheat growers objected to the buying of Asian wheat to divert toward the war in Afghanistan, Congress convinced them to take "the patriotic long term view" (Kaufman 2001). In addition, this patriotic capitalism led to the inauguration of new lines of products ranging from the more generic red, white, and blue Christmas lights and decorations and God Bless America signs to a "flag-clothing explosion," which included flag-themed prom and wedding dresses, disposable diapers, and tongue studs (Whiteside 2002)![20] Bookstores saw new lines of children's books celebrating the United States. For Halloween, there were reports of costume store runs on police officer, firefighter, Uncle Sam, and Statue of Liberty costumes. Sales of G.I. Joe action figures were boosted by post-9/11 patriotism and the military buildup after that (Brown 2003).

It is this context of the enormous rallying around the national tragedy of September 11 that gave rise to what has been both cele-brated and condemned as "The New Patriotism." Robert Putnam, who had chronicled and lamented the decline of civic associations in contemporary American society in his widely popular *Bowling Alone: The Collapse and Revival of American Community,* found that in the aftermath of September 11, Americans are now "bowling together." They are not just trusting the government and the police more, but also becoming more interested in politics, attending more political meetings, and working together more on community projects. Even more importantly, Americans trust each other more, from neighbors to strangers, across ethnic and social divisions, so that " . . . we have a more capacious sense of 'we' than we have had in the adult experi-ence of most Americans now alive. The images of shared suffering that followed the terrorist attacks on New York and Washington suggested a powerful idea of cross-class, cross-ethnic solidarity" (Putnam 2002).[21] It is this newfound sense of community that President George W. Bush invoked in his 2002 State of the Union address: "None of us would ever wish the evil that was done on September the 11. Yet, after America was attacked, it was as if our entire country looked into a mirror and saw our better selves. We were reminded that we are citi-zens, with obligations to each other, to our country, and to history. We began to think less of the goods we can accumulate, and more about the good we can do" (Burke 2002).[22]

While many commentators have remarked on how the war on terror and in Iraq distracts from domestic politics (in particular the economic recession), it might be as important to note that these ren-derings of community and unity in the face of "national" crisis builds the kind of horizontal solidarity that detracts from the many forms of vertical asymmetries (accentuated even more with the economic and social policies of this administration) that plague the national space. The imagined nations, as Anderson points out, present themselves as "communities" "because regardless of the actual inequality and exploitation that may prevail in each, the nation is always conceived as a deep, horizontal comradeship" (Anderson 1983, 16). President Bush's approval ratings reached "unprecedented heights" after the September 11 attacks and remained very high for a very long time thereafter: the current rally being "remarkable, even when set against the whole history of presidential approval" (Gaines 2002, 531).

Indeed, while U.S. charities promising to help the victims of the 9/11 attacks were inundated with funds, charities that regularly help the poor such as food banks and other local agencies were starved for resources as donors shifted their priorities (Skocpol 2002).

Along with celebrations of community, this resurgence of patriotism led to many kinds of repressions occurring at many different levels of the state and society. At the top, the suppression of free speech has sometimes taken directly coercive forms, most pointedly in the expanded powers of the infamously titled USA PATRIOT Act to spy, interrogate, and detain, as well as in the use of barricades, designated "protest zones," and force to control expression in public areas. But the "patriotic vigilantism" that has emerged throughout U.S. society owes itself more to the discourse emanating from the administration. The binary "either you are with us or you are with the terrorists" rhetoric that came from many political leaders in the aftermath of September 11 set certain limits on acceptable speech and conduct, especially when combined with then White House spokesperson Ari Fleischer's comment to the American public to "watch what they say." For those protesting such suppression of free speech, Attorney General John Ashcroft had these harsh words: "To those who scare peace-loving people with phantoms of lost liberty, my message is this: Your tactics only aid terrorists." As Anthony Romero, executive director of the ACLU, points out, these kinds of remarks from the government's top leaders have granted ordinary people the license "to shut down alternative views."

The discourse emanating from governmental channels has been joined by the output from a jingoistic media, especially the widely disseminated, but more and more centralized and tightly controlled broadcast media. Fox network's Bill O'Reilly labeled the progressive *Los Angeles Times* and *The Nation* columnist Robert Scheer a "traitor," and defense adviser Richard Perle called the investigative reporter Seymour Hersh "the closest thing American journalism has to a terrorist"(Solomon 2003). Military experts questioning the planning for the war on Iraq were criticized for endangering troops in the field, with Joint Chiefs of Staff Richard Myers even publicly questioning their "agenda" (Solomon 2003). Scholars were branded as "traitor professors" on a television talk show (Foner 2003).

Patriotic vigilantism has permeated many aspects of society, and ingrained itself in ordinary peoples' daily lives. Universities and colleges around the country have witnessed various kinds of limitations. Middle East studies scholars have been scrutinized for their positions on the Iraq war and on the Israeli-Palestinian issue. An aggressive, highly organized campaign led by the newly founded organization "Campus Watch" has conducted virtual witch-hunts, posting "dossiers" on individual professors and branding them as "apologists for Palestinian and Islamist violence"(Solomon 2003).[23] ACLU affiliates around the country reported cases of students being punished for expressing antiwar views (Solomon 2003). Local authorities and "private patriots" have felt free to shut down any expressions of dissent, from the arrest of a man wearing a "Peace on Earth" T-shirt in an upstate New York mall to country music fans crushing Dixie Chicks CDs because the lead singer said she was ashamed of the president[24] (Solomon 2003). It is this patriotic context within which the U.S. peace movement emerged.

2. The Terms of Opposition

> ... Many commentators, both in and out of the government, seem to view freedom of expression as at best an inconvenience and at worst unpatriotic. The incessant attacks on dissenters as traitors are intended to create an atmosphere of shock and awe within the United States, so that those tempted to speak their mind become too intimidated to do so.
>
> (Foner 2003, 13)

The patriotic context created in the aftermath of September 11 narrowed the space for the expression of dissent. With Democrats assuring the president, in the words of the ranking Democrat on the House International Relations Committee, Tom Lantos, of "solid, unanimous support" in the war on terrorism, it is unsurprising that any official opposition to the war would occur within fairly limited parameters (Solomon 2003). In a context in which a mild comment made by Tom Daschle on the president's failure to find a diplomatic solution to the Iraqi crisis elicited not just right-wing talk-radio vitriol (from Rush Limbaugh for example), but also a statement from House Speaker Dennis Hastert hinting that Daschle came "mightly close" to giving "comfort" to the enemy, it is unsurprising that the dubious connection of the war against Iraq to the war on terrorism went uninterrogated by politicians of both parties (Solomon 2003).

But more surprising was the prevalence of patriotic discourse in the unofficial opposition—that is, the peace movement.[25] The widespread use of the flag was often combined with renditions of "America the Beautiful" to interpellate protestors as "Americans."[26] A critic of

Bush's foreign policy and firmly opposed to the war on Iraq, Todd Gitlin called on "post-Vietnam liberals" to free themselves of their "60's flag anxiety and . . . reflexive negativity" and "embrace a liberal patriotism that is unapologetic and uncowed (Gitlin 2002). Indeed, protestors, in an attempt to both reject the right-wing definition of patriotism and to appropriate it for their own purposes, portrayed themselves as the "true patriots."

The peace movement either responded to or appropriated the patriotic impulse generated in the wake of 9/11 by using at least four strategies. The first strategy, an attempt to distance itself from the label of "Saddam lovers," was to condemn Saddam Hussein at the same time as opposing the war against Iraq. Second, and after the war started, all opposition voices felt it necessary to combine their critique of the war with the assertion of "support[ing] the troops." The third strategy, which has also been used by previous peace movements, was to distinguish the "American government" from the "American people," claiming in effect to be the better representatives of the latter. Finally, the most commonly used strategy was the distinction made between American "ideals" and "practice," claiming an exemplary American past (America as essentially a land of liberty, freedom, and justice) based on certain founding myths of what "America truly is" and arguing that the practices of the current administration were in fact betraying those ideals.[27] This final strategy involved appropriating "the right to dissent" as an American ideal and hence as patriotic.

In itself the first strategy should have been unnecessary. The critiques of Saddam Hussein's regime are amply documented and well-known, and the opposition to Saddam Hussein's brutal dictatorship by human rights groups had been strongly voiced long before he ceased being an ally of the United States. Other than a few very isolated instances of "rallying around Hussein" in some parts of the world (more to make a provocative point than support him), peace movements around the world had not voiced any sympathy for the man or his regime. But that it was felt necessary by the U.S. peace movement to articulate such a clear opposition to Hussein was an indication of how politically charged and accusatory the climate in which this war was being opposed had become. It is the last three strategies that are particularly interesting for my purposes here. Each of these strategies is ridden with problems and based on certain untenable distinctions. Moreover, each of them is predicated on certain self–other constructions that are intrinsic to nationalist discourses, distinctions that are at the heart of the vision of empire the peace movement has attempted to critique.

3. When Are Americans Complicit?

It has been a common tactic of the peace movement to draw a distinction between the "American government," especially as it is embodied in the form of the Bush administration, and the "American people," and to argue either that the public is unaware of or generally unsupportive of U.S. foreign policies. Even otherwise unforgiving critics of U.S. foreign policy such as Edward Said, Noam Chomsky, and Arundhati Roy make this distinction between the public and the government quite regularly, thereby imbuing the American people with a quality of "goodness" or "innocence" while the government is projected as "militarist" and "evil." As Vinay Lal argues quite persuasively:

> While it may make sense to argue for an immense gulf between government and people in political regimes where representative democracy has been disavowed, what import can any such claim have about a country which has been peddling "free elections" to the rest of the world? And why, at a time when academic work has nearly sanctified the notion of people's agency, should Chomsky, Roy, and others be prepared to argue that Americans are led astray like sheep and that their fundamental goodness should not be doubted? What does it mean to rely effortlessly on such clichéd formulations when one is speaking of the most well-connected country in the world, where no one can plead ignorance? If the American people are not complicit in varying degrees with the policies carried out in their name by their representatives, how can we possibly explain that one poll after another has shown—in the recent war with Iraq as in previous exercises in US militaristic adventurism—extraordinarily high levels of support for the policies of successive American administrations.
>
> (Lal 2003, 139)

Unlike other countries in the world, the American public has been largely supportive of the war effort. Indeed, of all publics in the world, even among the "coalition of the willing," the American public has been the most willing of all. Criticism of both the current administration and the rationale for war was widely available, even if it sometimes required a little extra effort to bypass the mainstream media's jingoistic coverage, and American citizens, who are usually notorious for being disinterested in international affairs, have after all since 9/11 found a new interest in foreign policy. Most important, to refer to an unsullied and uncorrupted American public is to disavow the complicity of any public in a war initiated by its state, especially in a functioning and stable democracy[28]. To lay the entire responsibility for a war on a particular figure (such as Bush) or a cabal (such as the neoconservatives) is to ignore the complicity of Americans in enabling, in a variety of ways, the militarism and aggression that has made possible the campaign in Iraq.

"Supporting the troops" while opposing the war erases another kind of complicity, one that is presumably even more serious. It is true that people join the military for all sorts of reasons and that those in the combat zones in the Iraq war are disproportionately drawn from minority communities who have few other outlets for economic mobility. It is also true that there is a sense in which U.S. soldiers are just ordinary people perfoming their jobs. But simply "doing one's job" does not exempt one from the ethical criteria that attaches to any practice, and especially to a practice that involves the institutionalized taking of lives. It is revealing to interrogate the conflations implicit in the plea to "support the troops," whether that comes from those supporting or opposing the war.

At the most basic level, we are asked to identify American troops as both soldiers and as persons but to empathize with them first and foremost as persons. Of course, we must retain their status as soldiers in our understanding because to see them only as persons would be to regard them as engaged in murder. Nevertheless, we must also see them as persons since soldiers are also persons with families, from families, with specific biographies. The state first tries to eliminate these biographies via the considerable investment of time and resources it expends in basic training, and it then re-presents them to a voracious public through extravagant media spectacles. Re-presenting their biographies humanizes them, vivifying soldiers from the abstractions of war making. But the nationalist script through which soldiers are humanized as particular persons —the signifier "troops" increasingly helping to conflate soldiers and persons—invites us to identify them as that part of "us" (read American) that is willing to do "our" dirty work of killing "them." In short, we are asked to accept that as extensions of the state, "our" soldiers are killing in order to execute foreign policy but then to see the person within that shell called soldier as an extension of our own specificity (which is articulated in the idiom of the nation). At the same time, we are asked to ignore this same maneuver for the Iraqis so that their soldiers, rather than also being persons, remain mere empty shells of the Iraqi state. "Support our troops" then not only dehumanizes others (both "their troops" and those killed by "our troops"), it also humanizes our soldiers so that killing by them is not murder but a necessary duty they perform on "our" behalf. Moreover, it humanizes them by inscribing their sameness to "us" and their/our difference from "others."

To oppose a war while supporting those carrying out the war, especially in the context of a voluntary army where "conscientious objection" is a difficult, but real, possibility, leaves no room for attaching moral responsibility to the actions of those most directly participating in the practice of war. But in the post–September 11 political climate, "opposing the troops" was considered far too unpatriotic. Assistant professor of anthropology at Columbia University Nicholas de Genova's attempt in a teach-in to "contest . . . the notion that an effective strategy for the antiwar movement is to capitulate to the patriotic pro-war pressure that demands that one must affirm support for the troops" (as he stated in his interview in the *Chronicle of Higher Education*) was met by so many death threats that he had to move out of his home and teach under the protection of security guards (Solomon 2003).[29]

4. *American Idealism Inscribes American Exceptionalism*

It was also common for the peace movement to draw on certain foundational myths about America's exemplary past to make the case that the drive toward war was a betrayal of the ideals of the nation, and in that sense "un-American." Along with the tendency to invoke "America's age-old traditions" of "freedom," "liberty," and "justice," it was also common to claim dissent as patriotic. In general, the contradictory impulses of expressing dissent and suppressing it have characterized every significant war in American history, including the American Revolution, the Mexican-American War, the Civil War, World Wars I and II, the "hot" wars of the "cold war" (including the Vietnam War), and the first Gulf War. But even those who otherwise recognized the historical repression of dissent in the United States found it unproblematic to say that "to dissent is to be American."[30] Eric Foner recognizes that "an equally powerful American tradition has been the effort by government and private 'patriots' to suppress free expression in times of crisis," but still claims that "few traditions

are more American than freedom of speech and the right to dissent".
(Foner 2003, 13) But if dissent has historically been as "American" as
the suppression of dissent, then to claim "the right to dissent" as an
"American right" (rather than a fundamental "democratic right") is
to distort the many contradictory impulses of American democratic
history by laying recourse to an essentialist conception of the nation.[31]

Similarly, to claim American traditions of "freedom," "liberty,"
and "justice" is to forget the long history of U.S. military aggression
and foreign intervention. Indeed, many of these interventions, as
in the case of Iraq, have occurred in the name of "freedom" and
"liberty," even as they have subverted democracies and quashed liberties in a routine fashion. The "manifest destiny" phase of nineteenth-
century American expansionism gave way to the Spanish-American
War of 1898 that brought Cuba, Puerto Rico, Guam, and the
Philippines into the U.S. ambit. This expansionist impulse continued
with amendments to the Monroe Doctrine that proclaimed the United
States's right to intervene anywhere in Latin America. World War II
saw the formal occupation of Germany and Japan, but also, and much
more widely, coercive interventions in many states during the Cold
War in the name of anticommunism. This latter has included U.S. support of right-wing dictatorships in Turkey, Indonesia, the Philippines,
Argentina, Guatemala, Iran, Iraq, Zaire, and so forth; assistance to
counterrevolutionary groups in leftist countries— including UNITA in
Angola, RENAMO in Mozambique, the Contras in Nicaragua, and
the mujahideen (later to become the Taliban in Afghanistan); and
covert actions or proxy wars in many other countries as well.
Democratically elected reforming governments have been overthrown
by military forces aided by the United States, for example, in
Guatemala, Chile, Argentina, Greece, and the Congo. Since World
War II, the United States has undertaken military actions in Vietnam,
Laos, Cambodia, North Korea, Lebanon, Grenada, Panama, Libya,
Afghanistan, and now, most recently, Iraq. Again, that long and troubled history might indicate that the ideals of "justice" are as American
as are the ideals of "genocide" and "militarism". To claim the former
as essentially American is to reflect a troubling amnesia with respect
to the latter.

Claiming an exemplary American past or ideal in general leads to a
form of "American exceptionalism" that can be disabling as a form of
effective critique since it conceals and renders unproblematic a complicated history and politics. It is precisely this kind of uncomplicated,
unnuanced American exceptionalism that the administration taps into

to make empire appealing to the American public.[32] As Rhodes points out, the attempt of the West Point speech and the NSS is

> to tap into the deep liberal vein running through American history and the American psyche. In the first place, he [George Bush] appeals to American beliefs that there is, and always has been, something special about America's role in the world. For America, interests and values are not in tension: what is good for America is also good for the world, and making the world safe for America will make the world a better place. Second, he appeals to Americans' liberal faith in progress.
>
> (Rhodes 2003, 138)

But for Rhodes, the aggressive, unilateralist, universalist (i.e., "imperial,") vision of the NSS is in tension with the "liberal" desire to create "democratic, rather than autocratic or totalitarian governance" in Bush's foreign policy (Rhodes 2003, 137). This tension between the liberal-democratic vision and imperialism is taken for granted by all opposition voices that claim America's exceptional liberal values to offer their critique of the case for war against Iraq. It is this that makes it possible for the *Economist,* worrying about the long-term consequences of the occupation of Iraq, to argue that "imperialism and democracy are at odds with each other," and as people protest the imposition of power, even in its benevolent forms, the ensuing pain will be felt by Americans, not just in terms of budget deficits or war casualties, but as "a blow to the very heart of what makes them American—their constitutional belief in freedom. *Freedom is in their blood;* it is integral to their sense of themselves. It binds them together as nothing else does, neither ethnicity, nor religion, nor language. And it is rooted in hostility to imperialism" (*Economist* 2003, 21; my emphasis).

Yet historically, liberalism and imperialism have never quite been at odds, in America or elsewhere. Indeed, as Uday Mehta convincingly shows, imperialism (in its British form, in his analysis), far from contradicting liberal principles or reflecting an unfinished chapter in the story of liberalism, is a constitutive part of it (Mehta 1999). The unabashed celebrations of liberalism's universality have always depended on liberalism's "other" for sustenance. Currently, and in the context of U.S. policy in Iraq, that "other" on the world stage is Iraq. To celebrate an "American exceptionalism" that claims freedom, liberty, justice, or democracy as fundamentally American is to misunderstand the nature of this constitutive relationship. Indeed, that so many advocates of imperialism are crawling out of the woodwork, from all over the political spectrum, is evidence of how close to the surface of liberalism the ghosts of imperialism have stalked. As the previous section demonstrates, many of the advocates of imperialism are indeed "liberal idealists" and their idealism is not tainted, but *constituted,* by their imperial imaginings.

The *Economist* concludes its rosy celebration of American liberalism on the note that "Empire is simply not the American way" (*Economist* 2003, 21). Yet if one was to take seriously the long history of American expansionism and the wide currency of the imperialist vision currently being formulated, one would be hard pressed not to say that empire is as much the American way as is democracy. The neoconservatives have been called both "democratic imperialists" and "imperialistic democrats"—what we cannot call them is "un-American."

The Limits of Patriotic Resistance to Global Empire

Studying the peace movement during the first Persian Gulf crisis, Roberta Cole (2002) found that the Military Families Support Network (MFSN)—one of the two peace organizations she studied—was unusual among peace movements in that it characterized itself as patriotic. Cole attributes the peace movement's generally uninviting constructions of national identity as partially responsible for its failure to appeal to the general public. Using a Gramscian analysis of resistance, Cole goes on to argue that "the peace movement may need to co-opt some of the elements of dominant discourse so that it resonates with the larger public and offers them a national identity that unites them as Americans, calls them to collaborate in virtue, yet redefines the virtue."[33] As necessary as it is for any social movement to appeal to a broad-based constituency, there are also serious risks in coopting elements of the dominant discourse, especially in a time of "crisis." Which elements and how they are co-opted matters a great deal for what kind of opposition is ultimately possible. Focusing on the national controversy over the Wisconsin School Board's decision to not require students to recite the pledge of allegiance or play the national anthem in the patriotic post–September 11 context, and the subsequent labeling of supporters of the decision as unpatriotic some of whom were even threatened, Michael Apple notes: "The populist notes being struck here are crucial, since hegemonic alliances can only succeed when they connect with the elements of 'good sense' of the people," pointing out that along with the populist and social democratic impulses that have marked a large part of Wisconsin history, there also exists "an authoritarian populism" that comes to the fore in times of crisis (Apple 2002, 304–305). Even if the patriotic posturing of the peace movement was a strategic maneuver to resonate with the common sense of ordinary people, that it occurred in a hypernationalistic context has meant that the "authoritarian populism" of the current climate has circumscribed the terms on which it could offer its opposition[34]. Why does "patriotism" appeal and what possibilities does it foreclose?

The call to patriotism resonates partly because it is largely understood as a positive valuation, a celebration of community, rather than a form of "othering." "What the rest of the world understands as 'nationalism' is recast in America as 'patriotism,' and perhaps not accidentally: love of the idea of America must supercede love of the nation-state, even if nowhere else do the flags and yellow ribbons come out as quickly as they do in America" (Lal 2003, 143). As Lal points out, while nationalism can evoke negative connotations, "patriotism engenders a more politically satisfying idea of transcendence: thus, the evils perpetrated in the name of the American nation-state can ultimately be overlooked on the assumption that they do not violate the core idea of America as the repository of social and cultural goods" (Lal 2003, 143). Indeed, Minxin Pei finds it paradoxical that a highly nationalist American society does not see itself as nationalist. Pei attributes this to the kind of prevalent nationalism in the United States—an American nationalism "defined not by notions of ethnic superiority, but by a belief in the supremacy of U.S. democratic ideals"—so that while Americans see themselves as "patriotic," defining patriotism as "allegiance to one's country," they do not see themselves as "nationalistic," defining that as "sentiments of ethno-national superiority" (Pei 2003).[35] While the distinction between the two forms of nationalism is important for some purposes, it might also conceal how civic nationalisms, to the extent that they become premised on certain moral absolutes (as they do in the forms of American exceptionalisms identified above), function much like ethnic nationalisms. And any call for community predicated on "moral absolutes," as nationalism/patriotism is prone to do, is othering in its effects and has grave political consequences.

"Patriotic pride," Martha Nussbaum is correct to point out, is "morally dangerous" (Nussbaum 1994). All forms of nationalism, and certainly the forms that are premised on some version of American exceptionalism, are predicated on certain self–other distinctions. In a very fundamental and constitutive sense, it is this "self–other" logic that makes it so easy to invoke, rationalize, and build empire, and all in the name of liberal values. Whether in its negative form to mark the distance of the self from the other, or in its positive form to cohere the self around certain fundamental values, nationalism and ethnocentric particularism are closely intertwined. It is the kind of othering that is etched deep into the soul of American exceptionalism that makes it so easy to invoke American freedoms in the service of empire, and that makes it so dangerous to invoke that idealism in the opposition to it. The perhaps unintended consequence of speaking to patriotic pride by claiming American exceptionalism is to awaken yet another kind of common sense about the "American self," and in this particular historic moment, the "Islamic other."

"The war on terror," argues Mark Salter, "represents a rearticulation of an American 'civilizing' mission," a rearticulation that accepts the logic of Samuel Huntington's "clash of civilizations" thesis as it wages war on Islamic civilization/barbarism even as the Bush administration goes to considerable effort to publicly repudiate the thesis (Salter 2003, 116). Indeed, the civilizational logic of Huntington's arguments is useful and appealing because it taps into a very long history of Anglo-European constructions of the "Islamic other" (Said 1978; Kabbani 1986; Southern 1962). It is this "knowledge" of the barbaric, fanatical, evil Muslim (so readily translated into the images of Osama bin Laden and Saddam Hussein in the current context) that enabled colonialism and the building of nineteenth-century empires. For leaders like George Bush and Tony Blair, who rely heavily on polls and focus groups for every domestic initiative, it is only in the sphere of foreign policy that there are opportunities to draw on such colonialist imagery of self and other and "to project a self-image of purpose, mission and political clarity." This is because in addition to the already existing "common-sense" about non-European others, "the vast inequalities of power and lack of accountability involved in foreign interventions facilitate the expression of clear and strident ethical values, as opposed to the vagaries of compromise and political pragmatism inevitable in domestic policy" (Chandler 2003, 112). It is this unspoken, taken-for-granted civilizational logic that makes it possible for even liberals such as Joseph Nye to invoke America's vulnerability to the "barbarian threat" in order to make a case for U.S. hegemony, albeit one established through international cooperation using "soft power" (Nye 2002). Indeed, the Western/non-Western distinction has once again become fashionable in polite international relations conversations. Opposition to war that lays claim to essentialist nationalist categories also unwittingly reproduces such self–other binaries.[36]

Conclusion: A Peace Movement with a Global Ethic?

According to Schell, one of the similarities between the military campaign against Iraq and the campaign opposing war is that "both are global—the United States seeks to demonstrate its self-avowed aim of global military supremacy, and the peace movement is equally determined to reject this" (Schell 2003). But how can an oppositional movement that is predicated on nationalism and American exceptionalism mount an effective critique of empire and be truly "global" in a significant manner at this particular historical moment? Eager to appropriate patriotism from the political Right and appeal to people's common sense, the opposition to war has failed to develop the means to adequately respond to the global imaginary that is at the heart of the administration's foreign policy. What then would it mean to develop an oppositional ethic that does not rely on such distinctions? I would like to tentatively sketch out the contours of an oppositional movement that is predicated on a global ethic.

"We should regard our deliberations," Nussbaum argues, "as, first and foremost, deliberations about human problems of people in particular concrete situations, not problems growing out of a national identity that is altogether unlike that of others" (Nussbaum 1994, 4). It is certainly true that many social movements on the Left—such as those waged against class, race, and gender inequalities–in the United States have made use of nationalist rhetoric, making demands in the name of nationalist ideals (Kazin 2002). But in order to oppose empire, it seems imperative to move beyond the limited boundaries of a nationalist position, to create an ethic that can put the well-being of Iraqis as full and complete subjects prior to the need to reclaim American goodness. This requires the cultivation of a moral worldview in which the unjustness of the war is predicated on its consequences for Iraqis (and also Americans) as *human and concrete* subjects rather than on a betrayal of some essential American ideals. At the most basic level, it calls with utmost urgency for the development of a truly global ethic, the cultivation of a cosmopolitan consciousness, "a more international basis for political emotion and concern" (Nussbaum 1994, 3).

Indeed a discourse of freedom, democracy, justice, and human rights, without such a serious commitment to a global ethic, is meaningless to secure the full and complete dignity of all human subjects. In a sense, all of those terms are empty signifiers that can be marshaled by both pro- and antiwar advocates, as they were in the war against Iraq. In the name of "Operation Iraqi *Freedom*," it becomes possible to "kill innocent Iraqis" in order to "save innocent Iraqis." The logic of a nationalist ethic privileged over a global ethic makes it possible to violate the dignity of "others" in ways that would not be considered acceptable for the "self." In a context in which there is no mechanism to make the actions of the world's most powerful states accountable to the citizens of the poorer third-world states in which they feel free to intervene, it is not surprising that such violations have found ways to legitimize themselves through the language of "benign imperialism" (Chandler 2003).

In order to create a global, cosmopolitan consciousness and ethic, peace movements will also have to join together with global justice movements that have emerged with strong force in the form of antiglobalization voices. The ideological precepts of neoliberal globalization remain central to empire building, and while it is easy to focus on the more visible military face of aggression, political economy and security imperatives are always much more closely intertwined than international relations scholars are in general wont to admit. Lately, this connection between political economy and security has come to be acknowledged in the argument for developmental aid that has become fashionable in some liberal quarters on the grounds that poverty and underdevelopment are breeding grounds for terrorists and hence pose security risks—an argument once again premised on security to the "self" rather than justice for the "other." "The greatest struggle Americans face is not terrorism," says Henry Giroux, "but a struggle on behalf of justice, freedom, and democracy for all of the citizens of the globe (Giroux 2002, 341). Without prioritizing issues of justice over issues of order, oppositional voices are bound to remain ineffective in confronting empire.

The recent antiwar movement has been largely held together by its opposition to the war against Iraq, and even more so to the figure of Bush. But the motivations for empire are much larger and deeper than can be captured by a focus on a single leader or administration or a particular war, important as those are. What is striking about the current historic moment is the brashness with which empire is being resuscitated and established. But more important, this arrogance is made possible by deep-seated and unexamined prejudices about "others" on the global stage. Still, there is a way in which this naked justification and exercise of power also creates an opening, an opportunity, for a global, public, open dialogue—a reaching out from

America to the world (and vice versa) in the search for shared interests, understandings, and ethics. In that sense, an anti-imperialist strategy must at the very least be committed to a global ethic and to global justice. For the American peace movement, that would mean interpellating Americans as global citizens.

Notes

1. I borrow the term "intimate enemy" from Ashis Nandy (1983).
2. The first edition was written in 1989 just before the first Gulf War under the pseudonym Samir al-Khalil. The more popular revised edition updated the changes in the regime since that war.
3. See for instance Ajami (1998).
4. George Packer traces the genesis of the neoconservative position to a 1996 *Foreign Affairs* article by William Kristol and Robert Kagan called "Toward a Neo-Reaganite Foreign Policy." They argue for the revival of America's sense of mission and purpose after the end of the Cold War by a dramatic increase in America's military spending and the expansion of America's influence all over the world–resulting in the establishment of a "benevolent global hegemony" (Packer 2003).
5. "The hidden hand of the market will never work without a hidden fist . . . McDonald's cannot flourish without McDonnell-Douglas, the designer of the U.S. Air Force F-15. And the hidden fist that keeps the world safe for Silicon Valley's technologies is called the United States Army, Air Force, Navy, and Marine Corps" (Friedman 2000, 464).
6. At the same time, Marxist journals such as the *Monthly Review* have seen a new spate of articles both pointing to the economic underpinnings of the new empire and critiquing the use of the term "imperialism" bereft of its associations with capitalism and exploitation.
7. See also Max Boot (2002).
8. Notice how effortlessly this commentator speaks of the "void" created by the demise of old European imperialist powers to be now filled by the United States, as though the colonial administration of the third world is the "natural" state of affairs.
9. I am less interested here in the dynamics and logics of, as well as the different kinds of interests at stake in, empire building, although these are of course very important questions that will have to be examined in some depth to build and sustain an effective mode of resistance. While I do believe that a narrow focus on this particular administration that misses the larger structural dynamics in empire building is inadequate, I remain unpersuaded by the structural-determinist explanations emerging from different quarters—both in Robert Jervis's "hegemonic stability theory" version (examining the U.S. war on Iraq as part of a larger project in "the establishment of U.S. hegemony, primacy, or empire," Jervis attributes this exercise of power less to "accidental" "personalities and events" and more to a logical extension of international systemic dynamics [Jervis 2003, 83—84]), or in its teleological Marxist

version (reviewing the continuities as well as the differences in the different phases of imperialism, the editors of the Marxist journal *Monthly Review* find the new U.S. doctrine of world domination to be a product not of a particular administration, but rather "the culmination of developments in the most recent phase of imperialism" [*Monthly Review* 2002]). There is also of course the debate among international relations scholars about the extent to which Hardt and Negri underestimate the place and role of the United States at the heart of empire, or the extent to which empire is underwritten by the international competition and economic self-interests that underlie what Callinicos calls the "inter-imperialist rivalries" between "unequal rivals" (U.S., Europe, and Japan). See Hardt and Negri (2000) and the debate inaugurated about the book in the pages of the journal *Millennium* on the nature of Empire. See Barkawi and Laffey (2002), R. B. J. Walker (2002), and Callinicos (2002). See also Vltchek (2002) for an argument about the complicity of Western Europe in empire. For a particularly compelling Marxist account of the material underpinnings of empire, see Harvey (2003).

10. Copies of the West Point speech and the NSS document can be found at www.whitehouse.gov. Extensive analyses of these documents are available in Bromwich (2003) and Rhodes (2003).

11. As the above quote hints at, Gaddis believes that "the Bush strategy is right on target with respect to the new circumstances confronting the United States and its allies in the wake of September 11" (Gaddis 2002, 56).

12. I would add that there is another version of "idealism" that has emerged in the stridently proglobalization camp, and, as among the previous idealists, there is a close connection between the "liberal imperialist" and the "free-market imperialist" camps. I will return to the twin imperatives of security *and* political economy discourses in the logic of empire.

13. The national coalition at the heart of the February 15 protest was United for Peace and Justice (UFPJ).

14. This was organized by Win Without War, an entity made up of thirty-two organizations including the National Council of Churches and MoveOn.org.

15. The vigils were organized by MoveOn.org.

16. The prowar rallies were mostly organized by Clear Channel Worldwide Inc., the largest owner of radio stations worldwide and owning over 1,200 stations all over the United States.

17. Leading to the infamous rumors of new flags having to be ordered from China!

18. The United States Postal Service was affected by the unrelated, but associated in the public mind, Anthrax scare.

19. Many corporations initially pulled out their ads but then found more "effective" ways to package their products. Waiting for nine days after the attack, General Motors' red, white, and blue campaign called "Keep America Rolling" (based on extensive polling to find the "right balance") was answered by Ford's "Ford Drives America" (Piore 2001).

20. Patriotic clothing, like other patriotic products, have always had a market in the United States, with companies like American Eagle Outfitter and Tommy Hilfiger that have always banked on patriotic imagery to sell their products. The aftermath of September 11 saw the explosion of that market.

21. Analyzing the budding of community in the aftermath of 9/11, Apple and Giroux attribute what they think of as the desperate longing for community in the United States to the "unattached individualism of the market" (Apple 2002, 305) and "the ethic of neoliberalism with its utter disregard for public life, democratic public sphere, and moral responsibility" (Giroux 2002, 335).

22. Keep in mind, as indicated above, that the president was also simultaneously urging Americans to accumulate more goods in the name of patriotism.

23. In April 2002, Bush nominated Daniel Pipes, a long-standing anti-Islamic ideologue and founder of Campus Watch, to join the board of the United States Institute of Peace, an organization designed to promote the peaceful resolution of international conflicts.

24. Stations owned by Clear Channel, the country's largest radio chain reaching 54 percent of all American adults under age 49, dropped the Dixie Chicks from their play lists in March.

25. It is important to point out here that I am referring to the U.S. peace movement as a monolith, even though, needless to say, there were many different peace movements, attended by people with very different kinds of motivations and values. For the purposes of this chapter, I am examining the *dominant* motifs in most variants of the peace movements—rallies, demonstrations, public commentary, and so forth—as observed and studied by this researcher.

26. Once again, this is unsurprising as those critical of unthinking flag-waving patriotism were reprimanded. Indeed, the resurgence of patriotism among those associated with the Left (such as Democrats and students at Berkeley) was claimed as "victory" by right-wing commentators. See for instance Emery, "Look who's waving the flag now: as democrats rediscover patriotism, the anti-American left sulks," *Weekly Standard*, October 15, 2001, 31–33. I am using the word "interpellate" here in the Althusserian sense of "being hailed into a subject position."

27. As Coles (2002) shows, some of these were also part of the rhetoric of the peace movement during the first Gulf War. What was different was claiming "patriotism" as a virtue in relation to these.

28. It is common practice now to invoke the moniker "innocent" to refer to any publics not directly involved in governmental actions, such as in the widespread use of the term "the innocent victims of September 11." Yet although many, even most, of the people who died in the September 11 attacks were not direct participants in the making of U.S. foreign policy (alleged by the terrorists as the reasons for the attack), nor deserving of the kind of violence directed at them by the terrorists, their "innocence," as citizens of the United States (for those who were), is a more complicated issue that also requires the interrogation of what constitutes complicity and agency.

29. De Genova's brash but provocative statements, that he hoped Iraq would defeat the United States and that he wished for "a million Mogadishus" were unsurprisingly, in the prevalent patriotic context, met with great hostility.

30. See, e.g., Greg Shafer (2003, 14–19).

31. Making clear that the demonstrations would not affect his position on the war, Bush used the opportunity to confirm "American superiority" by celebrating the basic freedoms allowed to American citizens to dissent that are denied to citizens in Iraq and North Korea.

32. It is precisely because of this taken-for-granted American exceptionalism that the Abu-Ghraib prison abuses evinced such shock from the American public (but not in the rest of the world) and made it possible for the administration to dismiss the events as largely aberrant. At the congressional hearing, Secretary of Defense Donald Rumsfeld called the abuses "fundamentally un-American," Army General Lance Smith termed them a "distasteful and criminal aberration," and Democrat Joe Lieberman said "Americans are different," the abuses were "not the real America . . . They are not who we are" (Barber 2003, 17).

33. Cole makes the point that some of the characteristics drawn on by Bush's rhetoric, characteristics that were part of the "dominant common sense" and hence appealing and credible, were "generic" in that they could be co-opted by both pro- and antiwar discourses. The significance of this point will become apparent a little later in the chapter.

34. Reports that the FBI was gathering extensive intelligence on the identity, tactics, training, and organization of antiwar demonstrators, using the expanded powers vested in them by the PATRIOT act, made the potential material consequences of "disloyalty" even more frightening (Lichtblau 2003).

35. While Pei understands that the "psychological and behavioral manifestations of nationalism and patriotism are indistinguishable, as is the impact of such sentiments on policy," he takes both the basic distinctions between the ethnic and civic form of nationalism at face value, as well as the civic basis of American nationalism. Further, he sees the American state as absent in the reproduction of national identity, unlike "authoritarian regimes" where "the state deploys its resources, from government-controlled media to the police, to propagate "patriotic values," thus missing entirely the enormous investments of the state in any liberal democratic state, including the United States, in producing and reproducing particular narratives of the nation (Pei 2003).

36. It might be interesting to point out here that Putnam's new analysis that revealed that Americans are now "bowling together" also finds that trust toward Arab Americans is lower than toward other ethnic minorities and that Americans are now more hostile to immigrant rights (Putnam 2002).

Bibliography

Ajami, Fouad. 1998. *The dream palace of the Arabs: a generation's odyssey*. New York: Pantheon Books.

Editors. America and empire: manifest destiny warmed up? 2003. *Economist*, August 16, 19–21.

Anderson, Benedict. 1983. *Imagined communities: reflections on the origin and spread of nationalism*. London: Verso.

Apple, Michael W. 2002. Pedagogy, patriotism, and democracy: on the educational meanings of 11 September 2001. *Discourse: Studies in the Cultural Politics of Education* 23 (3): 299–308.

Ayers, William. 2003. The banality of terror. *Humbolt Journal of Social Relations* 27 (2): 36–51.

Bacevich, Andrew J. 2002. *American empire: the realities and consequences of U.S. diplomacy*. Cambridge, MA: Harvard University Press.

Barber, Benjamin R. 2003. *Fear's empire: war, terrorism, and democracy.* New York: W. W. Norton.

Barkawi, Tarak and Mark Laffey. 2002. Retrieving the imperial: empire and international relations. *Millennium: Journal of International Studies* 31 (1): 109–127.

Boot, Max. 2002. *The savage wars of peace: small wars and the rise of American power.* New York: Basic Books.

————. 2003. Neither new nor nefarious: the liberal empire strikes back. *Current History* 102 (667): 361–367.

Boyd, Andrew. 2003. The web rewires the movement. *The Nation,* August 4, 13.

Bromwich, David. 2003. Acting Alone. *Survival* 50 (1): 19–23.

Bronski, Michael. 2003. Supporting the troops: a code word for "supporting the war". *Z Magazine,* May, 42–44

Brown, Patricia Leigh. 2003. Enthusiasts gather to salute g.i. joe, a man of action. *New York Times,* June 30, 1.

Burke, Amy. 2002. Patriotism and community. *Dissent* 49 (2): 44–46.

Callinicos, Alex. 2002. The actuality of imperialism. *Millennium: Journal of International Studies* 31 (2): 319–326.

Chandler, David. 2003. The dynamics of empire: the need for a new analysis of imperialism. *Global Dialogue* 5 (1): 105–115.

Chen, David. 2002. A subdued hurrah for 2002 in a patriotic Times Square. *New York Times,* January 1,1.

Coles, Roberta. 2002. War and the contest over national identity. *Sociological Review* 50 (4): 586–609.

Connolly-Ahern, Colleen and Lynda Lee Kaid. 2002. Corporate advertising as political advertising: patriotic messages in the aftermath of 9-11, *Journal of Political Marketing* 1 (4): 95–99.

Editors. 2002. U.S. imperial ambitions and Iraq. *Monthly Review* 54 (7):1–13.

Emery, Noemie. 2001. Look who's waving the flag now: as democrats rediscover patriotism, the anti-American left sulks. *Weekly Standard,* October 15, 31–33.

Falk, Richard. 2003. Will the empire be fascist? *Global Dialogue* 5 (1): 22–31.

Ferguson, Niall. 2003. *Empire the rise and demise of the British world order: lessons for global power.* New York: Basic Books.

Ferguson, Niall. 2004. *Colossus: the price of America's empire.* New York: Penguin Press.

Ferguson, Niall. 2006. *The war of the world: Twentieth-Century conflict and the descent of the West.* New York: Penguin Press.

Foner, Eric. 2003. Dare call it treason. *Nation,* June 2, 13.

Foster, John Bellamy. 2002. The rediscovery of imperialism. *Monthly Review* 54 (6): 1–16.

Friedman, Thomas. 2000. *The lexus and the olive tree: understanding globalization.* New York: Anchor Books.

Gaddis, John Lewis. 2002. A grand strategy of transformation. *Foreign Policy* (133): 50–57.

Gaines, Brian. 2002. Symposium: civic engagement in the post-9/11 world. *PS* 35 (3): 531–536.

Gibbs, David N. 2001. Washington's new interventionism: U.S. hegemony and inter-imperialist rivalries. *Monthly Review* 53 (4): 15.

Giroux, Henry A. 2002. Democracy and the politics of terrorism: community, fear, and the suppression of dissent. *Cultural Studies—Critical Methodologies* 2 (3): 334–342.

Gitlin, Todd. 2002. Liberalism's patriotic vision. *New York Times,* September 5.

———. 2003. America's age of empire: with barely a debate, the Bush doctrine has set out a radically, new-and dangerous-role for the United States. *Mother Jones,* January–February, 34–39.

Goldwasser, Amy. 2001. Pledging allegiance to the season. *New York Times,* December 13, 4

Hardt, Michael, and Antonio Negri. 2000. *Empire.* Cambridge, MA: Harvard University Press.

Harvey, David. 2003. *The new imperialism.* Oxford: Oxford University Press.

Ignatieff, Michael. 2002. Nation-building lite. *New York Times Magazine,* July 28.

———. 2003. The burden. *New York Times Magazine,* January 5.

Ikenberry, G. John. 2002. America's imperial ambition. *Foreign Affairs,* September/October.

James, Caryn. 2002. Critic's notebook: singers smoothly merge politics with patriotism. *New York Times,* February 4, 9.

Jervis, Robert. 2003. The compulsive empire. *Foreign Policy* (137): 82–87.

Kabbani, Rana. 1986. *Europe's myths of orient.* Bloomington, Indiana: Indiana University Press.

Kaplan, Lawrence F. and William Kristol. 2003. *The war over Iraq.* San Francisco: Encounter Books.

Kaufman, Leslie. 2001. Ledger allegiance: my bottom line, right or wrong. *New York Times,* December 2, 4.

Kazin, Michael. 2002. A patriotic left. *Dissent* 49 (4): 41–44.

Lal, Vinay. 2003. Empire and the dream-work of America. *Global Dialogue* 5 (1): 135–144.

Lichtblau, Eric. 2003. F.B.I. scrutinizes antiwar rallies. *New York Times,* November 23, 1.

Makiya, Kanan. 1998. *Republic of fear: the politics of modern Iraq.* Berkeley: University of California Press.

Mallaby, Sebastian. 2002. The reluctant imperialist. *Foreign Affairs* 81 (2).

McAdam, Doug, and Yang Su. 2002. The war at home: antiwar protests and Congressional voting, 1965–1973. *American Sociological Review* 67 (5): 696–721.

Mehta, Uday Singh. 1999. *Liberalism and empire: a study in nineteenth century British liberal thought.* Chicago: University of Chicago Press.

Misztal, Barbara. 2003. Negative capability or dealing with the complexity of the Iraqi war. *Sociological Research Online* 8 (3).

Moskos, Charles. 2002. Reviving the citizen-soldier. *Public Interest* 147 (Spring): 76–85.

Nandy, Ashis. 1983. *The intimate enemy: loss and recovery of self under colonialism.* Delhi: Oxford University Press.

Nussbaum, Martha. 1994. Patriotism and cosmopolitanism. *Boston Review* 19 (5): 3–6.

Nye, Joseph. 2002. *The paradox of American power: why the world's only super-power can't go it alone.* Oxford: Oxford University Press.

———. 2003. U.S. power and strategy after Iraq. *Foreign Affairs* 82 (4): 60–73.

Packer, George. 2003. Paved with good intentions: the Bush administration says its push toward global dominance is driven by high-minded ideals. But that's part of the problem. *Mother Jones,* July–August, 28–34.

Parenti, Michael. 2003. Rulers of the planet: why US leaders intervene everywhere. *Global Dialogue* 5 (1): 91–104.

Pei, Minxin. 2003. The paradoxes of American nationalism. *Foreign Policy* 136: 30–37.

Piore, Adam. 2001. Red, white and what a deal. *Newsweek International,* Nov 26, 59.

Putnam, Robert D. 2002. Bowling together. *The American Prospect* 13 (3).

Rhodes, Edward. 2003. The imperial logic of Bush's liberal agenda. *Survival* 45 (1): 131–153.

Said, Edward. 1978. *Orientalism.* New York: Vintage Books.

Salter, Mark B. 2003. The clash of civilisations and the war on terror(ists): an imperialist discourse. *Global Dialogue* 5 (1):116–125.

Schell, Jonathan. 2003. The world's other superpower. *The Nation,* April 14, 11–12.

Shabani, Smid A. Payrow. 2002. Who's afraid of constitutional patriotism? The binding source of citizenship in constitutional states. *Social Theory and Practice* 28 (3): 419–444.

Shafer, Greg. 2003. Lessons from the U.S. war on Iraq. *Humanist* 63 (4): 14–19.

Simes, Dimitri K. 2003. America's imperial dilemma. *Foreign Affairs* 82 (6).

Simon, Roger, Lisa Huriash, and Hohn Slania. 2001. A nation, in pain, rallies. (Various types of patriotism in wake of terrorist attacks). *U.S. News & World Report,* October 12, 60.

Singer, Mark. 2001. I pledge allegiance: a liberal town's school system meets the new patriotism. *The New Yorker,* November 26, 54

Skocpol, Theda. 2002. "Will 9/11 and the war on terror revitalize American civic democracy?" *PS,* 35:511–540, no. 3, 537–540. [AU: SHOULD THIS READ: '...*PS* 35 (3): 537–540'?]

Solomon, Alisa. 2003. The big chill. *The Nation,* June 2, 17–22.

Southern, R. W. 1962. *Western views of Islam in the middle ages.* Cambridge, MA: Harvard University Press.

Vltchek, Andre. 2002. Western terror: from Potosi to Baghdad: origins of the culture of terror. *Z Magazine,* December, 30–34.

Walker, R. B. J. 2002. On the immanence/imminence of empire. *Millennium: Journal of International Studies* 31 (2): 337–345.

Whiteside, Rob. 2002. Through the perilous fight: when Americans suit up in the flag. *Harper's Magazine,* July, 64–66.

Zizek, Slavoj. 2004. Iraq's false promises. *Foreign Policy* (140): 42–50.

Chapter 5

Déjà Vu: The Fantasy of Benign Military Rule in Pakistan

Ayesha Khan

Prologue

Pakistan is a country about which the world knows relatively little, but about which many assumptions have been made. Since its creation in 1947, the West has perceived it more often than not as a moderate Muslim state. The government has variously permitted increasing or decreasing influence of the religious right in its affairs. During the 1980s this influence was at its peak, but despite this it still retained the reputation of being more open to Western influence and persuasion than Afghanistan, Iran, Saudi Arabia, and Iraq.

This perception was clouded after Saudi Arabian terrorists led an attack on U.S. soil on September 11, 2001. Pakistan's intelligence links with the Taliban and al-Qaeda operatives seriously threatened the way the international public viewed this country of 160 million people. It was only when the military leader General Pervez Musharraf immediately promised to cooperate with the United States in its efforts to break the terrorist networks that Pakistan could begin the process of rebuilding its international image as a moderate Muslim state.

But for most Pakistanis, with an eye on the shifts in domestic politics, the assumptions made by the West about their country are so narrow and so self-serving that they are not taken seriously. The Pakistan we know is an entirely different place altogether, where the government's moves are not representative of the will of the people at all, and in fact the people themselves in all their diversity are mostly mysteries to one another. Just as the government remains ignorant and suspicious of its own people, so also the different ethnic, religious, and linguistic groups lack a comfortable familiarity with one another. Each of the four provinces that make up Pakistan has its own story to tell, featuring an unhappy relationship with either the federal government, or another ethnic group, or the military.

The consequences of oversimplifications, which are characteristic of analyses of global events since 9/11, are, as usual, devastating for the people of Pakistan and their aspirations for a more prosperous and just society. The government's new alliance with the United States and its antiterror agenda has as its first casualty the very political and social enfranchisement that has been promised in rhetoric. An urgent response to the discourse of this new alliance is required. This task starts with a closer look at how the Pakistan government is exercising its power in the name of national interest.

Introduction

Pakistan's international position after 9/11 has transformed utterly, yet little has changed domestically. Although international focus remains on the overt transformations that took place in Pakistan's foreign policy—the about-face on the Taliban and the reining in of home-grown terrorists exporting their skills in neighboring countries—on the domestic front the implications of world events since 9/11 remain sorely unexamined. These implications need to be interpreted in terms of the most deep-seated political questions in Pakistan, which are unresolved but remain as important as they were when the country was created in 1947. What should the role of the military be in the governance of Pakistan? Is Pakistan a secular state for Muslims and others, or is it an Islamic state defined by its religious identity? If we want democratic governance, what form of it will accommodate our diverse ethnic and linguistic groups, ensure representation of an uneducated majority, and control violence and ideological extremism?

The aftermath of 9/11 has given observers a false sense that these questions are now being answered seriously. Pakistani politicians, journalists, and activists warn that the country's new international importance as a support to the United States's "war on terror" will serve as a cover to further the military's historic agenda of entrenching its political and economic hold on the country. Similarly, the rise of the Mutahida Majlis-e-Amal (MMA),[1] particularly in the North-West Frontier Province, is seen in some circles as a success of the religious right toward establishing a theocratic state, thus beating out the secularists from the ideological debate once and for all. In yet other circles, which include politicians and the military to some extent, this phenomenon is viewed as a cynically engineered development, serving to enhance the army's grip on power by supplying international detractors with an alternative worse than military rule.

These are the kinds of issues that concern Pakistan and its people, particularly because they remain divisive, emotive, and easily manipulated for short-term political ends. When the United States turned its gaze and guns toward Pakistan after 9/11, and the country's military-led government promised to cooperate with the superpower, a fountain of rhetoric sprung up as if from nowhere. Suddenly Pakistan was going to tackle the question of religious extremism and come down hard on the side of secular rule. Suddenly the military rulers were more committed to democracy than any elected government ever had been or could be. Suddenly General Musharraf was the only possible leader who could save us from being overrun by Taliban supporters (never mind the fact that many citizens didn't mind the idea at all). If any Pakistanis ever believed any of this rhetoric, they were ignorant of their country's history and the role of the armed forces in suppressing political culture and institutions. That too is not surprising, as every successive government, military or not, has demonstrated a strong distaste for examining the past.

The New Dominant Discourse

Pakistan has a complex social, cultural, and political landscape, and it would be incorrect to ascribe to its people any unified set of attributes or beliefs about themselves. In the post-9/11 scenario, we can identify a set of beliefs and propositions about current ideological and political divides that are espoused by international observers, particularly in the United States, and by the Pakistani government, presumably because they suit their immediate goals in the "war on terror." They enjoy significant popular support as well, being subscribed to by influential elements among the establishment, elite classes, ethnic groups, and even across gender and social divides. They are reflected in domestic and international electronic and print media coverage of Pakistan. Although some analysts vehemently oppose these beliefs, a sincere wish persists among sections of the people that they were true.

For example, from a global perspective it is valid to believe that the United States is a friend to Pakistan. Even some Pakistanis share this belief. Related to this is the belief that the current military regime is benign; it is certainly not a despotic regime that the international community would reject and that Pakistanis themselves should agitate against. In fact, the regime is not only benign but it also understands the threat of a violent Islamist politics that uses terrorism as a tactic in its war against the infidels. It is assisting the United States in defending itself and also clearing Pakistan of the enemy on its own soil. Best of all, in the process, the regime is turning Pakistan into a real democracy, which over time will prove to be worth the price of quelling the political rights of the people in the short term. My discussion examines these beliefs.

1.   *The United States is a Friend to Pakistan*

There was enormous public sympathy for Musharraf after 9/11 when he faced the ultimatum from U.S. president, George W. Bush to decide Pakistan's role in the "war on terror." There was also wide agreement that, in the interest of the nation, he could have selected no other path than joining United States in its war. After all, who would choose confrontation with the United States? Later, criticism would be raised in the press that the government took too literally the American's power of persuasion ("You are either with us or against us") and missed an opportunity to negotiate for more economic support and benefits before agreeing to their terms. There may be truth to that, as at least one account reveals that the U.S. government was not at all sure whether Pakistan would agree to its terms (Clarke 2004, 23). Nonetheless, when Musharraf agreed to cooperate with the United States, he began to be scrutinized at home for his ability to manage both the Americans and domestic issues. As the months went by public sympathy faded.

With cynical resignation Pakistanis recognize that the United States favors military rulers in their country. The bias began with Field Marshall Ayub Khan (1958–1969), who built the country's economy on a U.S.-inspired model of modernization, and cultivated close diplomatic ties with U.S. leaders in the early years of his rule (Talbot 1998, 170–2). It was reflected again in the fall of the elected leader Zulfiqar Ali Bhutto in 1977, a vocal supporter of the Non-Aligned Movement and unpopular with the Americans. It worked in favor of General Zia ul-Haq (1977–1988), whose brutal military dictatorship received international legitimacy when the United States decided he was an invaluable ally in its covert anti-Soviet war in Afghanistan. And finally this bias also saved General Musharraf, whose military takeover from civilian rule in 1999 earned him international opprobrium (Pakistan was expelled from the Commonwealth) but became legitimized once again when the United States turned to him for assistance in its "war on terror."

Civilian governments, in contrast, have not enjoyed this kind of unqualified support from the United States. While the United States turned a blind eye to Pakistan's growing nuclear program during the Zia years, as soon as Benazir Bhutto was elected, the U.S. Congress imposed sanctions on Pakistan under the Pressler Amendment. This marked the beginning of disengagement by the United States from Pakistan, once a frontline ally in its covert war against the Soviet occupation of Afghanistan. Military and development aid alike came to an end, the United States showed little interest in the dilemmas of a potentially nuclear South Asia, and it totally forgot the chaos that emerged in neighboring postcommunist Afghanistan. Now the United States regrets that it did not maintain any engagement with Pakistan and promises not to repeat the same mistake.

Before 9/11, Pakistanis could be forgiven for enjoying a spring mood of optimism that this new regime would bring Pakistan stability and prosperity. Historically there has been little active engagement of the public in determining the kind of rulers they have in Pakistan. By now the country has been governed by unelected military regimes for thirty-two of its fifty-eight years of existence. Whenever elections have been held, either for puppet parliaments to serve the military or for direct civilian rule, they are marred by accusations of corruption. If a civilian government is in charge, it is held responsible for rigging elections, and usually for numerous other counts of corruption during its rule. As a result, the electorate has not had the opportunity to gain substantial experience with the electoral process, nor has it developed much faith that it is a fair one. Further, it is assumed by the general public that governments act in their own interest (usually financial) and have little consideration for the so-called electorate. Corruption charges, leveled by other power brokers outside of government, become the justification for a sudden dissolution of government or military takeover.

Nawaz Sharif, the last elected prime minister, was deposed in a military coup in October 1999. The coup took place at a time when Nawaz Sharif was attempting to accumulate for himself almost dictatorial powers by manipulating parliamentary politics and bulldozing legislation through the assemblies to enhance his powers. His business interests were well known, and his political cronies were also under suspicion of personal corruption. The country had just emerged from a military fiasco in the remote and disputed mountainous Kargil region in May 1999 that brought Pakistan to the brink of a full war with India. Both the civilian establishment and the army emerged humiliated from the ill-planned adventure. It came almost as a relief when the military, led by Chief of Army Staff General Pervez Musharraf, stepped in to redress the situation and bring order where political chaos was impending. Musharraf's role as aggressor in the Kargil attack was either ignored, or used by some avid supporters as an example of his ability to be a courageous leader of the nation.

At first the public and media alike focused on the differences between President Musharraf and his civilian predecessor. His reputation as a benign dictator, not to be excessively feared by the West or the liberal sections of Pakistani society, spread fast. Musharraf posed for press photographs with his family, dressed in civilian clothing to play down his military role. Western diplomats and journalists breathed a sigh of relief that they would not be doing business with an Islamic fundamentalist, of which there were held to be many in the military.

In fact, so did women, who heard positive policy statements in favor of protecting their rights and reconsidering discriminatory legislation. If nothing else, still argue activists with the women's movement, Musharraf does not use the state to oppress women. The legacy of General Zia and his protégé, the twice-deposed prime minister, Nawaz Sharif,[2] caused women's rights organizations to be harassed by the state in an effort to maintain the support of the religious right for the government's politics.[3] Pakistan's first woman prime minister, Benazir Bhutto, was expected by many of her educated supporters to reverse the legacy of Zia during her two brief stints in power, but she was either unwilling or too weak to change discriminatory legislation against women and take other policy decisions.

Musharraf's personal popularity drowned out opposition voices within the country and also the concerns of Western governments eager to be seen to be supporting democracy. The argument made by some political critics, that the low caliber of our civilian politicians and the weakness of civilian-led democracy was a direct fallout of eleven years of military rule under General Zia ul-Haq, was largely ignored. One important reason for this was that disappointment in the popular former prime minister Benazir Bhutto cut deep. Her father had been Pakistan's most popular elected leader, deposed in a coup d'état and executed in 1979 as General Zia tried to consolidate his power. Benazir had come to power twice through elections after Zia's death, and both times found her government dismissed by the army under allegations of corruption. Perhaps it was embarrassing for Pakistanis to recall that they sustained themselves through the difficult years of Zia's rule by believing falsely in the potential of democracy.

Not long after the initial enthusiasm for his rule, comparisons between Musharraf and his civilian predecessors stirred serious debate in the media and among political commentators on how to protect constitutional rule despite the obvious demerits of civilian rule. These voices dimmed after 9/11. Pakistan suddenly entered the international limelight, and the fresh scrutiny drew no praise from the outside world. After all, the military and civilian rulers had conspired together to support the Taliban, and how was Pakistan going to live that down? It seemed that the regime had no choice but to embrace partnership with the United States yet again.

It was only in Pakistan's short-term interest, if at all, that it allied itself with the United States in a war whose terms it had not defined. And it was a short-lived bout of public sympathy that buoyed the government when it made that decision. Today, there is yet another friendship between the United States and a military regime lacking electoral credibility, in which the latter is unable to define the terms of the relationship, and uses it to extend its own power. The United States has been complicit in this by arguing that at this juncture Musharraf is good for Pakistan. In fact Musharraf himself now believes this to be true, as do his supporters and members of the political party he created to support him in Parliament.[4] Should the U.S.-Pakistan alliance collapse for any reason, as it has more than once in the past, the military will be left vulnerable and unpopular in its own country.

2.   The Current Government Is a Kind of Benign Military Regime

Pakistan's political landscape is determined by so many factors that it is facile, as it would be in any country, to judge its actual stability or progress by how long Musharraf stays in power or how well liked he is internationally. There is now growing evidence within the country that his rule is hardly benign, and that the sidelining of so many representatives of the people in a military-controlled democracy will create more long-term problems than it will solve. Hence no real progress may be taking place at all, but rather a kind of déjà vu during which the damaging legacy of military rule will unfold again and make it impossible for civilian governments to function in the future.

Public sympathy for General Musharraf's rule eroded in large part due to the ongoing violence in Afghanistan and in Pakistan's tribal territories, and the unpopular war in Iraq. Hence the refrain in the media, both local and international, about Musharraf's delicate balancing act between controlling "extremists"[5] at home, at some risk to his domestic support, and appeasing international pressure. The U.S.-led war on "terror" has lost its thin support in Pakistan through the excessive use of force, inability to bring closure to the theaters in Afghanistan and Iraq, and refusal to address the demands for political justice in the Arab world. This in turn has further eroded Musharraf's credibility, as demonstrated by the surprising success of the MMA in the elections. The MMA was the only political platform that openly condemned the government's support for U.S. actions in Afghanistan. Today Pakistanis of any persuasion are hard-pressed to explain Musharraf's support for a war that is producing suffering and instability in Iraq and Afghanistan, not to mention hundreds of deaths due to army incursions into Pakistan's own tribal-controlled areas in search of al-Qaeda members. Anti-U.S. sentiment is widespread, even among members of the elite who are reluctant to challenge Musharraf's power.

But there are plenty of other moves by the military government that have stirred up political opposition at home. While such moves may seem unimportant in the wider context of the war on terror and international power politics, that cannot be allowed to become the prime criterion for judging the success of a government. The direct analogy is to U.S. support for military dictators in Latin America during the Cold War. Sustaining military regimes was rationalized by reference to U.S. national interest, but it was entirely damaging to the prosperity and political enfranchisement of that southern continent. Unfortunately the case is not being made vociferously enough that to view Pakistan through the short-term perspective of narrow U.S. interests is unjust, dangerous, and does not serve the long-term interest of its people.

The Okara Military Farms in the Punjab are an important symbol of how the military government is positioned in relation to the common man. These farms, covering 25,000 acres, were leased by the military from the provincial government and worked by the peasants on a crop-sharing basis with the army. The British colonial rulers originally devised this arrangement in 1913 when they ruled the Punjab and needed dairy and crops to feed their soldiers. In 2000, the army tried to change the cultivators' status from sharecroppers to that of tenant farmers, with no rights over the land they had cultivated for over a century. A rebellion broke out, resulting in the birth of a farmer's organization and unprecedented cooperation between both Christian and Muslim peasants in the Punjab. But paramilitary forces repressed it over the course of the next four years, after numerous arrests and even the shooting of farmers by the forces.

The military flexed its muscles and brought in soldiers to surround the villages and lay siege to them until the resistance broke down. In the process the forces shot at least seven cultivators, and the story got brief but extensive press coverage.[6] The Punjab provincial government, although it wished to have the land brought back under its control, was powerless to resist the army's decision. The army displayed contempt for the process of negotiation or compromise building and also protected its growing economic interests in its handling of the rebellion. This phenomenon alone lays to rest the argument that it is a soft military regime that will bring Pakistan back on track to democracy.

In fact, the military has acquired such significant economic interests that it is now a major stakeholder in all segments of the economy, including agriculture, service, and manufacturing industries. Whereas historically the military managed to lay claim to a great amount of state resources in the name of upholding national security, now it not only benefits from a large defense budget but its commercial interests grew in the 1990s to give it control of a financial empire worth approximately Rs. 130 billion. One estimate is that the military-owned businesses today control about 23 percent of the country's total assets in the corporate sector (Siddiqa 2004, 3).

As the military expands its economic empires through a network of small and medium enterprises, large public sector enterprises, and large-scale private sector ventures, it has a growing interest in maintaining a policy environment that protects its investments. Its enterprises tend to be limited to the local market in areas with few major competitors. They do not generate significant employment or income gains, yet enjoy preferential access to capital, land, and of course policy benefits if the military is in power. (Sayeed and Nadvi 2004, ii) In short, if the military enjoys the benefit of its muscle and firepower when it assumes political control and elbows aside political parties, so too does it now enjoy the ability to threaten and diminish the struggling private sector in Pakistan. If the military remains in power, then, it is able to protect and nurture its growing economic interests.

Pakistan's tribal areas, located in the northwest of the country close to Afghanistan, have enjoyed semiautonomous status since the time of British colonial rule. Its people are heavily armed, ethnically Pathan, and were supportive of the counter-communist war in Afghanistan in the 1980s as well as of the subsequent Taliban rule in the mid-1990s. While the government and intelligence agencies used the tribal areas for giving training and support to the mujahideen and later the Taliban, after 9/11 it had to do a complete about-turn. As if it wasn't difficult enough to extricate the deep intelligence links with religious armed parties, the government was subsequently persuaded by the Americans to send its own forces into some of these areas to track down suspected terrorists in hiding.

In effect the government is doing what the United States is not capable of doing directly, since it lacks intimate knowledge and its own intelligence contacts in the tribal areas, and since it must be careful not to arouse domestic anger by engaging in military action in Pakistan. The result of the ongoing army action was the bombing of villages in South Waziristan, stifling of the local economy, deaths of women and children, arrests of so-called foreign militants, and of course dozens of dead soldiers as well. There were efforts by government representatives to negotiate with the tribesmen to hand over any foreign militants under their protection, but they were doomed to failure largely because of the confusion created by the sudden about-turn in policy.

There will obviously be serious consequences for the state after this military action. Citizens of Pakistan have been killed by their own army and starved of their economic lifeline in the name of largely U.S. interests. The action may breed antistate insurgency at some point, and possibly also increase support for violent religious-based organizations as well. The ethnic factor is not to be forgotten, since much of the support in the western provinces of Pakistan for the Taliban grows from a shared Pathan culture, in addition to a common religious and political outlook.

The case of Balochistan is the more historic example of what happens when the state turns against its citizens. Thirty years ago that poverty-stricken province launched its own nationalist movement to demand more from the Pakistan government. The Baloch people have not forgotten that in the early 1970s their Leftist movement incurred the wrath of the then-civilian government, which put it down through a campaign of bombing and army operation that left thousands dead. Today the beginnings of a renewed insurgency have already swept across that province.

The Balochistan Liberation Army (BLA) has launched violent action against state institutions accused of launching large infrastructural projects in that resource-rich province without allocating adequate control or employment to local people. Violent attacks of bombs, grenades, rockets, and more occurred almost on a daily basis from January to June 2004, and there is no indication that the matter is being resolved politically. Instead, small, secret, army operations are underway to root out insurgents and close their training camps. BLA's key demand is backed by Balochistan's political parties. That is, they want participatory decision-making processes to arrive at an agreement about future arrangements and access to resources of the province (*Herald* September 2004, 50–63). They are demanding an effective devolution of power, not one controlled by the military from Islamabad.

The violent suppression of people's movements and the economic entrenchment of the military are just some examples of what Pakistan is bound to face in the aftermath of this current era of military rule. Time and again, civilian governments have been unable to manage the legacies of such violence and have ultimately colluded in similar tactics. In 1971, when East Pakistan broke away to form an independent Bangladesh, the blame was put on the elected prime minister, Zulfikar Ali Bhutto, but it was the military regime of Field Marshall Ayub Khan that laid the foundations of the civil war. In the 1980s, the military regime of General Zia led the covert war against the Soviet occupation of Afghanistan at the behest of the United States, leaving Pakistan with a legacy of politically relevant religious extremists, an extraordinarily empowered intelligence agency, and a highly armed society with a serious domestic drug abuse problem. Whatever the legacy of the current military regime will be for Pakistan, one knows it cannot be benign.

3. *All Muslims Are Potential Terrorists, Unless Proven Otherwise. Pakistan's Leader General Musharraf Is Helping to Prove Otherwise for His Country*

The hysterical aftermath of 9/11 has legitimized false dichotomies as a way to make sense of world events. Huntington's thesis of a clash of civilizations between the Christian West and the Muslim East was a warning to wary Muslim countries as they observed the emergence of the United States as the only superpower in the 1990s. When Bush intoned that "you are either with us or against us," in the post-9/11 world, it seemed that the battle lines were indeed drawn on the basis of religion, with the Muslims behind enemy lines.

Muslim scholars in the West have attempted to resist this thesis.[7] But in Muslim countries such as Pakistan, which have little representative voice in the West and whose people have been put on the defensive by an international media that knows little about them, it is easy to fall into the trap of feeling that Muslims are on the other side of a new ideological battle. International political developments since 9/11 have borne out this view, and given further shape to the domestic belief that the United States is working against the interests of Muslims.

The first development that strengthened a sense among Pakistanis that they were now vulnerable to attack was the U.S. war on Afghanistan. Many observers in Pakistan doubted that the United States would actually invade Afghanistan because it would remember the catastrophic history of the British and Soviets when they made their unsuccessful forays into that country over the last 150 years. But they were proven wrong. America's old friends quickly turned into enemies. Afghan *mujahideen* and Saudi *jihadis* like Osama bin Laden, who were once close allies of the United States in its covert support for their resistance to Soviet occupation,[8] became the new targets.

This new enemy was so compelling that the United States went to war in Afghanistan, while Pakistanis watched aghast as history was set aside and the latest superpower tried its luck at subduing that poor but unconquerable land. Those Pakistanis who were ethnically Pathan themselves, or who had become familiar with Afghan refugees and immigrants in Pakistan, felt the attack was shockingly close to home. Three hundred thousand refugees from Afghanistan's eastern provinces poured over the border in response to the U.S. campaign, bringing the total number of Afghan refugees in Pakistan up to 3.3 million (UNHCR 2004, 8). These ethnically Pathan refugees were under suspicion for supporting the Taliban. Times had changed, and they received none of the welcome accorded to their predecessors in the 1980s who had fled the Soviets in Afghanistan and received food and shelter from aid agencies across the border. The Pakistan government wanted to maintain its policy of no longer accepting Afghan refugees, no doubt partly because so many of them came from former Taliban-controlled areas and because the government wanted to show the United States that it had turned its back on its former friends.

The Pakistan government allowed the United States access to military bases inside the country, adding to the growing unease that Musharraf had no control over his new friendship with the United States. Rumors abounded that the U.S. military had assumed control over Pakistan's air space. The new photographic equipment that appeared at airport immigration was there to collect data for the Americans, or so immigration officials apologetically admitted to concerned travelers. Karachi residents living near the coast thought they heard fighter aircraft from U.S. warships as they flew above into neighboring Afghanistan. It soon became common among the chattering classes, taxi drivers, storekeepers, and students alike, to observe that the United States had killed more innocent Afghans than al-Qaeda had killed civilians in the 9/11 attacks. Sympathy for the United States after 9/11 gave way to a sharp sense that all Muslims were fair game now, including Pakistanis, no matter how much unelected rulers like General Musharraf tried to pretend otherwise.

The veracity of this view was further confirmed by the U.S. attack on Iraq in March 2003. There was little surprise that the Americans went to war, and even less when the charges that Iraq possessed weapons of mass destruction proved unfounded. Pakistanis now ask each other quite seriously whether they are next in the line of Muslim states to be attacked by the new imperialists. Even some peace activists grudgingly share the common view that if Pakistan had not possessed nuclear weapons, perhaps it would already have met the same fate as Afghanistan and Iraq.

When Dr. A. Q. Khan, a metallurgist who participated in Pakistan's nuclear program and assumes full credit for Pakistan's nuclear capability, was exposed in early 2004 (allegedly because of U.S. intelligence) as a leading salesman in the underworld of trade in nuclear weapons technology, public response was mixed. It was hard to believe that the United States sprung this news on the Pakistan government without using it as leverage to extract more support for its war on terror. Pakistan found itself once again in the awkward position of having to prove that it did not support terrorism, particularly the kind that spreads nuclear technology in the Muslim world, and the government could not respond from any position of strength. It was rumored that a deal was struck. The United States refrained from prosecuting Khan and exposing the military links in his underground network. In return for the favor, the Pakistan government agreed to conduct its own army operation in the tribal areas to search for al-Qaeda fugitives, a move it had long resisted.

Whether or not this was indeed the case cannot be proven, but such conspiracy-tinged theories illustrate how Pakistanis view themselves in relation to Western powers. It is arguably a tendency among the weak to use such theorizing to illustrate their vulnerability. One outcome of this nuclear scandal was that public sympathy for Khan remained largely unscathed, and a major corruption story was buried partly because the public became defensive in the face of alleged U.S. manipulation. Another outcome of was that the military stood to benefit by avoiding serious investigation. In the end, both the U.S. government and General Musharraf got their way.

The domestic press regularly covers stories about Muslims, especially Pakistanis, who have been detained or deported from the United States under its tightened immigration and surveillance procedures. Businessmen, even wealthy ones who have traveled regularly to the United States for many years, exchange stories of at least one person they know who has been detained for questioning—usually without access to a telephone—upon arrival in the United States. The United States is suddenly a less attractive place to visit, the visa procedures seem too cumbersome, and the possibility of enduring humiliating cross-questioning is greater than many potential travelers wish to endure. Students from elite schools are thinking again before applying to U.S. colleges; suddenly Canada, Australia, and even the United Kingdom seem more comfortable options. Whether we like it or not, observes one analyst, we have all become "Muslims" after 9/11.

The tussle for control of Pakistan is being portrayed as one between extremist Islam and seriously weakened forces of moderation, represented by this government. The threat of things getting worse only strengthens the international credibility of General Musharraf. In fact, the more he is seen as trying to control the renegade *madrassas,* arrest extremists, and make friends with Afghan president Hamid Karzai, the more believable it is meant to be that without him in power the country would be run over by the Pakistani version of the Taliban. In truth, the collaboration between the government and right-wing religious parties runs very deep and has a long history. The army cannot shed its role overnight as covert supporter of *mujahideen* and *jihadis* sent by religious political organizations to the conflicts in Afghanistan and Kashmir.

The army and the religious right wing are actually on the same far-right of the spectrum, both ultimately authoritarian in their own way. Hence, the current international discourse that places Muslims in the difficult position of having to demonstrate their secular credentials actually works in favor of the military at home. It can sell itself as the convincing alternative to the "fundamentalists," who claim that only a *jihad* could stop the United States in Iraq (*Dawn*, March 31, 12). The government could have scripted these words because they so perfectly fan the fears that secure U.S. support for General Musharraf. Pakistan is pitching itself against the "Muslim terrorists" on the international level, when at home it is more closely allied with the politics of religious extremism and not the interests of the people of Pakistan.

4. Democratic Processes and Institutions Are Taking a New Foothold under the Controlled Elections and Parliamentary Experiment Led by Musharraf

Whenever the military comes to power it fully exploits the idea that, in a developing country with low literacy and high poverty levels, democracy needs to be slowly and gradually nurtured. The stability of the country becomes synonymous not with democracy but with national security, and the regime claims that it is best placed to guarantee the latter. What is ignored is the reality that the conditions for social, economic, and political stability are fast eroded under military rule in Pakistan because it lacks any electoral credentials and ultimately relies on force for establishing its writ of power.

After a successful military coup d'état in October 1999, Musharraf declared himself president in June 2001. He then assumed extraordinary powers for the president, who, according to the country's constitution, has only a nominal role as head of state. Musharraf formed the National Security Council (NSC), with himself as its chairman, comprising all three heads of the armed services and all four provincial governors. He alone has the power to select and dismiss its members, whose role it is to advise him on a wide range of political, security, and ideological issues. As such the president immediately accomplished two things: first, he assumed many of the constitutional powers of the prime minister and second, he institutionalized the political role of the military through the new NSC.

Musharraf held a referendum in April 2002 to ask the people of Pakistan whether or not they wanted him to be their president. This move was not only illegal, as he was an unelected president, but also violated the constitutional requirements for the holding of a referendum, which do not permit it to substitute for electoral procedures. "I'm a democrat by instinct," he said after it was over and he had won.[9] The referendum was termed a farce by the public, and after Musharraf accepted its results in his favor he was forced to go ahead and apologize for doing it in the first place.

Then he held elections a few months later, which only rubbed salt in the wounds of a humiliated electorate. There was actually little domestic political pressure to hold elections, because a movement for the restoration of democracy was slow to take root in the wake of the distraction provided by the new "war on terror." In a country of mainly illiterate voters, one did not need to be educated to think that elections were being forced on an unprepared population at the behest of the Americans, who needed to increase the international legitimacy of their new friend.

The president followed close in the tradition of his military predecessors by using old tactics of threat and coercion exercised through the intelligence agencies to foster a political party that would stand in the elections and go on to serve the regime. The "King's Party," as it is known, is the Pakistan Muslim League (Q) (PML [Q]), comprising some new politicians and primarily defectors from Nawaz Sharif's Muslim League. Not only that, but the leaders of the two most popular political parties in the country, Benazir Bhutto, whose Pakistan People's Party (PPP) still maintains enormous grassroots support in tracts of the country, and Nawaz Sharif, who also enjoys strong popular support in his home province of the Punjab, were in exile at the time and could not contest the election.

In October 2002, Pakistan held elections to local councils, provincial assemblies, and the National Assembly. The elections were held under the Legal Framework Order 2002, which gave the president discretionary powers to dissolve the National Assembly, extended his presidential term by five years, and validated all his acts and decrees prior to the Order. It was amended just hours before the election to permit independent election candidates to join any party within three days of the announcement of the election results. (UNDP 2005, 4)

The PML (Q) won the elections, to no one's surprise, with the press and public alike sharing stories of how the votes had been rigged. The newly elected assemblies led by the PML (Q) were quick to endorse Musharraf's legal maneuvers and passed the 17th Amendment Bill to the Constitution. Now the General had a semblance of democratic legitimacy for his enormously undemocratic decisions before the elections.

The historical precedent that came to mind among observers and media commentators was Ayub Khan's Basic Democracies, another controlled electoral experiment held in the 1960s. Under the Basic Democracies, elections to local government bodies, separately in the east and west wings of the country, were held on a non-party basis under military rule. The intent was to build a cadre of civilians at the local level who would support the government and forestall any mass political movement. The model failed when mass student and union-led protests succeeded in toppling the regime in 1968. But the idea remained in the memory of the military, prompting General Zia to hold non-party elections in the 1980s and General Musharraf to take half steps of his own in the democratic direction early in his political career.

There are ongoing criticisms that people's political rights, freedom of expression, and press freedom are under attack by the military, even in the new so-called democracy. While they may be true to a certain extent, these restrictions pale in comparison with those imposed by General Zia[10] and therefore aroused only sporadic protest from civilian society until 2004. Meanwhile Pakistan's press and electronic media are enjoying a kind of boom as private channels and radio stations proliferate, and talk shows on even controversial subjects are aired. Government pressure is subtler, as anecdotal evidence suggests that military intelligence officers do not make their views known crudely, but prefer to pressure editors of publications privately to ensure that coverage of the government remains of an acceptable kind. One example of this, for the ordinary observer, is the manner in which the media, the press in particular, has failed to publish detailed exposes of the activities of Dr. A. Q. Khan and his international trade in nuclear secrets, preferring to accept the government statement that the man acted alone without any military or government support. He is neither in jail undergoing trial nor is he permitted to meet the press under his house arrest, both signs that the media is being prevented from exploring the matter further.

The military has made some concessions to democratic institution building, and this has served to appease the U.S. government's fears that General Musharraf lacks sufficient international credibility. Pakistan was readmitted to the Commonwealth in 2004, reversing its expulsion after the military takeover. Pakistan has also been allotted the status of a non-NATO ally by the United States, in recognition of the government's cooperation not only in the war on "terror" but also in its attempt to institute some democratic reforms. The manner in which the military has manipulated political leaders to create a semblance of parliamentary democracy does not appear to have prevented it from receiving this recognition.

Despite this unhappy situation, these reforms are still worth mentioning in some detail because in isolation they do appear to mark important milestones in the process of increasing the peoples' representation in government. It is likely that they will increase the sense among voters that political empowerment begins at the grassroots level and that the political system is indeed responsive to the people. What remains to be addressed, of course, is how much these reforms are undermined by the larger context in which they have been made.

Women's political participation

An affirmative action measure to increase women's political participation was decreed by presidential ordinances[11] in the run-up to the elections. A similar provision existed in the Constitution, but it lapsed and was ironically not renewed during the last bout of civilian rule in the 1990s. Its restoration and improvement was a long-standing demand of the women's movement in Pakistan, which in fact had developed the modalities for implementing a provision reserving 33 percent of seats for women at all three tiers of elected government: the national assemblies, provincial assemblies, and local bodies. The restoration of reserved seats was also recommended by the Inquiry Commission on the Status of Women 1997, a body comprising legal, religious, and feminist experts that were respected across the country.

The government supported national-level mobilisation campaigns launched by NGOs to encourage women to contest the elections. A record 67,512 women filed nominations for 35,963 reserved seats at all three levels of the local government (UNDP 2005, 4). There are 188 women in the National and Provincial assemblies and seventeen have been nominated for the Senate seats reserved for women. Another nine women were directly elected on general seats to the National Assembly (HRCP 2003, 234). Elections on reserved seats took place through an indirect process in which the political parties with the majority of seats in an elected body could nominate their women representatives to the reserved seats.

This is the first time so many women participated in any form in the country's electoral politics and it possible for them to begin to change the face of Pakistan politics for the better if they use their power effectively (UNDP 2005, 1). For this affirmative action measure to succeed, the state has to enact more gender equity measures that support women's entry into electoral politics. The broader indicators for women's development remain among the lowest in the world, and the state has historically taken few measures to reverse the prevalent discrimination against women in society (Khan 1998). These steps would include the repeal of discriminatory legislation, legal and police measures to prevent violence against women, and support for women in the workforce.[12]

It also means addressing poverty issues seriously, since the current incidence of poverty is 33 percent up from 23 percent in 1987–1988.[13] We also know that women and children suffer the most, both materially and socially, among the poor.[14] The ongoing increase in poverty in Pakistan has been blamed on inappropriate policies and poor governance.[15]

It comes as no surprise that at the local government level, elected women are experiencing extreme gender bias and resistance from their male colleagues, who are unaccustomed to working with women in the public sphere. At the national and provincial levels this translates into pressure on women to simply follow their party's position and avoid any independent contributions. Civil society organizations, on the other hand, are attempting to provide more comprehensive support to women in the elected bodies, including gender sensitization and orientation training to both men and women, helplines, and resources centers for women councillors and legislators.

Yet the government of Pakistan has already instructed the provinces to amend their local government ordinances in December 2005, just prior to the second round of local elections to be held under the rule of General Musharraf. They reduced the total number of seats in the union councils from 21 to 13 and brought the number of reserved seats for women down from 6 to 4.[16] The total number of reserved seats for women in local councils is now 28,582 compared to the previous total of 40,049 (Aurat Foundation 2005, 3). The government's commitment to enhancing the number of women in politics is already diminished, probably because it has decided that the political engagement of people at the local level had become too broad and representative and had to be slashed after one round of elections only.

Devolution of Power

A long-standing governance issue in Pakistan has been how to share power between the center, the provinces, and the local districts. The Constitution recognizes three tiers of government, although the modalities of how they should function in daily administration remains a major point of contention for everyone engaged in politics. One view of military regimes has been that historically they have empowered the third, or local tier, by ensuring that local and district councils are filled with their supporters so that the seeds of a constituency for the dictator in power are sown. In contrast, civilian governments and political parties have overemphasized the power of the National and Provincial assemblies and have tended to neglect the local bodies and underfund them in their effort to consolidate their hold on the center of government.

General Musharraf attempted to reform the system by developing an ambitious devolution plan, the Local Government Plan 2000, that was implemented, ingeniously, through the promulgation of ordinances in the absence of elected provincial governments. The plan served many purposes, not the least of which was to increase his base of support by fostering local bodies as a political base for his "king's party," but also to please the international donors and financiers who fund much of the development work in Pakistan and echo the demands of activist organizations by insisting that governance become less centralized. Now that the election process is complete and the reorganized local government bodies have had a chance to function, some analysis is emerging of how effective and democratic these reforms have actually been.

The precedents to this experiment both took place under previous military regimes, those of Ayub and Zia.[17] They did not achieve the stated results by empowering local government; rather they consolidated the grip of the central government (in both cases unelected and military) while weakening the provincial governments by reducing their funds and access to the local bodies. Under Zia, local bodies' elections were held on a nonparty basis in 1985, meaning that political parties could not contest as such and a cadre of personalized favorites of the regime entered this grassroots tier of government. While members of political parties could run on an individual basis, most refused to participate in these polls.

The current devolution plan once again did not allow local elections to take place on a party basis. If a fundamental aspect of democratic institution building is the closeness and accountability of political organizations to the people they represent, then at the outset this plan has ensured the exact opposite. According to the new rules, local council members are directly elected in a constituency. They in turn have the power to elect their district *nazim,* a person who in turn represents all the constituencies in the district as a whole. This powerful position, therefore, is determined on the basis of an indirect election, and the *nazim* may be someone who does not even enjoy the support of a majority constituency.

The plan, then, exacerbates the already tense relation between the local tier of government and the provincial governments. The latter can exercise control over a district *nazim* mainly through their bureaucratic powers alone, and thus reduce the *nazim's* ability to deliver any meaningful change in a district despite the fact that he enjoys access to more funds to spend than ever before. Historically the provincial elected assemblies have been the mainstay of civilian governments, who depend on their majorities in the provinces to keep their grip on power in the center, where an ever-watchful army has stood ready to assume power when it can. The military, in turn, continues to cultivate the support it requires at the grassroots level through bypassing the provincial governments and accessing the local constituencies through partially empowered local bodies. The growing insurgency in Balochistan, for example, is fueled in part by anger that the federal government is controlling the decisions of the new district governments and bypassing the provincial assembly altogether.

Although there are other positive elements to the devolution plan, which include a reduction in the size of electoral constituencies and also guaranteed representation of women and minorities in the local councils, it is dangerously close to being dismissed as an expensive effort by the government to extend its control at the grassroots level. There may be some prodemocratic outcomes in the long run, particularly the political experience gained by women councilors and *nazims*. But if it is proven to be a tool of manipulation used by the military, whenever a representative civilian government returns to power the whole idea of empowering the third tier of government will be pushed onto the back burner once again. The fact that the number of local council seats was arbitrarily cut from 21 to 13 for the last round of elections in December 2005 only confirms suspicions that the military does not take local democratic institution-building seriously.

Possibly the final blow to any illusion that somehow democracy is being strengthened under military rule was the announcement in July 2004 that the next prime minister of Pakistan would be a man who had yet to be elected to Parliament. Not surprisingly, the U.S. government showed no concern about the manner of this appointment. (It did express more concern, however, when rumors were afoot earlier that there may be a plot to overthrow Musharraf. "We would not be supportive of any effort to change the government of Pakistan in a way that is not part of the political process or constitutionally," said Secretary of State Colin Powell).[18]

Equally unsurprising was a suicide bomber attack on the proposed premier, finance minister Shaukat Aziz, as he ended a day of campaigning in one of the two constituencies where he proposed to stand for by-election to seats hastily vacated by members of the PML (Q). In short, the president of Pakistan sacked the sitting prime minister, a man selected through a parliamentary process, although a faulty one. He undermined his own claims to institutionalizing democracy by further selecting the new prime minister from among his unelected advisers, and even announcing that the man would run in a by-election (hastily organized) from two constituencies (where he had no obvious ties).

And in the last nonsurprise, Shaukat Aziz got a resounding victory in both constituencies and was promptly sworn in as prime minister. Although parliamentarians from opposition parties loudly protested this move, as long as the president of the country is also chief of army staff, it is not possible to effectively resist this kind of imposed political process. A leading political monthly, meanwhile, places Aziz's face on its cover with words, "Can He Deliver? Beholden to his military patrons and with no political base, will Shaukat Aziz be able to walk the walk...."[19]

The opposition parties demanded from the start of military rule that Musharraf resign either his army leadership or his role as president, but not retain both posts. That was the understanding with which some parties, particularly the MMA, agreed to cooperate to some extent with the regime. The deadline for his shedding of the uniform was December 2004. Yet Musharraf announced in September 2004 that "a vast majority of the Pakistani people want me in uniform," citing internal terrorism and the need to be strong for the nation as reasons to renege on his agreement with the politicians (Hasan 2004, 1).

The United States observed the heated developments coolly. The State Department spokesman said:

> Pakistan's long-term interest continues to be in a transition to a fully functioning democracy. We do expect to see continuing progress towards this goal, which is central to Pakistan becoming a moderate and modern Islamic state . . . [President Musharraf's] vision for his country he describes as one of enlightened moderation. This is a vision for Pakistan that we fully share." (Daily Times, September 18, 2004)

The new prime minister stated clearly in September 2004, that he and his cabinet requested the president to retain hold on both positions. He said that it was necessary for the country's "stability and solidarity." It required some maneuvering to make this possible, since the Constitution of Pakistan does not allow for the president to keep two offices unless subject to law. This caveat opened the way for the National Assembly to vote in favor of the legislation in October 2004, thus allowing Musharraf the option to retain his uniform. It would be up to the Supreme Court of Pakistan to assert that the law violated the spirit of the Constitution, which does stipulate that the chief of army staff remain apolitical. As one columnist summed it up, the situation "indicates that the decision to change the fundamental federal and parliamentary base of Pakistan's democratic structure is being firmly laid under the fourth spell of military rule, contrary to the repeated declarations of the founder of Pakistan that Pakistan would be a modern democracy" (Akhtar, September 19, 2004, 3). As expected, General Musharraf held on to his uniform and retains both his army and political positions to this day.

While all these political manipulations create distress and distraction for the public, the gravest questions currently facing political organizations and the government are still not being seriously debated at all. That is, what form of democratic rule is best suited to the country when social indicators remain so low and the attraction to politics of ideological extremism remains so strong in some parts? How can we improve upon the 1971 Constitution to ensure that it never gets suspended again and that the people's right to elect their own rulers remains intact?

The regime has made a clumsy attempt to settle the question by consolidating its own power and weakening the power of political parties, but that is no long-term answer. It has violated the Constitution, set up a flawed and weak democracy, and in fact increased the power of the military in Pakistan. In effect, it has given the nation its answers to the questions posed above.

Summary

The oldest political questions in Pakistan are still begging for answers—not from the army but from the people. The current political situation, both domestically and internationally, does not bring clarity to this difficult process. The current government puts the military at the center of power brokerage and management of a compliant democracy in the long run. It also makes the military a key corporate player in the economy for the first time, thus requiring it to maintain a political role to protect its interests.

Further, while the regime insists that it holds a moderate position on issues of Islam, governance, and international relations, there is little evidence that this is any more than a rhetorical gesture in times of crisis. Civil society organizations and the media do encourage discussion on the role of Islam in politics and identity of Pakistan, but in sharp contrast, the controlled elected assemblies resist opening up the topic. Meanwhile, the Constitution of Pakistan is a document much twisted and amended in the name of religion, and General Musharraf has backed off from removing laws that discriminate against citizens on the basis of religion. In his efforts to play politics and keep as many groups on his side, he has tried to appease religious organizations in his running of government rather than antagonize them by stating a clear secular position.

A military regime by its very definition and nature cannot build the foundation for democratic governance, because that would be its own undoing. It can, however, accomplish whatever is necessary to ensure that it stays in power in the short term, even hold elections and implement a plan of power devolution. But we have seen that these moves were motivated by decidedly undemocratic impulses and supported by the United States, which had its own national interests at stake. This is not to say that civilian governments represented authentic democratic governance either, but their weaknesses lay more in the realm of corruption, nepotism, and overcentralized governance. The threat of military takeover looms largest on the political horizon of Pakistan, so much so that it has impeded the healthy growth of civilian rule time and again. Pakistani rulers have only partially explored the type of democracy that best suits Pakistan, and even when they have done, the military seems to have set the parameters. But ultimately lack of experience on the part of the voters and politicians alike has held the country back from resolving this issue—to the benefit of the military once again.

So what has the post-9/11 world brought Pakistan? It has brought Americans—their aid, international backing, and military presence. It has favored a military regime to the detriment of the growth of our political culture and chances for democratic rule once again. It has deepened the power of political Islam in the aftermath of U.S. military campaigns. There has been no meaningful resolution of some of the most serious questions facing the nation. A ray of hope, however, that relations between Pakistan and India will improve as peace negotiations begin, may be one area of positive change ahead, but it is too soon to tell.

The "war on terror" has changed the discourse of international relations. By presenting the situation from a domestic perspective and showing how the military, the most powerful political player in Pakistan, is using the situation to its own advantage, I hope to introduce some sober analysis into this new discourse. We know that the military's grip on economic and political power is being consolidated. History will show that precious time has been wasted yet again, time that could have been devoted toward evolving an effective and responsive democracy in this complex nation. Finally, what will negatively affect the lives of millions will no doubt have less-than-positive international consequences as well. Unfortunately, in the rush to win the "war on terror" this possibility has not been taken into adequate consideration.

Notes

1. The Mutahida Majlis-e-Amal (MMA) is a coalition of religious political parties that ran as one during the 2002 elections and became the largest political party in the provincial assembly of the North-West Frontier Province and Balochistan. Both provinces border Afghanistan. The unprecedented collaboration of these parties, who otherwise have deep ideological and religious differences, was prompted by their shared antipathy for the U.S. invasion of Afghanistan in 2001 and General Musharraf's support of the Americans. Some of the MMA member parties were also direct supporters of the Taliban.
2. Nawaz Sharif was the chief minister of the Punjab, Pakistan's most populous and powerful province, during the tenure of General Zia. He went on to win elections as head of a coalition of political parties after Benazir Bhutto was deposed in 1990, only to find himself dismissed by the president less than two years into his term. Bhutto won the next elections, and when she was dismissed by the president yet again, Nawaz Sharif was reelected prime minister as head of the Muslim League (Nawaz) in 1996 and was deposed by coup in October, 1999.
3. For details on General Zia's policy on women see Mumtaz and Shaheed (1987). For details of Nawaz Sharif's efforts to continue with Zia's process of Islamization and discrimination against women, see Shahla Zia (1998) and Omar Asghar Khan (2001).
4. This is called the Pakistan Muslim League (Q). The party won the majority in the 2002 national elections. It comprises members of other national political parties, particularly the Pakistan Muslim League group run by former prime minister Nawaz Sharif.
5. In the Pakistani media the term "extremist" refers to a person who takes up arms to fight for a political ideology and makes a demand from the government. It includes the supporters of religion-based violent political organizations, as well as ethnic and nationalist groups fighting for political rights in Pakistan's provinces or in Kashmir. In the international media the term is used with reference to Pakistan's *jihadi* groups that support a holy war in favor of spreading their view of political Islam, and as such is indistinguishable from the other term, "terrorist."
6. See the website www.anjumanmuzareen.com.pk; also see Rizvi (2003).
7. Abdul Rauf Faisal's *What's Right with Islam is What's Right with America* (2005) and other publications illustrate this effort.
8. For details on this relationship see Cooley (2001).
9. "I'm a Democrat by instinct: Musharraf," Friday, May 10, 2002. www.newsarchives.indianinfo.com/spotlight/mushabid/10musha.html (accessed November 21, 2005).

10. The first public lashing organized by his government took place under a martial law regulation permitting the flogging of journalists.
11. At the local level, the local government ordinance provides for 33 percent reserved seats for women to be directly elected in the local bodies. The Legal Framework Order 2002 is an extra-constitutional law enacted by the military government to revive the provincial and federal parliaments. It includes some controversial provisions, such as discretionary powers to the president to dissolve the National Assembly and a five-year extension of his presidency (UNDP 2005, 4).
12. A full set of detailed recommendations for the empowerment of women can be found in *Report of the Commission of Inquiry for Women* (Islamabad: Government of Pakistan, 1997), 126–147.
13. *Social Development in Pakistan Annual Review 2004* (2004), 57. The incidence of poverty quoted here is determined by the number of people below the poverty line, which means those who lack sufficient income to procure the minimum amounts of the basic necessities of life, including food, clothing, education, and health care (56).
14. If the definition of poverty includes deprivation in well-being, then it is more clear how women in particular suffer. They are deprived in terms of their income-generation capacity, ownership of land and productive assets, access to labor market, access to economic options, social services and security. Further, the high rate of maternal mortality (350 per 100,000 live births) reveals the severe deprivation in access to health care. See *Pakistan National Report Beijing+10* (2005), 5, 23.
15. *Human Development in South Asia 2002: The Gender Question* (2002), 15
16. *The Sindh Local Government Ordinance, 2001, No. XXVII, Updated Version*, December 2005, Chapter VIII Union Council, 51.
17. This brief discussion on the devolution issue is based on the findings of Cheema et al (2003).
18. Iqbal (2004).
19. *Newsline,* September 2004.

Bibliography

Akhtar, Hasan, "Shaukat Aziz on the uniform issue," *Dawn,* September 19, 2004.
Aurat Foundation. 2002. *Citizen's campaign for women's representation in local government in Pakistan* (September 2000–October 2001).
———. 2005. *Women in Local Government 2005.* Islamabad: Aurat Publication and Information Service Foundation.
Cheema, A., S. K. Mohmand and Asad Sayeed. December 2003. "Local government reforms in Pakistan: legitimising centralisation or a driver for pro-poor change?" Mimeo. Collective for Social Science Research, Karachi.
Clarke, Richard. 2004. *Against all enemies.* New York: Free Press.
Cooley, John K. 2002. *Unholy wars: Afghanistan, America and international terrorism.* London: Pluto Press.
Daily Times. 2004. "Musharraf has not taken decision on uniform: US." September 18 [staff report].
Dawn. December 30, 2003. Text of the 17th Amendment Bill.

————. 2002. "Jihad only option to halt US: MMA." March 31. Bureau Report.

Faisal, Abdul Rauf. 2005. *What's right with Islamis what's right with America.* San Francisco: Harper.

Government of Pakistan. 1997. *Report of the commission of inquiry for women.* Islamabad.

Hasan, Khalid. 2004. "I'm still feeling the people's pulse: Musharraf." *Daily Times,* September 18, 1.

Herald. September 2004, 50–63.

Human Rights Commission of Pakistan. 2003. *State of human rights 2002.* Lahore: Human Rights Commission of Pakistan.

Indiainfo.com website. 2002. "I'm a democrat by instinct: Musharraf." May 10. www.news.indianinfo.com/spotlight/mushabid/10musha.html. May 10. [accessed November 21, 2005].

Iqbal, Anwar. 2004. "US won't support change of government in Pakistan: Powell." *Dawn,* May 30.

Khan, Ayesha. 1998. *Women and the government of Pakistan: a brief policy history (1975–1998).* Islamabad: Gender Unit, United Nations Development Programme.

Khan, Omar Asghar. 2001. "Critical engagements: NGOs and the state." In *Power and civil society in Pakistan,* edited by Anita M. Weiss and S. Zulfiger Gilani. Karachi: Oxford University Press. 275–300.

Mahbub ul Haq Human Development Centre.2002. *Human development in South Asia 2002: the gender question.* Karachi: Oxford University Press. 15.

Ministry of Women's Development, Government of Pakistan. 2005. *Pakistan national report Beijing+10.* Islamabad: Ministry of Women's Development. 5.

Mumtaz, K., and F. Shaheed. 1987. *Women in Pakistan: two steps forward one step back.* London: Zed Press.*Newsline,* September 2004.[cover page]

Rizvi, H. A. 2003. "Land allotments and the military." *Daily Times,* August 28.

Sayeed, A., and K. Nadvi. 2004. Industrial capital and pro-poor change. [unpublished report commissioned by the Collective for Social Science Research, Karachi, for the Institute of Development Studies, University of Sussex, and the Department for International Development, UK.]

Siddiqa, Ayesha. 2004. The politics of military's economic interests. [unpublished report commissioned by the Collective for Social Science Research, Karachi, for the Institute of Development Studies, University of Sussex, and the Department for International Development, UK.]

The Sindh local government ordinance, 2001, no. XXVII, updated version. December 2005. Chapter VIII Union Council. 51.

Social Policy and Development Centre. 2004. *Social development in Pakistan annual review 2004.* Karachi: Social Policy and Development Centre. 57.

Talbot, Ian. 1998. *Pakistan: a modern history.* London: Hurst & Company.

UNHCR. 2004. Challenges to return. Geneva: UNHCR.

United Nations Development Programme (UNDP). 2005. Political and legislative participation of women in Pakistan: issues and perspectives. Islamabad.

Zia, Shahla. 1998. "Some experiences of the women's movement: strategies for success." In *Shaping women's lives: laws, practices & strategies in Pakistan,* edited by Farida Shaheed Lahore: Shirkat Gah. 371–414.

Chapter 6

Bewildered? Women's Studies and the War on Terror

Monisha Das Gupta

question that I encountered repeatedly from my students and numerous colleagues at Syracuse University in the wake of 9/11 was, "Why did this happen?" On a predominantly white campus in upstate New York, which immediately kicked into patriotic overdrive, I heard the plaintive need for clarity on a world that to them had suddenly become opaque and uncertain. While many were not entirely comfortable with the declaration of a war without an end on terrorism, they felt the overwhelming need to be safe in the face of this newly perceived vulnerability.

Institutionally, little thought was given to my apprehensions about my safety as an Indian citizen working in the United States. In marking this, I am not gesturing toward the backlash against people of South Asian and Middle Eastern origin in the United States within hours of the collapse of the twin towers of the World Trade Center (WTC). I would hear those painful stories in the months that followed when I was called in to document the impact of 9/11 on yellow cab drivers in New York City (Das Gupta 2004, 2005). Rather, I am talking about that sickening fear in the pit of my stomach for my loved ones thousands of miles away. Most of my family lives in India, and in the days that immediately followed 9/11, the thought of a war in Afghanistan and its impact politically and economically on the region brought back panic-stricken memories of strife and insecurity. I remembered the blackouts, sirens, and the deafening sound of fighter planes in my Kolkata neighborhood during the 1971 freedom struggle that gave birth to Bangladesh, at which time I was ten years old; the flood of refugees in Delhi following the 1979 Soviet invasion of Afghanistan when that word "mujahideen" entered our vocabulary; and the 1984 assassination of then prime minister of India Indira

Gandhi, which was avenged by taking thousands of Sikh lives—a time when it seemed as if everything associated with the word "human" was suspended. I do not think that my students or colleagues were articulating their bewilderment at the WTC attacks with any inkling of this history of political turmoil that I carry in my body. But they had a vague intuition as they asked the question of each other (and of me) that people like myself might have an explanation for the rude shattering of their cocoon.

Efforts over the last two decades to open the U.S. academy to perspectives of and scholars from what we now call the economic South have been inadequate in answering why 9/11 happened. Productive struggles have opened up institutional spaces like Women's Studies to epistemologies and histories of the South. Yet, many U.S. feminists failed to responsibly answer the question as to why the 9/11 attacks happened. I will dwell on this inadequacy because, if we, collectively as feminists, cannot answer the question, we cannot clearly respond to 9/11 and the "war on terror." The war has put this nation in crisis and, more importantly, opened up parts of the world to direct, unabashed, and violent U.S. military intervention on the basis of cultural understandings that turn on such binary oppositions as good and evil, us and them, and civilized and barbaric.

Looking specifically at Women's Studies and more generally at the social sciences in the United States, I argue that Women's Studies continues to be an imperial site implicated in the American state's long history of empire building. Globalization, in Women's Studies as well as in disciplines such as sociology in which I am trained, continues to be treated as a specialization rather than as something that touches every American's life and therefore needs analysis in teaching and writing about so-called domestic issues. This neat compartmentalization of the "domestic" from the "international" has two effects. First, as people living in the United States, we remain blind to the many ways in which the economic North and South interpenetrate and in which our lives are connected through unequal relations of power to the lives of those in the South. I argue that the current dominance of the race, class, and gender paradigm[1] in Women's Studies, as powerful as it is, has interfered with a systematic pedagogic and scholarly attention to imperialism. As I explain below, the paradigm restricts our gaze to the domestic by dropping from it analyses of the intersection of imperialism with race, class, and gender, which the black and third-world feminists it invokes have consistently theorized. The blindness is further perpetuated as mainstream feminists who study the American state have continued to characterize it as a welfare state instead of a restructured "warfare state" (Gilmore 2002) or "an advanced colonial/capitalist state" (Guerrero 1997). Second, the compartmentalization of the domestic and international has given rise to an academic division of labor in which people who look like me—scholars from newly independent countries in the South who do their intellectual and sometimes political work out of the U.S. academy—are expected to teach and write about international phenomena while Americans focus on the domestic.

When Robin L. Riley, coeditor of this volume, invited me in November 2001 to speak for a series of panels she was planning to organize on gender and war, I wanted to tackle that insistent question of why 9/11 happened, especially in light of the fact that this was the first initiative on campus to offer an alternative to the jingoistic cries of mostly male speakers hosted by Syracuse University's Maxwell School, well known for producing diplomats and CIA officers. Even as I clearly saw my task as a manifestation of the division of labor I have just alluded to, I also spoke to my audience of the hope in my heart that 9/11 had the potential to disrupt that division. The urgent need that U.S.-born members of the audience had to make sense of the 3,000 people dead in the ruins of the WTC and the lives lost and to be lost in Afghanistan (and later in Iraq) might mean that Americans could no longer inure themselves to what the United States did and does in the world. It would mean that my American colleagues would need to learn, teach, and write about that world in terms of connections, deeply problematic as they are, rather than oppositions.

I carried this hope to the University of Hawai'i, where I am now part of Women's Studies. Hawai'i is a key site within the United States to think about imperialism. Hawai'i was annexed without a treaty in 1898 after its government was illegally overthrown by a U.S.-backed coup in 1893. It was a U.S. territory between 1900 and 1959 and was admitted to statehood in 1959 on the basis of a plebiscite that did not offer independence as an option as it should have under international mandates (McGregor 2002; Trask 2000). Native Hawai'ian activists fighting for self-determination, along with their allies, feel everyday the impact of the United States, which has historically exploited their lands and seas, and currently promotes tourism and military bases as the state's twin economic engines. Citing concerns about national security following the 9/11 attacks, the army, in October 2001, negotiated to resume live-fire training in O'ahu's Makua Valley, the home of at least forty-five endangered plant and animal species and a hundred sacred native sites (Kakesako 2001). This decision rolled back the gains of community-led legal action that ordered the army to suspend its exercises after a misfired mortar ravaged 800 acres of the military reservation in September 1998 (Earthjustice 2004).[2] From 2002 onward, activists have been resisting the U.S. military's initiative to takeover 25,663 acres of additional lands and further destruction of Hawai'i's already fragile ecosystem for military exercises (Blanco 2004; Not in Our Name 2003). These exercises involve Strykers, armored assault vehicles, which have been designed to be deployed "just in time" to quell urban unrest in the Pacific and Southeast Asia. Those fighting for self-determination here in Hawai'i know how it feels to be occupied. Hawai'i, thus, provides a unique location to critique imperialism. The University of Hawai'i's Women's Studies' focus on Asia, the Pacific, and on the faculty's commitment to fight the militarization of the islands distinguishes it from other such programs or departments in the country. Yet, even in this new environment, the question of imperial academic feminism did not lose its salience.

In January 2004, I attended a Women's Studies colloquium given by an Iranian feminist Farideh Fahri (2004), who was tracing how such unlikely actors as the widows of martyrs created spaces for the women's movement in Iran after the 1979 revolution. These spaces were opened up because of the women's willingness to work with the possibilities as well as constraints of a theocratized state to demand their entitlements. The talk invited the audience to rethink in complex ways the simplistic opposition between women's rights and Islamic fundamentalism, an opposition that has been mobilized again and again in the case of women in Afghanistan as justification for invading the country. But what happened in the room was quite the reverse. Fahri's examples of postrevolutionary measures such as lowering the age of consent to marriage, legally treating marriage as a contract, discouraging girls from playing sports, and excluding women from judgeships and the office of the president—developments that Iranian women had to navigate—left the audience, including some feminists, alternately amused and revolted. By contrast, other examples of the advances Iranian women have made in education, especially in law school, and their entry into politics drew murmurs of approbation. Later, when I asked one of my colleagues to explain these reactions, she said that laughter was a way of coping with the strangeness with which she and the audience were confronted.

In all this hilarity, the point about Iranian women's activism emerging from two contradictory regimes of the theocratic state—one that legalized discriminatory practices against women and the other that provided educational, political, and economic opportunities to women—was lost. The audience, some of whom were feminists , made its point by constituting and asserting a Western, modern, secular self for which the practices of the Iranian state were shocking, ridiculous, and unintelligible until some of the effects of these practices, like an increase in women in higher education, started to resemble what that self could identify as women's liberation. After this familiar exercise in imperialism that Chandra Mohanty (1986) diagnosed nearly two decades ago as thinking-as-usual in Western feminism, the audience turned to discussing with Fahri the Bush administration's folly in Iraq, where it was trying to put in place a transitional government without any clear understanding of the country's complicated sociocultural formations. The audience shifted uncritically from exercising imperialism to attacking it. Yet, the audience and the Bush administration shared normative ideas about civilization and democracy that demarcated "us" from "them" and allowed both entities to assert the superiority of Western values and subjectivity. The problem with Women's Studies and how it should respond to the war on terror in its institutional practices lies precisely in the seamless and unselfreflexive shift from the imperial to the critical.

In her influential essay, "Under Western Eyes," Mohanty (1986) argues that Western feminists deploy a colonizing discourse when they engage in cross-cultural work by casting women in the "third world" as homogenized victims of patriarchy while simultaneously positing themselves as self-conscious subject-agents. By asking Western feminists to be attentive to the representational and material politics of cross-cultural research and to abandon a universalizing account of women's oppression as the method of building global sisterhood, Mohanty offered firmer grounds for solidarity based on differences among women, which in turn, redefined narrow conceptions of feminist issues as seen through Western eyes.[3]

Feminist Pedagogies: Mapping the Domestic and International

Revisiting her concerns in the essay nearly two decades after it was written, Mohanty (2003) finds feminist scholarship and pedagogy caught in the universalism/particularism conundrum in which differences are treated as so profound and irreducible that they prevent any vision of common action. The antagonism between the universal, and therefore a historical, and the historicized particular maps onto the partitioning of the domestic from the international to which I have been referring. Interestingly, local, U.S.-centered feminist issues and frameworks—race, class, gender, and sexuality as privileged analytical categories—remain universal, untouched by international feminist frameworks, which are particularized. In Women's Studies, this compartmentalization is reflected in curricular strategies to incorporate international women's issues and struggles by "producing a multicultural bazaar of international feminisms for the globally conscious [but locally anchored and stable] undergraduate consumer" (Lal 2003, 2).

Analyzing three models—the feminist-as-tourist, the feminist-as-explorer, and comparative feminist studies—that internationalize Women's Studies curricula, Mohanty (2003) identifies the first two efforts as the least effective in providing comparisons between the United States and other parts of the world and in breaking down the opposition between the universal and the particular. The feminist-as-tourist pedagogical model internationalizes an otherwise U.S.-based syllabus by visiting women in other cultures to learn about the sexist practices that oppress them and, in some cases, women's resistance to them. While the domestic and the international are juxtaposed, they remain separate, with the international being a distant site of excessive misogyny expressed in practices such as veiling, "honor" killings, genital mutilation, femicide, arranged marriages, and wife burning (see also Lal 2003). In this model, the originary and superior place of Western feminism remains intact and no analytical tools are offered to examine the imbrication of the domestic and international as a result of the eighteenth- and nineteenth-century phase of colonialism and the contemporary phase of global capitalist and U.S. military expansion. At the University of Hawai'i Women's Studies colloquium, Fahri's audience slipped into the touristic mode by refusing to see any parallels between challenges facing U.S. women and feminists and their Iranian counterparts, and in so doing, enacting their disavowal in terms of horror or approbation. Horror enforces notions of the unbridgeable particular while approbation underlines the universalization of Western feminist values.

Unlike the feminist-as-tourist pedagogical model, the feminist-as-explorer model makes no reference to the United States but focuses solely on the international. Like its counterpart, the feminist-as-explorer model promotes the discreteness rather than the relationality of the two areas. Thus, for example, one might become conversant with discourses of third-world development without fully understanding how the

United States has become increasingly instrumental in defining that discourse and how it rehearses and refines the tropes of development with similar effects on domestic groups. Be it development or structural adjustment and its accompanying package of economic reforms determined by the International Monetary Fund and the World Bank, no account in this approach links these international strategies that undermine the self-determination of postcolonial nation-states to U.S. corporate, trade, and military policies. As a result, globalization as "an economic, political, ideological phenomenon that actively brings the world and its various communities under connected and interdependent discursive and material regimes" (Mohanty 2003, 521) remains obscured.

Courses focussing on third-world women or on international development, which Women's Studies offers to correct parochial frameworks and to prepare students to live in a globalizing world, are often taught by third-world scholars. The division of intellectual labor promotes the sharp demarcation of the domestic and international. This division is analogous to the way in which Women's Studies courses about women of color provide "a racial alibi, and the bodies of knowledge produced by and about women of color are less important than the hailing of 'women of color'" (Lee 2000, 86). In a similar move, the labor of teaching about globalization, colonialism, neoimperialism, and development is too often "offshored" to third-world bodies within Women's Studies or other departments. With this offshoring, faculty members who teach about domestic issues no longer need to learn and teach about international issues (even though, they, like their students, also live in a globalizing world). So, for example, the vocabulary of structural adjustment as a globalized economic strategy, rarely crosses over to understandings of poverty, degeneration of health care and education, and cuts in public spending in the United States. The combined effect of separating bodies of knowledge and the bodies responsible for them results in the perception in Women's Studies that theories and analyses produced by third-world women or women of color "are plausible and carry explanatory weight only in relation to our *specific* experiences, but they have no use value in relation to the rest of the world" (Alexander and Mohanty 1997, xvii). Despite its desire to internationalize and diversify its frameworks, Women's Studies, through this mode, reproduces the parochial/imperial duality.

The third approach that is relational and responsible is available within Women's Studies curricula. Mohanty calls this the feminist solidarity or comparative feminist studies model in which the domestic and the international are not territorially fixed and distant but mutually constituted. It encourages examination of "relations of mutuality, coresponsibility, and common interest"(Mohanty 2003, 521) by taking into account connecting global forces that differentially impact women, their families, and their communities while opening up grounds for alliances among women in the economic North and South.[4]

Disavowed Dependencies

It is easy to see how the first two approaches that create the United States as a bounded sealed-off space separated and separable from the rest of world could foster my U.S. students' and colleagues' bewilderment at the WTC attacks. Many academics had a difficult time connecting the United States to such a "distant" and "little-known" place as Afghanistan when it started to get news coverage. Capturing the sense of bewilderment, Carolyn Ellis, professor of communication and sociology at the University of Southern Florida, in an autoethnography in which she records her responses to 9/11, notes:

> The revenge talk. Suspected Muslims. Suicide missions. Afghanistan. Osama bin Laden. Taliban. I am embarrassed that I don't even know who Osama bin Laden and the Taliban are. I doubt that I could point to Afghanistan on a map. I realize how isolationist I have been, we all have been. How innocent and complacent. I listen closely and try to understand what has happened. How? Why? And what for? We should find those who are guilty and blow 'um off the face of the earth. I don't know who 'um' is exactly, but the vague picture in my mind is of dark-skinned men with turbans, long robes, and beards. Not until later will I think about the complexities of racial profiling . . . I get some inkling of what a privileged life I have led and how little collective grief I have felt." (Ellis 2002, 388–389)

In contrast, South Asian taxi drivers in New York City who witnessed the second plane hit the tower, though equally shaken and traumatized, grew immediately apprehensive, quite correctly predicting the backlash that was to follow within hours against Muslims, South Asians, and people from the Middle East. What enables these two distinct subject positions informed by their distinct yet connected histories—one that falters toward an awakening and another that is knowing and ever-vigilant?

Ellis's confession of conjuring up a racialized, yet unknown space, rings descriptively true but analytically she conflates innocence with complacence. Innocence implies not knowing. Complacency stands for a satisfied state of knowing that encourages inaction. The tension between being able to imagine a highly racialized picture of territorial violation, while not being able to place who these people might be or where they might come from or why they might take such action is not a sign of innocence. Rather, it implicates one in an imperial project that encourages citizens to ignore multiple modes of internal and external colonization while enjoying the fruits of such subjugation, whether they be cheaper clothes and shoes, cheaper gas, cheaper fruits and vegetables, poor people and immigrants as stock scapegoats, the United States' international standing as superpower, or the doors that a U.S. passport opens. By invoking innocence, Ellis and disoriented academics like her absolve themselves from taking responsibility for their willful ignorance. When I ask Women's Studies to examine itself as an imperial site, I am concerned with the disavowal of connections forged in unequal terms between the so-called domestic and the international at home and abroad. I am concerned with accountability that must precede any effort toward transnational feminist alliances.

Since I am writing at a time of openly declared war, I am compelled to reformulate Mohanty's argument about "common differences" as the basis of "transnational feminist solidarity." My argument here revolves around recognizing the fact that commonalities between the North and South are often structured through the dependence of the North on the South. Thus, unlike Mohanty, I am less interested at this moment in mutuality, interdependency, coresponsibility, and coimplication. In answering the question of why 9/11 happened, we need to understand the *politics* of commonalities. Hélène Cixous (2002, 432) strikes a note of hope when she says, "I think the horrifying ordeal of September 11 has already given birth to a new foundation. A consciousness of what there is in common between the diverse living elements of an immense population." I, too, believe this, but I also believe that the foundation cannot be sound unless Americans can responsibly answer the following question. How do problems experienced by different groups in different spaces become common struggles? Commonalities are often understood as the suspension of power relations, even though Mohanty (2003, 521) prefaces her elaboration of the third and more effective pedagogical model by saying that it must pay attention to the "directionality of power" as it seeks to relate the local to the global and the particular to the universal.

The coresponsibility that she hopes that the third model can foster needs to come out of the recognition that those who live in the North are fully implicated in the crisis in security and sustainability in the North and the South.

If vulnerability, collective grieving, and the lack of safety now become issues Americans have in common with the people on whom their government wages the war on terror, what power-laden processes give rise to those commonalities? For decades, American security and complacency depended on the insecurity of many at home and others thousands of miles away. The feelings of invincibility and safety that 9/11 shattered for many Americans rested on the daily exposure to violence, economic sanctions, scarcity of basic goods and services, and the loss of loved ones of those who live in Palestine, Afghanistan, Pakistan, the Philippines, Iraq, and Cuba, to name just a few places. Until 9/11, the United States had managed to outsource the distressing experiences of war to marginalized pockets within its borders and other parts of the world. Post-9/11, internally, some Americans have tried to rebuild their sense of safety at the expense of the safety and security—physical, psychological, and material—of immigrants from South Asia and the Middle East, many of them working class. And, even before 9/11, poor people of color within domestic borders were rarely safe having daily felt the heavy hand of what they experience as a police state. In the United States today, we need to recognize common cause not just because we have a set of experiences stemming from very different roots that allows us to empathize with people who have experienced what we have but because we recognize that we are responsible for those experiences with which we now empathize.

Reterritorializing the United States: Black and Third-World Feminist Analyses of Imperialism

Interrogating Women's Studies after 9/11 involves asking not only how it has internationalized its curricula (i.e., interpreted its task as looking elsewhere) but also how it understands the domestic. In the 1980s, radical women of color named their epistemology "Black and Third World feminism." This move reterritorialized the United States by asserting that the third world could not be located "out there." There was a third world inside the United States. Transnationalizing domestic space, these feminists re-membered the United States by recalling a long history of internal colonization of Native nations and of extra-territorial interventions that led to undocumented and documented immigration, which brought the elsewhere home. The examination of borders, nation building, militarization, and the many faces of U.S. imperial expansion lay at the core of these feminist analyses.

The civil rights movement and the movement against the war in Vietnam required an understanding of Western imperialism and anticolonial struggles in Africa, Asia, and Latin America. Second-wave feminism grew out of these social movements. Yet, as Becky Thompson (2001) has shown in her account of multiracial feminism, women of color and white women, who were anti-imperialist and antiracist, did not find a receptive home in (predominantly white) feminism until writings by feminists of color created the space in the 1980s. If we go back to the Combahee River Collective's "A Black feminist statement" (1983) that serves as a blueprint even today of the issues that animate black and third-world politics, we find the Collective declaring: "We realize that the liberation of all oppressed peoples necessitates the destruction of the political-economic system of capitalism and imperialism as well as patriarchy" (Combahee River Collective 1983, 213). This statement constituted a call to feminists to analyze the gendered processes of capitalism and imperialism so that we do not mistake patriarchy to be a singular form of oppression and so that we could simultaneously develop an anti-imperial and anti-capitalist consciousness.

A still older work, Angela Davis's *Women, Race, and Class* (1981), critiques the early twentieth-century phase of the suffragist movement for its dual and linked investment in white supremacy and imperialism. Davis writes, "The last decade of the nineteenth century was a critical moment in the development of modern racism . . . This was also the period of imperialist expansion into the Philippines, Hawai'i, Cuba and Puerto Rico. The same forces that sought to subjugate the peoples of these countries were responsible for the worsening plight of Black people and the entire U.S. working class" (117). As a matter of fact, in Hawai'i, the business-political-missionary complex, when drafting the Republic of Hawai'i constitution in 1894, drew on the "Mississippi laws," designed to disenfranchise blacks, so as to keep Native Hawaiian from voting and participating in government (Silva 2004, 136–137). White suffragists, responding to public debates on the continent over how to establish an electoral process in Hawai'i and the other newly acquired territories, were concerned not about imperialism but the extension to their "new possessions" of what

Susan B. Anthony called the "half-barbaric" practice of white male enfranchisement (Davis 1981, 117). Whether black and third-world feminists were historicizing the shortcomings of the women's movement in the United States or writing a manifesto to guide their contemporary struggles, they considered imperialism to be an integral part of the problem of racism, poverty, and sexism in the United States.

The writings of Angela Davis, Audre Lorde, June Jordan, bell hooks, and Gloria Anzaldúa consistently make this point. I mention these particular names because their essays, excerpts from their larger works, or poetry can be found in most introductory Women's Studies texts. Their works are also included in upper-division, topics-based Women's Studies courses. Yet, how many of us teach Audre Lorde's essay, "Grenada revisited"(1984a), written after the U.S. invasion of her island home, in our Women's Studies classes? How many of us talk about Angela Davis's internationalism and her contemporary revisioning of that ideology or about June Jordan as an African American voice that fearlessly advocated Palestinian self-determination? Do we spend much time explaining why bell hooks in all her works insists on decolonizing our minds, actions, as well as material reality? How many of us flesh out Anzaldúa's (1987) complex story of Mexico's colonization by the United States politically and economically in the very first chapter of *Borderlands/La Frontera?*

Within this Women's Studies canon, Pacific Island feminists, who offer trenchant analyses of imperialism, and Asian American feminists, who have critiqued U.S. nationalism and citizenship for being exclusionary, are relatively marginalized.[5] Unless a course incorporates issues of Pacific Island women, our students are less likely to encounter the writings of the Native Hawaiian feminist Haunani-Kay Trask (1999), who offers one of the clearest accounts of the contemporary effects of the United States' colonization of Hawai'i on native peoples in the form of land theft, rapacious tourism, militarization, and relentless Americanization.

Asian American feminists, on their part, have made crucial connections among border controls, national identity, and immigration. In these times when the war on terror justifies the profiling of immigrants, Mitsuye Yamada's "Asian Pacific women and feminism" (1983), written soon after the outcry against Iranians in the United States following the 1979 Iranian hostage crisis, serves to remind us how quickly immigrants to the United States come to embody threats to the U.S. border and national security. By noting, "I know they speak about me" in response to her students' animosity against those Iranians "who overstep our hospitality by demonstrating and badmouthing our government," Yamada (1983, 75) stretches our memory back to the internment of first- and second-generation immigrants of Japanese ancestry. At this moment, her essay could be productively read, for example, with Native American writer Leslie Marmon Silko's "Border Patrol State,"(1997)[6] in which Native Americans, such as Chicana/os, Mexicana/os, or Asian Americans are criminalized as outsiders through the militarization of domestic space. Such connections help us concretely grasp that "domestic militarism and international militarism go hand in hand," an observation made by feminist geographer Ruth Gilmore (2002), as key to understanding the current war on terror. The imprints of U.S. imperialism are also covered up by excluding from the central concerns of Women's Studies the history of feminist participation in the Central American solidarity movement in the 1980s, although we see enough references to Latina women, a group identity that homogenizes the different histories of migration in relation to U.S. foreign policy.[7]

The occlusions I have just discussed enable Women's Studies to promote the hegemonic and distorted idea that, we, in the United States, have lived mostly in peace since World War II. Women's Studies has been part of spinning the cocoon of safety and security despite evidence offered by feminists of color of the havoc the United States has wrecked on vulnerable groups of people within and without. Had we paid attention to the workings of imperialism, we would have realized that the United States has actually been continuously at war as M. Jacqui Alexander (2002) pointed out in her inventory of U.S. military engagements since 1945. Historical memory would show that empire building has been a long and systematic process that was set in motion in the decades preceding the current war on terror. Since Women's Studies is one site at which this memory has been repressed, we as feminists find ourselves in a different position than many of our sisters in the 1980s. Pointing to feminist and lesbian contributions to the Central American solidarity movement, Becky Thompson (2001, 248) notes:

> This was partly made possible by multiracial feminism, which included significant attention to the United Sates as a colonizing country–a critique brought home in part by feminists of color from previously colonized countries (such as Trinidad, India, and Argentina) now living and active in the United States . . . This analysis, along with the anti-Vietnam war protests that many women had been involved in through the early 1970s, readied them to stand up against U.S. imperialism in Central America in the 1980s.

At the turn of the twenty-first century, what has Women's Studies, as one arm of the women's movement, done to ready itself to combat the current incarnation of U.S. imperialism?

The RCG Paradigm: The Declining Significance of Anti-imperialism

Since the late 1980s, scholarly developments and the hiring of women of color in academe have successfully moved Women's Studies away from its focus on gender and its sexual politics as the sole axis of oppression by emphasizing the centrality of race and class as intersecting analytical categories. Patricia Hill Collin's (1986; 1991) foundational work on the intersections of race, class, and gender has led to efforts to institutionalize the treatment of these intersecting categories as basic to social analysis. This shift has been so significant that it is no longer acceptable to leave out racial and class differences when researching or teaching about women in the United States. The attention to race and class is an indispensable corrective to the idea that gender inequality can be understood without locating women in the racial and economic order. While research and pedagogic strategies vary in the degree to which they are successful in treating oppressions as simultaneous (Combahee River Collective 1983) rather than additive, the race, class, and gender, or the RCG, approach has become a dominant (and undeniably important) paradigm in Women's Studies and in feminist scholarship in the social sciences and humanities.

The exclusive attention to race, class, and gender has, however, obscured the nation-state as an equally central analytic. Indebted as this approach is to the insights of the same radical black and third-world feminists who tenaciously foregrounded U.S. imperialism, it works with few tools that can theorize the ways in which nation-states shape and are shaped by race, class, gender, and sexuality. This analytical vacuum is being filled by interdisciplinary feminist political economists (Alexander 1994; Alexander and Mohanty 1997; Bannerji 2000; Carty 1994, 1999; Chang 2000; Guerrero 1997; Jayawardena 1986; Sudbury 1998; Yuval-Davis 1997; Glenn 2002; Lubiano 1998) many of whom are identified as transnational feminists, who have further developed the theorizations of the 1980s radical black and third-world feminists to understand the contemporary nature of states and capital. As a theoretical-methodological approach, transnational feminism analyzes how state processes depend on national ideologies about race, gender, sexuality, and class to determine who can be a citizen—legally and ideologically—and what rights a citizen can have. In the current phase of globalization, capital relies on state sanctioned restrictive notions of citizenship to cheapen and deskill migrant labor in the North. Class and class mobility, thus, get reconstituted in the dual context of cross-border movements and racialization in the United States. New forms of gender oppression arise as a result of state processes that categorize immigrants into legal and illegal. From a transnational perspective, cross-border flows deterritorialize the United States creating intimate dependencies between the domestic and international even as they reterritorialize the nation that seeks to seal these porous borders. While this group of transnational feminists use intersectionality as a method and attend to the political economy of race, class, and gender reformulations, those ensconced in the RCG paradigm tend to see questions of the state, nation, and citizenship as either extraneous or additional variables.

Partly, RCG has been successfully assimilated within Women's Studies because it in no way disrupts its cartography of the domestic and international. Immigrant women from the South become assimilated and domesticated as women of color and their stories are told through the limited, though important, lens of U.S.-bound constructs of race and class. The RCG paradigm understands differences among women along class and race lines and often contains these differences within a nationalist framework that lumps women with different national histories into U.S.-centric racial-ethnic groups. The "American" in African American, Asian American, Euro-American, or Mexican American is rarely called into question. Until recently (see Glenn 2002), the differences among these groups had not been recounted through the gendered and raced story of U.S. citizenship. The presence of Asian, African, Caribbean, and Central and Latin American women is rarely investigated to discover why they are here and what the United States' relationship with their countries of origin might be. Poverty and underdevelopment, the two powerful tropes for these regions, are enough of an explanation. The RCG paradigm has a difficult time grappling with the restructuring of race, gender, and class in cross-border movements—a fact we are confronted with post-9/11. Consequently, the management techniques that the state deploys to code bodies and spaces as well as its transformations remain hidden from view.

Not all feminists dealing with domestic issues have overlooked the state. Mainstream feminists who study and research domestic public policy have examined the American state as a welfare state, trying to hold it accountable for its failure in the last four decades to provide a safety net in the face of the injuries of capitalism. In fact, feminists critical of the surveillance and inadequacies of the welfare state retreated from their position to defend the existing policies when, under the Clinton administration, welfare was restructured as a way of forcing welfare-entitled women to work.[8] The fact that the most restrictive welfare and immigration policies since 1965 were passed under a Democratic administration should have alerted these feminists that the policies were not simply functions of particular governments and their party politics. What these feminists continue to characterize as a welfare state had, starting in the 1970s, restructured itself into a neoliberal one, a development I have discussed elsewhere (Das Gupta 2003). In the 1980s, the structural adjustment programs that have become so closely associated with the third world were tried out in the United States and the United Kingdom as these states retreated from their welfare commitments, slashed public spending, and became more proactive in facilitating the movement of capital at the expense of these countries' manufacturing sectors. The neoliberal state also reinvented itself as the "warfare state" (Gilmore 2002) as it became more punitive toward economically marginalized domestic groups. While its neoliberal ideology espoused smaller government, the warfare state rested on an ever-expanding, often privatized bureaucracy as its prison industrial complex grew at an unprecedented rate.

Mainstream feminist policy analysts had difficulty marking the radical transformation that the state was undergoing because they failed to connect the domestic to the international. They recognized dimly that the feminization of poverty that they were seeing in the United States in the 1980s (homeless women, women on welfare, and teenage mothers) was connected with a worldwide phenomenon. But how exactly were the expression of poverty here and over there linked? While they could quickly point to underdevelopment, the failure of development, or the impact of development in those other parts of the world, they did not think systematically about how these competing explanations were connected to a domestic economy that was structurally readjusting. Throughout the 1990s, those of us who taught development in the U.S. academy had to define what we meant by structural adjustment. The postindustrial economic landscape, the service economy, and degeneration of social indicators for those who were poor in the United States had yet to register with these American feminists as structural adjustment. The welfare state paradigm, thus, also circumscribed what could be legitimate feminist investigations of U.S. public policy and how the question of gender could be articulated vis-à-vis the (mischaracterized) state.

Terrain of Gender and War: Post-9/11 Feminist Inquiry

Given these paradigms, I turn to a roundtable on gender and September 11 in the Autumn 2002 issue of *Signs* as an indicator of the kinds of feminist analyses the war on terror has provoked. The short essays demonstrate the breadth of feminist frameworks and the thoughtfulness with which feminists, the majority based in the U.S. academy, have considered the question of gender and war. Though the essays were written before the invasion of Iraq, the questions about masculinity, femininity, sexuality, violence, trauma, and memory they raise bear application and elaboration in the context of the United States' occupation of Iraq. The articles represent three interlinked analytical themes: gendering the attack, the subsequent warmongering, and the war in Afghanistan; gendering the cultural construction of national memory and the domestic drama of rescue and protection; and subjecting to feminist critique the international politics of rescue in which the oppression of Afghan women became the justification for the war. These analyses ask us to examine the revived scripts of genocidal frontier lore as strategies of remasculinization used by the Bush administration (Brady 2002; Taylor 2002); the "continuing battle between competing versions of masculinity" (Radstone 2002, 459) that the Manichaean fantasy of good and evil stages; the displacement of normative heterosexuality and its quick restabilization in images of a sodomized WTC and a sodomized Osma bin Laden in which the body politic is penetrated and, in turn, penetrates (Freccero 2002); the recuperation of a heroic working-class masculinity long under assault from economic restructuring and under scrutiny for its sexism and brutal racism (Brison 2002; Sturken 2002; Lee 2002); and the partiality of remembering 9/11 through the filters of race, gender, and national belonging (Cvetkovich 2002; Lee 2002; Sanabria 2002). These analyses underline the urgency of being able to grasp and resist the construction of a violent, militarized, and racialized patriarchy in civil society, in statecraft, and in international politics. The self-examination, so necessary, revolves around understanding domestic gender and racial dynamics that subjugate the Other through war. Little is said about the political economy of dependency though the analyses point to the psychoanalytic dimensions of war, trauma, and violence that momentarily merge the Self with Other before disavowal and repression restablizes the opposition.

The third theme–how feminists should respond to the oppression of women under the Taliban and the cynical appropriation by the Bush administration of the status of Afghan women to justify its invasion of Afghanistan—represents the range of debates that engage critiques, such as those made by Mohanty (1986), over a colonizing Western feminist discourse. A number of essays straddle the tension between speaking out against the oppression of Afghan women and an ethical course of action to stop it without taking recourse to a colonial rescue script (Brison 2002; Cornell 2002; Haaken 2002; Winnett 2002; cooke 2002; Schweitzer 2002; Stone 2002). Like Ivy Schweitzer, many essayists confess to the complicated feelings evoked by stories and images of Taliban's gendered and sexualized violence against women in Afghanistan or by images of women lifting their burkas to expose their faces after U.S. occupation. Unlike Schweitzer, cognizant of Western feminism's investments in colonizing discourses, other writers center women in Afghanistan as agents, who built underground movements and made the Taliban's human rights violations internationally visible so that the international feminist community could debate how best to mobilize their governments. However, as Ranjana Khanna (2002) points out, part of the Left's failure to work meaningfully with much-publicized groups like the Revolutionary Association of Women of Afghanistan (RAWA) on ensuring justice for women in a reorganized Afghanistan, stems from the "navel gazing" about whether such moves would repeat imperialist dynamics. Reminding the Left and feminists in particular of the "recent and remote mutual imbrication of women's lives under colonialism and globalization," Khanna (465) calls for a transnational feminism that can "work *unsentimentally toward justice.*"

There is tension also in efforts to analyze and interpret the misogyny of the attackers. Two essays (Brison 2002; Stone 2002) dwell on the three men who went to a strip club at Daytona Beach the night before they embarked on their suicide mission and the promise of seventy "dark-eyed virgins in heaven" as a reward for martyrdom. How do Western feminists oppose gender oppression by other men at other sites without playing into that "civilizational binary that constructs the logic of empire" (cooke 2002, 470)? Strategically, both Brison and

Stone argue that neither the hijackers nor the Taliban have a monopoly on misogyny. The objectification and hatred of women also infuse U.S. culture. "It's easier to sell anything with sex [at Daytona Beach or in Kabul]," says Laurie Stone (2002, 474). And Brison (2002, 437) concludes that "all of us—including women who were kept out of firehouses, the 343 firefighters who were killed by the suicide hijackers, the Taliban and the Northern Alliance, and the lap dancers and the fighter pilots—are victims of oppressive gender norms."

Do these analyses return us to efforts at solidarity by arguing for the universality of patriarchy across cultures or do they invite us to explore "common differences" through an unwavering attention to specificities? At this point, if we were to remember that "in the United States one can no longer act as if one did not know that it is the United States itself that nourished raised, armed its own executioners," (Cixous 2002, 432) how can our analysis skirt the pitfalls of "is it the same or is it different" conundrum? Janice Haaken (2002) directs Western feminists to take responsibility for the United States' violent practices when she reframes the place of male violence in their imaginary—violence, which in Susan Brison's view not only affects Afghan women but a range of other actors including white American men. Haaken (2002, 455) rightly points out that "the role of U.S. foreign policy and international capital in generating the massive suffering on display remains at the periphery of our vision" when questions of gender in this war center on male violence and ignore state violence.

The *Signs* roundtable themes, their analytic possibilities and limitations, and interventions the scholars offer are indicative of the legacies of Western feminism and its encounters with third-world feminisms, its reworking since those initial encounters, and the investigative terrain that a topic such as gender and war opens up. It is in this context that I turn to Hannah Naveh's (2002) piece which struck me as an essay that came closest to answering the question that my colleagues and students asked: Why were Americans attacked? Naveh is not part of the U.S. academy. She is based in Tel Aviv University's Women and Gender Studies Program. In a gendered reading of the United States' proximity through globalization to areas that used to be distant and far-flung yet within its ambit of power, Naveh (2002, 452) perceptively observes:

> Obviously the other was reacting to some kind of understanding of having its own borders violated by American encroachment. The other has felt America's deterritorialization of its integrity within its borders to be

damaging. The other felt that its space was infringed on. The sheer magnitude and brutality of the reaction prevented understanding of its nature as a political "reaction" and posited it as an original sin against humanity, as a self-willed proactive strike against an innocent and (benevolent) entity; nevertheless, I believe we should take full account of the murderous blow as an insistence on borders by subverting America's prerogative to determine its distance from others.

I certainly don't want to suggest that this is the only way to look at and interpret 9/11. While I am attracted to Naveh's framing of American encroachment and the violent reaction as a "boy's game" of "push and shove over territory" that reflects a deep discomfort with proximity, I do not agree with her appeal to women's ethics of proximity that revalues closeness and permeability because it does not resolve the question of imperialism. But I do want to ask why this analysis had to be offered all the way from Tel Aviv. Is it symptomatic of the intellectual division of labor[9] in which U.S.-based American academics think primarily of race, class, and gender and "international" feminists, whether based in the United States or not, think about the gendered and raced restructuring of capital, states, and borders to trace the imprints of imperialism?

Conclusion

As I write, 500,000 activists demonstrate at the Republican National Convention in New York City. Even the mainstream media, to the extent to which they take notice of protestors, comment upon the immense diversity of issues that they bring to public view. A narrow reading of the demonstrations might interpret the activists as asking for a government that would turn to domestic issues instead of blowing billions of dollars on international military interventions and empire building. It could be read as a call to state managers to retreat, to reel in a runaway sovereignty, and to look inward. But a broader reading reveals how the 500,000 protestors and thousands of others they represent connect the war on terror to the simultaneous war on women, the war on the poor, the war on drugs (Brady 2002), the war on AIDS, the war on immigrants, and the war at the United States–Mexico border. The protestors have little doubt about how the wars and casualties within provide ammunition and training for the war without. These connections can and have been made within

Women's Studies, which needs to remember its life-giving connections with progressive social movements.

There is nothing inevitable about Women's Studies in the United States serving as a site of imperialism. The connections between wars at home and wars abroad and those between privileges at home and suffering abroad makes it necessary for those who have so far specialized in the domestic to become conversant with what it has imagined to be remote and, therefore, inconsequential. They should do this not simply out of self-interest because what used to be remote has now come home. While Ranjana Khanna's (2002) reminder to U.S. feminists about working unsentimentally toward justice is important to heed so as not to fall into the trap of crippling guilt or panicked self-interest, such work must engage the affective because 9/11 and its aftermath have had an emotional fallout and because understanding the relationality between the North and the distanced South must generate hope and the possibility of change.

Thus, scholars working within Women's Studies need to teach and write responsibly about the folding together of the domestic and international. As I have argued, this responsibility entails a radical shift in perspective. To teach or write about the North does not necessarily translate into gaining command over or speaking for the South—modes of epistemic subjugation that many U.S. feminists rightly renounce. Instead, a framework that reveals the United States' everyday dependency on the South invites U.S. feminists to present the connections, structured through unequal power relations, as ways of knowing *themselves*, not the Other. To realize that one is really learning about the self, located not only in the nationally configured grids of race, class, and gender but also in an international division of labor structured through multiple forms of imperialism, gives Women's Studies in the United States a powerful tool to do cross-border work, often interpreted too literally as actual alliances with social change organizations in the South. Ethically addressing the power-suffused dependence of the United States on the rest of the world in U.S. classrooms and in scholarship allows Women's Studies to construct an equally effective, and perhaps more achievable, agenda to secure justice.

Notes

I thank Ben Davidson, Cynthia Franklin, Linda Lierheimer, Laura Lyons, Keiko Matteson, Naoko Shibusawa, Ty Kawika Tengan, Becky Thompson, and Mari

Yoshihara for their careful comments on earlier drafts. Thanks to the editors for their thoroughness. Robin L. Riley's suggestions helped sharpen the chapter.

1. Sometimes the paradigm incorporates sexuality as a separate category that intersects race, class, and gender, and at other times it subsumes sexuality under gender.
2. Since the 1980s, community-based coalition groups such as Hui Malama o Makua and national environmental groups such as Earthjustice have taken legal action to protest military exercises involving incendiary weapons in the 4,190-acre Makua Military Reservation (Earthjustice 2004). A post-9/11 agreement between Malama Makua and the army allowed smaller scale live-fire trainings after a three-year suspension. The agreement, however, was violated five times as of August 2004 (Lum 2004). In 2003, a fire caused by a so-called controlled army exercise consumed over 2,100 acres.
3. Radical black feminists were also challenging the universalization of white middle-class experiences. Mohanty's critique draws and builds on these deconstructions.
4. Women of color made an analytic shift when they used the concept of "alliances" that could accommodate difference instead of "solidarity," a core principle in the Left, which underlined unity and subsumed difference (Lorde 1984; Reagon 1983). Alliances are strategic and bring different groups together for short periods of time to work on common issues. I prefer alliances to a notion of solidarity.
5. While it is common on the continent to treat Asian American and Pacific Islander feminisms together, Native Hawai'ian feminists and their Asian American allies resist this conflation and point to the differences in demands and issues of indigenous peoples and immigrants.
6. Silko's (1997) essay has been excerpted for the first time in a new introductory Women's Studies text coedited by scholar activists, Gwyn Kirk and Margo Okazawa-Rey (2004), who were part of the Combahee River Collective. Kirk is a British feminist, who was politicized in the squatters' movement in Britain in the 1970s and on coming to the United States has been part of antiracist and anti-imperialist struggles. Both Kirk and Okazawa-Rey have been active in organizing within the United States against military bases in Asia and Puerto Rico. It is not surprising, then, that their text, in taking on the politics of globalization as its conceptual framework, departs from the domestic preoccupations of Women's Studies and its carving out of the domestic and international.
7. For a multiracial rendition of the Central American peace movement in which Latino communities in the United States as well as Central American refugees are coactors see Thompson (2001).
8. The Personal Responsibility and Work Opportunity Reconciliation Act of 1996 restructured welfare.
9. I realize that Naveh's location in Israel, which with the backing of the United States encroaches upon Palestinians, complicates my schema of a North–South division of labor.

Bibliography

Alexander, M. Jacqui. 1994. Not just (any) body can be a citizen: The politics of law, sexuality and postcoloniality in Trinidad and Tobago and the Bahamas. *Feminist Review* 48 (Autumn): 5–23.

———. 2002. Decolonizing the academy. Paper read at African American Studies: Transnationalism, Gender and the Changing Black World, 19–20 April, Syracuse University.

Alexander, M. Jacqui, and Chandra Mohanty, T. 1997. Introduction: genealogies, legacies, movements. In *Feminist genealogies, colonial legacies, democratic futures*, edited by M. J. Alexander and C. Mohanty. New York: Routledge.

Anzaldúa, Gloria. 1987. *Borderlands/la frontera: the new mestiza*. San Francisco: Aunt Lute Books.

Bannerji, Himani. 2000. *The dark side of the nation: essays in multiculturalism, nationalism and gender*. Toronto: Canadian Scholars' Press.

Blanco, Sebastian. 2004. Strykers' island. *Honolulu Weekly*, 16 June, http://www.honoluluweekly.com/cover/detail.php?id=27.

Brady, Mary Pat. 2002. Quotidian warfare. *Signs* 28 (1): 446–447.

Brison, Susan J. 2002. Gender, terrorism, and war. *Signs* 28 (1): 435–437.

Carty, Linda. 1994. African Canadian women and the state: 'Labour only please'. In *We're rooted here: essays in African Canadian women's history*, edited by P. Bristow. Toronto: University of Toronto Press.

———. 1999. The discourse of empire and the social construction of gender. In *Scratching the surface*, edited by E. Dua and A. Robertson. Toronto: Women's Press.

Chang, Grace. 2000. *Disposable domestics: immigrant women workers in the global economy*. Cambridge: South End Press.

Cixous, Hélène. 2002. The towers: *les tours*. *Signs* 28 (1): 431–433.

Collins, Patricia Hill. 1986. Learning from the outsider within: The sociological significance of black feminist thought. *Social Problems* 33 (6): 14–32.

———. 1991. *Black feminist thought*. New York: Routledge.

Combahee River Collective. 1983. A black feminist statement. In *This bridge called my back: writings by radical women of color*, edited by C. Moraga and G. Anzaldúa. New York: Kitchen Table Press.

cooke, Miriam. 2002. Saving brown women. *Signs* 28 (1): 468–470.

Cornell, Drucilla. 2002. For RAWA. *Signs* 28 (1): 433–435.

Cvetkovich, Ann. 2002. 9-11 everyday. *Signs* 28 (1): 471–473.

Das Gupta, Monisha. 2003. The neoliberal state and the domestic workers' movement in New York City. *Canadian Woman Studies/Les Cahiers de la Femme* 22 (3–4): 78–85.

———. 2004. A view of post-9/11 justice from below. *Peace Review* 16 (2) 141–148.

———. 2005. Of hardship and hostility: The impact of 9/11 on New York City taxi drivers. In *Wounded city: the social impact of 9/11*, edited by N. Foner. New York: Russell Sage Foundation.

Davis, Angela. 1981. *Women, race, and class*. New York: Random House.

Earthjustice. 2004. *Biological and cultural treasures at Makua to be protected.* Honolulu: Earthjustice.

Ellis, Carolyn. 2002. Shattered lives: making sense of September 11th and its aftermath. *Journal of Contemporary Ethnography* 31 (4): 375–410.

Fahri, Farideh. 2004. Women and post-revolutionary politics in Islamic Iran. Paper read at Women's Studies Colloquium Series, 30 January, University of Hawai'i.

Freccero, Carla. 2002. "They are all sodomites!" *Signs* 28 (1): 453–455.

Gilmore, Ruth. 2002. Terror, structural adjustment, and the warfare state. In *Race, gender and the war on terror* (videorecording). Berkeley: Center for Race and Gender, University of California.

Glenn, Evelyn Nakano. 2002. *Unequal freedom: how race and gender shaped American citizenship and labor.* Cambridge: Harvard University Press.

Guerrero, Marie Anna Jaimes. 1997. Civil rights versus sovereignty: native American women in life and land struggles. In *Feminist genealogies, colonial legacies, democratic futures,* edited by M. J. Alexander and C. T. Mohanty. New York: Routledge.

Haaken, Janice. 2002. Cultural amnesia: memory, trauma, and war. *Signs* 28 (1): 455–457.

Jayawardena, Kumari. 1986. *Feminism and nationalism in the Third World.* New Delhi: Kali for Women.

Kakesako, Gregg K. 2001. Makua live-fire to resume. *Honolulu Star-Bulletin,* 4 October, http://www.starbulletin.com/2001/10/04/news/story1.html.

Khanna, Ranjana. 2002. Taking a stand for Afghanistan: women and the left. *Signs* 28 (1): 464–465.

Kirk, Gwyn, and Margo Okazawa-Rey. 2004. *Women's lives: multicultural perspectives.* 3rd ed. Boston: McGraw Hill.

Lal, Jayati. 2003. In spaces of globalization, new places for gender: Prospects for global feminism. Paper read at American Sociological Association, 16 August, at Atlanta.

Lee, Chana Kai. 2002. Memories in the making and other national fictions. *Signs* 28 (1): 438–439.

Lee, Rachel. 2000. Notes from the (non)field: teaching and theorizing women of color. *Meridians: feminism, race, transnationalism* 1 (1): 85–109.

Lorde, Audre. 1984. Age, race, class and sex: women redefining difference. In *Sister outsider.* Freedom, CA: Crossing Press.

———. 1984. Grenada revisited: an interim report. In *Sister outsider.* Freedom, CA: Crossing Press.

Lubiano, Wahneema. 1998. Talking about the state and imagining alliances. In *Talking visions: multicultural feminism in a transnational age,* edited by E. Shohat. New York and Cambridge: New Museum of Contemporary Art and MIT Press.

Lum, Curtis. 2004. Live-fire training to resume in Makua Valley. *Honolulu Advertiser,* 13 August, http://the.honoluluadvertiser.com/article/2004/Aug/13/ln/ln03a.html.

McGregor, Davianna P. 2002. Recognizing Native Hawaiian: a quest for sovereignty. In *Pacific diaspora: island peoples in the United States and across the*

Pacific, edited by P. Spickard, J. L. Rondilla, and D. H. Wright. Honolulu: University of Hawai'i Press.

Mohanty, Chandra. 1986. Under western eyes: feminist scholarship and colonial discourses. *Boundary 2* 12 (3): 333–358.

———. 2003. "Under western eyes" revisited: feminist solidarity through anti-capitalist struggles. *Signs* 28 (2): 499–535.

Naveh, Hannah. 2002. Nine eleven: an ethic of proximity. *Signs* 28 (1): 450–452.

Not in Our Name. 2003. What is the Stryker Brigade combat team? http://www.notinourname.net/downloads/stryker-hawaii.pdf.

Radstone, Susannah. 2002. The war of the fathers: trauma, fantasy, and September 11. *Signs* 28 (1): 457–459.

Reagon, Bernice Johnson. 1983. Coalition politics: turning the century. In *Home girls: a black feminist anthology*, edited by B. Smith. New York: Kitchen Table Press.

Sanabria, Ruth I. 2002. Now for the evening news. *Signs* 28 (1): 440–442.

Schweitzer, Ivy. 2002. Women: the canary in the mine. *Signs* 28 (1): 466–468.

Silko, Leslie Marmon. 1997. Border patrol state. In *Yellow woman and a beauty of spirit*. New York: Touchstone Books.

Silva, Noenoe. 2004. *Aloha betrayed: native Hawaiian resistance to American colonialism*. Durham, NC: Duke University Press.

Stone, Laurie. 2002. After the bodies fell. *Signs* 28 (1): 473–475.

Sturken, Marita. 2002. Masculinity, courage, and sacrifice. *Signs* 28 (1): 444–445.

Sudbury, Julia. 1998. *"Other kinds of dreams": black women's organizations and the politics of transformation*. London: Routledge.

Taylor, Diana. 2002. Ground zero. *Signs* 28 (1): 448–450.

Thompson, Becky. 2001. *A promise and a way of life: white antiracist activism*. Minneapolis: University of Minnesota.

Trask, Haunani-Kay. 1999. *From a native daughter: colonialism and sovereignty in Hawai'i*. Honolulu: University of Hawai'i Press.

———. 2000. Settlers of color and "immigrant" hegemony of "locals" in Hawai'i. *Amerasia Journal* 26 (2): 1–24.

Winnett, Susan. 2002. The memory of gender. *Signs* 28 (1): 462–463.

Yamada, Mitsuye. 1983. Asian Pacific American women and feminism. In *This bridge called my back: writings by radical women of color*, edited by C. Moraga and G. Anzaldúa. New York: Kitchen Table Press.

Yuval-Davis, Nira. 1997. Women, citizenship and difference. *Feminist Review* 57 (Autumn): 4–27.

Chapter 7

Trading Places: Juxtaposing South Africa and the United States

Hannah Britton

I naively thought that I could enjoy several months in South Africa, simply knowing that I was on a separate continent from George Bush. And then he arrived in Pretoria, only a few blocks away from the office where I was working.

George W. Bush made his first official presidential trip to the African continent in July 2003. The whirlwind tour of five African nations in five days was a dazzling display of imperial detachment, and it reinforced the perception that U.S. leaders do not view African states as viable members of the international community. The visit was never meant to build authentic relationships but rather was intended to unveil the current U.S. plan *for* Africa. Instead of dismantling the imperial legacy of resource exploitation, the visit reexpressed the Bush administration's need to utilize Africa's oil reserves. Instead of retreating from the pattern of using Africa as the physical location of Cold War violence, the visit re-presented the agenda of the Bush administration to use African states as staging grounds and their militaries as the frontline fodder for the coming "war on terrorism." Rather than providing unconditional assistance for fighting HIV/AIDS, the carrot of 15 billion U.S. dollars was used frequently to induce Africa's compliance with future U.S. military operations.

I wish to share with you the impact of U.S. imperialism and, more recently, the U.S. war on terrorism on Africa. Some of these conversations I have shared with friends and host families in South Africa during my five trips to the nation in the last fourteen years, some have occurred in the South African press and media, and others are happening within the academic circles of African studies literature. None of the conversations are exhaustive, nor perhaps are they generalizable. Nevertheless, they seem important to covey because they are not what we hear or talk about in the U.S. press.

I want to suggest that there are continuities between the impact of colonialism, the Cold War conflict, and the new age of imperialism after 9/11 that are critical for understanding the U.S. relationship with African nations. This chapter articulates ideas—some new and some tragically reminiscent—about what I believe needs to be discussed, debated, and understood in order to shift the terrain of struggle. It also expresses my personal observations about the shifting political terrain between South Africa and the United States, between repression and democracy, between the expression of freedom and the suppression of rights, between apartheid South Africa and apartheid USA.

1990: Apartheid, South Africa

In 1990, I went to South Africa as an idealistic, young, antiapartheid activist. I had been deeply troubled by all that I had read and studied about apartheid, the system that separated races and enforced discrimination against the indigenous black population and the mixed-race colored population. While there, I lived in townships and traveled into white areas. Townships were artificial creations of the apartheid government that housed black South Africans near urban centers so that they could serve in the white economy. Townships remain today as they did then, communities that are overpopulated and severely underresourced. My first night after the two-day flight was spent in Mamelodi, a township outside Pretoria. There was a poster hanging on the wall with a quote from Lilla Watson, an antiapartheid activist: "If you have come to help me, you are wasting your time. If you have come because your liberation is bound up with mine, then let us work together." This message set the tone for my engagement with South Africa: a clear voice from the antiapartheid struggle indicating paternalistic assistance and charitable condescension were not desired. This nation needed allies who recognized the need for mutual liberation.

In 1990, things started to shift politically, and democracy seemed almost possible. Still, although things were beginning to change, much remained static and violent. Yes, Mandela was now free, and political parties were unbanned. I saw his speech in Soccer City Soweto at the first South African Communist Party (SACP) rally—asserting again that he was not a communist but had deep allegiances to the goals of the SACP. Then there was the white-only referendum administered by de Klerk to gain the right to negotiate on behalf of the South African white population with the resistance movement, opposition parties, and labor unions. The stage was set for negotiations between the resistance movement and the white minority government.

But, as joyful a time as this was, I remained paralyzed by the police state that was South Africa in 1990. Everything was still separate—housing, transportation, schools, and lives. I lived in the townships, traveled into the white areas, marveled at the distance—so small topographically, so huge psychologically. The extremes were separated by a vast gulf—on one side abject poverty, on the other great wealth.

Then there were the armed military and police that walked most city streets. I mainly remember this in Pretoria—men with large machine guns, who claimed to patrol for safety and security, but left me feeling everything but safe and secure. The irony was that the apartheid system was designed to make me—a white person—feel safe in white areas. Yet, it was precisely in those white areas where I felt the least secure, because neither my politics nor my host families were at home or free in those spaces. Rather, life was free and space was safe in the townships.

Safe, that is, until the police came into the townships. My memories are scattered. There had been a national "stay-away" earlier that week. This nonviolent means of protest disabled the economy temporarily as the masses "stayed away" from work. Nonviolent mass action combined with an economic boycott was an essential tactic of the opposition. The government responded as it always did, with escalating violence—violence arrived in Mamelodi that weekend. The members of the Mamelodi community had a government-sanctioned meeting to discuss rent issues—rent on land that rightfully belonged, of course, to their people. Since the government had approved the meeting, there was a large turnout, and the elderly and children, too, attended. The police blocked the exits, dumped overwhelming amounts of tear gas into the stadium, and then watched. Injuries seemed endless. Several young men sacrificed their hands and lives holding down the razor wire so others could jump over the sides of the stadium. The police then terrorized the entire township—driving through the area, tear-gassing the streets, and using helicopters to patrol from above. Since then, I associate the sound of helicopters with fear, violence, tear gas, gunfire, and the police.

The child in the house where I was staying came in to tell us that his eyes and ears were burning—the tear gas was everywhere. We ran through the house, closing the windows and covering our faces with wet clothes. It was a world in which a three-year-old child knows how to respond to tear gas quickly. In my short visit of two months, this was still not the worst violence I would see.

In my naivety, my first response that day was, "This is horrible—we have to call the police!" I forgot that it was the police who had brought the tear gas. Only then did I begin to think about authority and power in a different light. My second thought was no less ideologically conditioned: "Well, we have to call the press at least." I phoned a local newspaper that had a national readership. They took down the information and said they would get someone there in a few days.

In a few days, the gas was gone, the victims were in the hospital, and the urgency had dissipated. I started to become aware of what it means to exist in a police state. In the next several months, I discovered again and again how the press and the government worked hand in hand to keep the reality of the townships and of the oppression from the eyes and ears of those in power and those for whom power was working. White South Africans could drive by townships and shantytowns and never see them—many of the walls were so high on the highways that you had to climb on top of cars to see over them. Nice, middle-class homes were built on the outskirts of the townships. If you merely drove by townships, you saw modest but fine homes. It was work to see beyond the physical and ideological walls.

When I emerged from the plane in Chicago, my first step back in the United States after months in apartheid South Africa, I went to the first newsstand and bought every magazine and newspaper I could. I was hungry for a "free press" and "fair reporting." I pored over the pages to see what had happened, and also to see if anything had been reported about South Africa. I felt calmer, if not safer, back in the States. Regardless, I instinctively fled from helicopters.

2003: Democratic South Africa

Thirteen years later, I returned for my fifth trip to South Africa, this time as an academic. The political landscape there and here in the United States had changed dramatically; in many respects they were switching places. Audre Lorde's essay "Apartheid U.S.A.," in which she outlined the chilling parallels between these two countries, rang so solidly true.[1] She wrote in 1985. I write in 2005. The post-9/11 context and more specifically the push toward war in Iraq unleashed both national policies and public attitudes that significantly limited public debate and discussion, discouraged dissent and protest, and chipped away at the bedrocks of freedom of speech, press, and movement. And these attitudes were equally infused with racial if not class ideologies that again are frighteningly similar to those in the apartheid era.

From May until late July 2003, I spent the better part of three months doing my research. I lived with four of the host families I have known since the early 1990s. Each had their response to the war in Iraq; but at the foundation of each response was an opposition to unilateral action. One family member wanted to raise money so that she could go to Iraq to become a human shield—even though she would be leaving children and a decent government job that she had fought so many years to obtain. Another advocated sanctions against the United States and their products. Both agreed that while such sanctions would not be economically crippling, they would be ideologically powerful. Another believed that the only way to challenge the U.S. administration was through nonviolent mass action—since clearly in his mind the electoral process in the United States could no longer be viewed as legitimate. Another feared that the Bush administration was responsible for 9/11, either directly as a means to quell criticism or indirectly by ignoring evidence of an impending attack. Regardless of their responses, no one could image how or why the administration would in fact launch this war with so little evidence, so little support, and against the advice of the international inspectors, their own military adviser, and the United Nations (UN).

I also found, however, that on the part of the South Africans with whom I interacted, there was an overwhelming desire to separate U.S. citizens from the actions of the U.S. government. These people remembered a time when their government took military action against their own people, and so they were clear in their assessment that the United States was entering a phase of apartheidlike suppression of dissension and debate. Almost everyone I met believed that when the evidence of manipulation of the U.S. press and public trust became apparent, the country would not elect Bush to a second term. I felt compelled to share my doubt: it was possible that no matter what was unearthed about weapons of mass destruction or the then alleged misrepresentation of evidence, people might again vote for Bush.

The only person I encountered who was supportive of the war was a white South African woman I met at a laundry mat. It was unusual that she was there. She explained that her young grandsons had come to visit after a long holiday in the game park. They had mountains of soiled clothes and she felt she needed to help her "domestic" to organize their washing. She discovered by my accent that I was from the

United States. Eventually, the discussion turned to war, as she asked what I thought of "Our General." It took me a moment to realize that "our general" was Bush. She stated that she supported a strong hand in the "Middle East," making clear her support for the war. Our conversation slowed, as usual, when she asked if I was staying with an "Afrikaans or English family?" When I explained that the family was Sotho and Ndebele, she became concerned for my safety. I always received this reaction in South Africa's conservative white circles. I sensed she was uncomfortable accepting that I was living in a world beyond her boundaries. We had gone from sharing a General to being divided by a gulf. After many weeks in the country the only vocal supporter of the war I met was someone who continued to benefit from the policies of apartheid. Are these the allies for which the United States aspires—the remnants of the apartheid state?

Although this was not widely covered in the U.S. media, South Africa did in fact try to stop the war in Iraq through diplomatic means. South African leaders had strong messages for both Bush and Blair; they sent government officials to intercede in the situation in Iraq and to discuss the South African model of disarmament. During the transition to democracy in the early 1990s, South Africa voluntarily pursued the destruction of its chemical, biological, and nuclear weapons programs that had been a bedrock of apartheid-era military defense and internal suppression. This denuclearization was started by the apartheid leaders and was supported by the African National Congress (ANC).[2] Then UN chief weapons inspector, Hans Blix, praised South Africa's disarmament and strongly encouraged Iraq to follow its example.[3] However, by the time Iraq welcomed the South African leaders in the spring of 2003, war was already a foregone conclusion.

The South African government's position on the war on Iraq was to pursue multilateralism and support the process of the UN. Any action taken without express UN mandate would be deemed regrettable and seen as a threat to global peace. President Mbeki supported the UN and a multilateral solution to the situation in Iraq and actively worked to extend disarmament guidance to Iraq. Government leaders from the ANC regularly voiced concerns that war in Iraq, particularly war without UN mandate, would destabilize the region and the world, bring political chaos and potential economic chaos triggered by oil prices that would hurt marginalized areas like Africa the most, and set a precedent that undermined the principle of sovereignty.[4]

Former president Nelson Mandela adamantly opposed U.S. action in Iraq, not because he was supportive of Saddam's dictatorship but because he was suspicious of U.S. motives. Speaking at the International Women's Forum in Johannesburg in January 2003, he accused both the United States and the United Kingdom of undermining the UN and pursuing war for oil—not freedom. Mandela argued that the motives of the United States and Bush were clearly not about weapons of mass destruction or violence of the leaders, because "their friend Israel has got weapons of mass destruction but because it's their ally they won't ask the United Nations to get rid of them."[5] He similarly posed the question of the U.S. use of nuclear weapons and Bush's disregard for working with the UN: "Because they are so arrogant, they [America] killed innocent people in Japan during Hiroshima and Nagasaki. If Saddam Hussein was not carrying out the UN instructions and resolutions . . . I will support them [the UN] without resignation, but what I condemn is one power with a president who can't think properly and wants to plant the world into holocaust."[6] His concerns were for the instability and destruction that the war would bring to the region and the world.

South Africa is a global player now. South Africans have earned their place because of their fearless pursuit of democracy, civil rights, and civil liberties. They have been heralded internationally for their efforts to dismantle authoritarian institutions and weapons. They occupy the unique position of being highly regarded by both developing and developed nations—and thus would be ideal in negotiating across nations. Indeed, there is much they can teach us and much we can learn.

Yet, we continue to think of them within paternalistic frameworks and interact with them in imperialistic ways. Such a posture is vividly expressed in three examples: the effect of Bush's visit to Africa in 2003, the impact of the U.S. war on terror on domestic policy agendas in Africa, and the regional reporting of the ill-treatment of prisoners in Guantánamo Bay. While these may seem unrelated at first, each presented me with opportunities to have or observe conversations in the press and in academic circles regarding the relationship between the United States and South Africa. In many ways the two seem to have switched roles—one going from pariah to a state that others look to for creative leadership and the other moving in the reverse direction.

1. George Bush Comes to Town

Bush's first visit to Africa as president was a whirlwind tour of five nations in five days—quickly to become known as Bush's "Five

Nation African Safari" in the South African press. For me and for many of my friends and families in South Africa, it was a remarkable trip. First, many in South Africa, and on the continent in general, were struck by the choice of the five nations: Senegal, South Africa, Botswana, Uganda, and Nigeria. Why these? The U.S. administration defended the selection of these nations as follows: Senegal and South Africa are seen as model democracies within the continent; Nigeria, Botswana, and South Africa are economic powerhouses within the continent; and Uganda has been heralded as a model for fighting HIV/AIDS under President Museveni's leadership.[7]

While all of this may be true, African press sources were also very much aware of the unstated but quite apparent strategic reasons for selecting these states. The *Mail and Guardian,* a progressive South African newspaper, reported, "Nigeria and Senegal are vital for future US oil supplies; South Africa's support is crucial because she's a regional power and an influential developing world country, while both Uganda and Botswana are paeans to the US free market agenda."[8] There are no secrets here. As the war on terrorism and the war on Iraq continue to escalate, access to new sources of oil is imperative.

And, where did Bush *not* go? Given the war on terrorism and where it has had the most impact in Africa, one would imagine that Kenya or Tanzania would be top priorities. The bombings of the U.S. embassies there in 1998 have been referred to repeatedly by the administration as the actions of al Qaeda network and Osama bin Laden. So, why not visit fellow victims of the terrorist attacks on U.S. targets? Perhaps because Kenya refused to support the U.S. war on Iraq, and instead "insisted on United Nations Security Council approval for any use of force against Iraq."[9] Even though they had experienced the pain of terrorism domestically, Kenya chose to support a collective, multilateral solution to the Iraq situation. If the UN Security Council had approved force, Kenya would likely have agreed. But without such approval, there were clear problems for Kenya. Not only would U.S. unilateralism work against a new world system based on multinational solutions and agreements, there was the strong chance that retribution and insecurity created by the war could indirectly lead to more dead bodies in Kenya.

Uganda was "the only East African nation that supported Bush during the Iraq War," and the U.S. administration also had an interest in Senegal as "a newfound friend since it drifted away from France."[10] Given the resistance by Kenya and France to the U.S.-led attack on Iraq, the choices of Uganda and Senegal become even more understandable.

In fact, Botswana and Uganda were "all important U.S. allies in the war on terrorism."[11] So there is a very clear message underlying Bush's new-found interest in Africa. Assistance and diplomatic ties are driven centrally by who is, as Bush stated soon after 9/11, "with us."

My friends and host families in South Africa were also concerned with the timeline of five days. Five days. Five states in five days. I can only speak personally from Pretoria,[12] where the streets were blocked a week in advance, where Bush's motorcade path was painstakingly cleared from all potential threats, where he went directly from the airport to the hotel to the Union Building, and where he bypassed townships and shantytowns. This may not seem so exceptional to the average U.S. reader: of course there should be security; of course he should only stay in urban, privileged settings. But how can he learn to understand the realities of the country in this way?

But understanding Africa was hardly the real purpose of this trip. Many would argue that his "African Safari" was a venue through which to extend U.S. strategic interests, economically and militarily. Five days is certainly enough time to do that, especially when the conversation is distinctly one sided.

Since coming to appreciate how Nelson Mandela handles his own security, I have had to rethink the security of government officials. On my previous research trips to South Africa in 1990, 1992, and 1996/97, I saw Mandela on numerous occasions in both small and large venues. Each time, I was struck by how accessible he was—security, if present, was not visible. Certainly, there were escorts, but not *security* in the sense we see with Bush. Children could easily approach Mandela and ask for a picture or handshake. There were no guards blocking the path. Someone once told me he had "invisible security," a claim that still remains a mystery to me. But in Mandela, I saw someone without fear of enemies —a man who after almost 27 years in prison decided to not be imprisoned again by walls of security. Instead, he acted on his need to meet people and understand the world around him. Contrast this to the layers upon layers of security accompanying Bush on his trip.[13] If Mandela has fewer enemies than Bush, it may be worth asking why.

Preparing the roads for an imperial visit is not a new occurrence by any means. Watching the streets blocked off in advance in Pretoria, and the path of the motorcade travel from one "safe" location to another, I was reminded of the British queen's visit to Antigua as recounted in Jamaica Kincaid's *A Small Place*.[14] The roads on which the queen might be riding in Antigua were "paved anew, so that the Queen might have been left with the impression that riding in a car in Antigua was a pleasant experience" (12). Colonial leaders usually prepared a shiny, trouble-free path for their imperial benefactors, and this pattern continues today. There is, for example, the now infamous story of Hillary Clinton's visit to South Africa, with its own colonial imprint.[15] One Robben Island[16] tour guide tells the story that Hillary Clinton brought an expensive touring coach for her trip to South Africa and Robben Island. But while transporting it the few miles from the mainland, the helicopter equipment carrying the coach broke over Table Bay. The coach rests at the bottom of the bay still.[17] Bush's tour duplicated this pattern. While the roads in South Africa were not paved anew for Bush's visit, there were no chances taken and the path was certainly cleared of anything unpleasant, including anti-Bush protests.

No protesters barred his way—even in South Africa, the pinnacle of public protest and active civil society. The massive protests that were prevalent throughout the country[18] were kept far away from Pretoria's Union Building, where the meeting between President Mbeki and Bush took place. The protests were supported by a far-reaching antiwar coalition, which ironically included President Mbeki's own ruling African National Congress.[19] According to Hopewell Radebe of *Business Day,* "People protesting against George Bush's visit to SA were kept so far away from the Union Buildings that the US president would be forgiven if he left the country believing that all South Africans welcomed him. In fact, the absence of shouting and toyi-toying activists left Bush's senior officials suspicious of intentions of both local and international media for whipping up public emotions for no reason."[20] I am reminded of apartheid-era days, when I became keen to look over walls to see what was hidden behind them.

This was only a taste of what was reported in the other nations. Troubling reports came from Uganda. The African Church Information Service reported the story of Goretti Kakaire, who had a small banana crop that was the basis of her livelihood and survival. Unfortunately for Ms. Kakaire, her banana trees were planted close to one of the roads on which Bush would be traveling while in Uganda. The U.S. security officials cut down the trees fearing they could be hiding places for would-be terrorists. This was a pattern throughout the visit, clearing trees and securing roads for Bush's visits, including "landmark trees" in Dakar.[21] There is a painful irony in destroying Ms. Kakaire's banana crop in order to facilitate a trip by Bush to advocate his vision for Africa's agricultural policy and free-trade initiatives.

Arrests predating the visit were widespread, including 1,500 in Dakar alone.[22] This massive detainment was combined with attempts to block protests in Uganda before they occurred.[23] Human Rights Watch called upon Bush to condemn the state repression that predated his visit to the countries.[24] Arrests, shootings, and beatings were some of the methods used by Nigerian police to clear the way and set the tone for Bush's visit.[25] These actions again raise the question of what type of message Bush wanted to send to Africa and its new allies in the war on terror. Is this war on terror really a war on civil dissent?

2. War on Terrorism

Bush's visit did little to quell accusations leveled at the United States' paternalistic and imperialistic attitude toward Africa. Instead, the choice of states and the agendas of the talks reinforced the U.S. need for both African resources, specifically oil reserves, and African compliance with the war on terror. Crucially, this compliance has had significant implications for the domestic policy agenda of African states. African states have quickly fallen in line as they proceed with discussions of their own antiterrorism legislation following the UN Security Council Resolution 1373, adopted on September 28, 2001. Resolution 1373 was in part a general condemnation of terrorism but was also a specific response to the terrorist acts in the United States in September 2001. Further, it was a strategy by the Security Council to develop a global response to terrorism. It established the Counter-Terrorism Committee (CTC) composed of the 15 members of the Security Council. The stated purpose of the CTC is to enhance the ability of member states to counter terrorist networks and thwart terrorist attacks. This has been accomplished by giving the CTC increased monitoring capabilities of member states' antiterrorism actions, by mandating the adoption of domestic antiterrorist legislation, and by receiving reports from member states about their antiterrorist activities. The U.K. representative to the UN, Jeremy Greenstock, first chaired the committee, and the CTC was known for a while in Africa as the Greenstock committee. The representative of Spain to the UN, Inocencio F. Arias, became the chair of the CTC in April 2004.

What has the CTC and Resolution 1373 meant in practical terms for African nations? Several patterns emerge. African nations have reported to the CTC on their new and existing measures for dealing with terrorist networks. Many states have asserted that their actions fall within the category of crime prevention and pre-9/11 antiterrorism legislation. Many states defended their own criminal law, and they have referred those pieces of legislation to the UN's Greenstock committee as ways of combating terrorism.[26] But several states have worked to create new antiterrorism legislation, including South Africa, Mauritius, and Kenya. And most others are under significant pressure to do so. As reported by the *Mail and Guardian*, "The Security Council used its powers to impose a mandatory duty on all member states to adopt laws and submit to a compliance reporting routine . . . the mandatory duties imposed on member states had no warrant in terms of the UN Charter."[27] This means regardless of the intention, the CTC and Resolution 1373 have given the Security Council, and indirectly the United States, significant oversight and influence in the domestic legislative affairs of sovereign nations.

There is no question that there was global political support for the United States following the 9/11 attacks, most often by states that had similarly experienced the pain of terrorist violence. Rather than using this sympathy and support to extend diplomatic ties and relations, the window of opportunity was used to extend U.S. policy abroad in a more paternalistic and supervisory manner. Rather than asking questions about why and how the 9/11 attacks happened and calling upon the international community for advice and assistance, diplomacy was replaced with international mandates.

This attitude and pressure has not played well in Africa, but many African states are finding it difficult to assert their opposition to the influence and expectations of the CTC. As the *Mail and Guardian* editors asserted, "The destruction of the Twin Towers was a terrible event. But the United States has an infuriating habit of assuming that its interests are the world's interests, and its national woes crises for the world. It has no right to internationalise its USA Patriot Act by expecting other states to introduce excessive security laws, in breach of human rights norms and unwarranted by their political conditions."[28] Yet, nations are compelled to report their work on these activities to the CTC, and they are under considerable pressure to demonstrate domestic compliance. There can be no underestimation of the profound difficulty for this new level of domestic counterterrorism action, given that so many of African nations are already deeply in debt and at risk financially. As Ajayi-Soyinka (2003, 607) argues, "[i]f the greatest democracy on earth finds it expedient in terms of national security to compromise its fundamental principles of democracy and freedom of speech and movement, what prevents African nations from sacrificing democracy at the alter of much-needed development aids - which ultimately will once again translate as national security?"

The push for antiterrorism legislation takes on additional weight in the context of postapartheid South Africa. After decades of struggle against the apartheid regime and its flagrant abuse of human rights, the 2003 Anti-terrorism Bill of newly democratic South Africa caused for all those who had lived in the shadow of the 1967 Terrorism Act of apartheid South Africa to experience a collective shudder. That act defined terrorism so broadly, that almost any act of civil protest could be deemed a terrorist act and "violators" could be held without charge or trial. The 1967 Terrorism Act was only one of the myriads of legislative acts to detain—and then often torture or murder—political dissidents. This legal framework was used to suppress free speech and assembly. The Terrorism Act, the Internal Security Act, and its precursor the Suppression of Communism Act worked hand in hand to limit even the most passive and limited expressions of dissent against the white-minority government.

Fewer than ten years after the first democratic elections in South Africa, held in 1994, the government continues to reform, prune, and expunge apartheid-era legislation to make room for the new human rights framework that governs South African society. This follows decades of struggle against a government condemned internationally for acts of terror against its own people. It is not surprising, therefore, that the South African 2003 Anti-terrorism Bill[29] met with such widespread skepticism and criticism. Organizations from across the political spectrum, but especially on the left, criticized the bill as a return to apartheid government control tactics, a challenge to hard-won human rights, and an implementation of U.S. policy and imperialism.

There is also no question that U.S. aid is given with purse strings connected to military and foreign-policy dictates. Take for example the decision by the United States to cut aid to African nations that opposed the U.S. position on the International Criminal Court (ICC). According to one South African reporter, "South Africa's generally positive relations with the United States were dealt a blow by the Bush administration's decision to end military aid to 35 countries, including South Africa, that opposed the U.S. demand for immunity for Americans in the International Criminal Court."[30] The Bush administration was working to foster bilateral agreements with signatories of the ICC treaty to "give immunity to Americans from prosecution and undermine the integrity of the court."[31]

Some will argue that this is of course what any nation might do—work to preserve their own self-interests and work to establish the most beneficial international agreements for their own self-preservation and enhancement. Yet, besides bringing into relief the shortsightedness of the United States' assessment of self-interest, it also underscores the difference between the rhetoric of the U.S. administration versus the reality of its actions.

What have we learned in the United States about making friends and extending military technology and training to regimes with a weak track record on democracy? It seems history is repeating itself when Bush minimizes internal problems of democracy and freedom for the nations that support the war on terrorism. The director of the Centre for Conflict Resolution in Cape Town, South Africa, Adekeye Adebajo (2003), argues that the actions of the Bush administration are nothing more than an extension of the colonial and imperial policies the United States has been utilizing throughout various regions of the world for decades or more. While the rhetoric of administration is that the United States is pursuing the war on terror to spread democracy, fighting the Saddam regime to topple autocrats, the reality is that the United States has not changed its policy of working with nations that support its economic and strategic interests regardless of the internal politics of those states. The imperialist practices of the United States in Latin America and the Philippines, the enslavement of African people during the Atlantic slave trade, and the conquest and forced assimilation of the indigenous population of the United States were only the beginning of the pattern of U.S. imperialism in the early twentieth century (Adebajo 2003, 175). This pattern continued throughout the cold war (which was a rather hot war in much of Africa) but flew under the flag of suppressing the spread of communism:

> Africa was flooded with billions of dollars of weapons provided to local proxies in countries like Angola, Ethiopia, Liberia, Mozambique, and Somalia. During the Cold War, the U.S. policy often ignored principles as basic as democracy and development and focused parochially on containing the "red peril" in Africa through protecting and providing military and financial assistance to often brutal and undemocratic clients like Liberia's Samuel Doe, Zaire's Mobutu Sese Seko, and Somalia's Siad Barre, in exchange for political support and military bases.
>
> (Adebajo 2003, 176)

I would extend this list to include apartheid South Africa. The United States took sides in many African conflicts, and our allies were not chosen for their democratic practices or beliefs, regardless of the rhetoric. Many of the conflicts in Africa today have been linked to the colonial patterns of divide-and-rule tactics. In addition, many of the current African conflicts are also linked to the use of the African continent as a battlefield of the cold war. The bodies of Africans and African land did not have the privilege to engage in a "cold" war, that is, in a mere ideological struggle. Like Vietnam and Afghanistan, most of the dying *and* most of the killing in the so-called cold war was outsourced to Africa's indigenous populations.

Despite calls for development, democracy, and decolonization that were consistent across several U.S. administrations, the foreign policy reality was one of covert operations with, and military assistance to, regimes that often had long-standing records of human rights abuses. This claim is not in dispute. However, we often lose sight of the fact that this pattern continued throughout the post–Cold War, pre-9/11 era. Adebajo (2003, 176) is equally critical of Clinton's African strategy:

> Clinton's democratization record in Africa was abysmal. Policy often resembled the Cold War era, as strategic rationales were found to justify the failure to support multi-party democracies in various African countries . . . "enlargement" of democracies was soon replaced by American support for a cantankerous warlord gallery that Clinton, during a diplomatic safari to Africa in 1998, arrogantly dubbed Africa's "new leaders": Uganda's Yoweri Museveni, Ethiopia's Meles Zenawi, Eritrea's Isais Afwerke, and Rwanda's Paul Kagame. None of these leaders could be accurately described as operating anything like a multi-party system, and most of them were thinly disguised autocrats. And as Clinton anointed them Africa's model rulers, these leaders quickly went to war against each other.

These failures of judgment were nothing compared with the foreign policy and humanitarian disasters of Somalia and Rwanda. At best these can be described as a complete misunderstanding of the history of these two nations, and at worst they were a flagrant negligence that cost hundreds of thousands of lives.

It is no surprise, then, that the Bush administration has not only followed Clinton's Africa strategy, it has deepened it. Indeed, many in South Africa are questioning Bush's attempt to create an Africa policy. As John Stremlau, a South African professor of international relations, charges, "The U.S. does not have an African policy; it has a war on terrorism policy."[32] The week before Bush was to visit Africa on his five-nation tour, even Defense Secretary Donald Rumsfeld questioned the U.S. involvement in Africa, indicating that the United States had "no vital interests" on the continent.[33]

Africa is seen only in strategic, military terms, which are currently defined as what is essential for the U.S. war on terror. Ironically, elements that are "not essential" include democracy, development, civil rights, and civil liberties. Since 9/11, the United States has chosen to work with African nations to develop their own domestic military strength and counterterrorism methods. Often these same methods are used by African autocrats on their own people to quell popular dissent and democratic protest, as seen in Morocco, Liberia, Eritrea, Tanzania, Ethiopia,[34] and, as indicated above, even South Africa.

I cannot count the number of times I have heard media and citizens in the United States explain their opinion that Bush is not experienced, or even bright, but that he has sufficiently surrounded himself with solid advisers. Let us look at his advisers and think about what they have done for South Africa. As Abedajo (2003, 182–183) reports, Bush's top foreign-policy experts have sent a clear message about their allegiances in the past:

> Dick Cheney voted against Nelson Mandela's release from prison as a Congressman in 1986, branding the African National Congress (ANC) a "terrorist" organization. Walter Kansteinner III, the current Assistant Secretary of State for African Affairs, opposed sanctions against apartheid South Africa in the 1980s and, as late as 1990, considered Mandela's ANC to be unrepresentative of the aspirations of the majority of South Africans . . . Powell's failure to attend, as scheduled, the UN's World Conference against Racism in Durban in September 2001, was a disappointing policy defeat . . . Condoleeza Rice has often been reported to be siding with the "hawks" in the Bush administration. During the debate on the Racism conference in Durban in September 2001, she insensitively dismissed reparations for Africans and their descendants in the Diaspora as an irrelevance of the past . . . Powell has identified with, and spoken out for, African and African-American causes . . . a controversial and notable exception was Powell's support for the misguided US policy of "constructive engagement" with apartheid South Africa, crafted by Chester Crocker, the prejudiced and patronizing Assistant Secretary of State for African Affairs under President Ronald Reagan in the 1980s.

Before we stop and think about what this list means, let us take a step back. Many have made the argument that the war on terror is merely a reimposition of the same methods of the Cold War and that the U.S. military missed the "good ole days" of the Cold War because of the "stability" of the us-versus-them mentality. This evidence for this claim is both palpable and haunting: in both the war on terror and the Cold

War, the United States sends military aid to "friendly" but not necessarily democratic regimes; in both, development aid is tied to military
interests; most of the military engagement occurs covertly or behind
the scenes; and for Africa both the war on terror and the Cold War are
hot wars fought through and on the African body.

Others have argued that the United States has undergone an
Israelification of their foreign policy. This is defined to mean that U.S.
foreign policy is now guided by a blinkered hunt for enemies on all
fronts, that terrorist activity is defined so broadly as to include democratic dissent and protest, that civil rights and civil liberties are
restricted in the name of security, and that preemptive strikes become
the expectation and not the exception.

That said, we can take a look again at the list of Bush's advisers.
Beyond the reimplementation of Cold War tactics, beyond the potential Israelification of U.S. policy, there is also a re-creation of
apartheid-era politics. The builders of the war on terror are not only
the same architects of the Cold War, they are the same proponents of
U.S./apartheid regime collaboration. These are the some of the same
people who did not take a stand against the internationally condemned terror-state of apartheid South Africa and some of the same
people who chose to pursue engagement with the white-minority government long after the UN and most of the world had strongly
denounced any such collaboration.

A week after Bush left Africa with his bag of promises for
HIV/AIDS and economic development tucked neatly under his arm,
the South African evening news showed the first tangible assistance
from the United States one night. I was sitting again with my host
family, watching the evening news—this one happened to be in
English—and it showed joint military-training operations between the
U.S. military and the South African defense force. Soldiers were rap-
pelling from helicopters onto rooftops. These tactics were billed as
counterterrorism training. Yet, these tactics were then used to fight
crime in Berea, Johannesburg. The bags of money are quick to flow
when they support military interests, but not to fight the poverty that
most often fuels the crime itself.

I am not opposed to fighting crime in Berea—having witnessed firsthand the violence in that particular area. But, perhaps, the best way to
fight crime in Berea is not expensive counterterrorist tactics financed
by the United States. Perhaps we could consider fighting the poverty
that is at the root of such crime, which might at the same time decrease
the situations that foster terrorism. In submitting their report to

parliament on the South African Anti-terrorism Bill, the South African Human Rights Commission makes this point: "Global security would not be possible in a world of increasing poverty. Indeed, there is no doubt that the absence of the rule of law and democracy, rampant poverty, violation of the rights of ethnic and minority groups, and political situations of domination and discrimination contributed to the frustration and hatred of people, leading them to acts of terrorism."[35] Additionally, they charge that the *war* on terror may be fostering the insecurity economically and politically that creates terrorism.

South Africa is not alone. Across Africa, U.S. military aid has been bountiful since 9/11. There has been a push to secure long-term contracts and agreements for the U.S. military to use bases across Africa. Troop deployment is increasing in Africa as well, with 1,800 U.S. soldiers in Djibouti alone. Joint military operations between the United States and Morocco have been occurring for the last several years. Surveillance of African "hot spots" has increased since Bush declared the war in Iraq finished, and this surveillance includes the use of satellites and aircraft that had been used in the war. Not only is the United States negotiating to use their bases for its troops and missions, it is supplying them with the tools of war as well, including a $6.5 million program with Mauritania, Mali, Niger, and Chad to supply military training, equipment, and the infamous Toyota pickup trucks (which were so useful in the genocide in Rwanda and the conflict in Somalia). The United States now has access to refueling in bases in Ghana, Senegal, Gabon, Namibia, Uganda, and Zambia. These are just a handful of the states engaged with some form of military collaboration with the United States. And many of the leaders of these African states are not opposed to these agreements, but enter into them eagerly.[36] The price tag for *just a few* of these programs is not insignificant. The West African Pan-Sahel Initiative is costing the United States $7.75 million; the East Africa Counter-Terrorism Initiative is costing $100 million. Both are part of the "low-profile spread of U.S. security efforts away from U.S. bases and NATO deployments."[37] We might wonder if the price tag for the war on terror isn't larger and less cost-effective than for a war on poverty?

3.   The View from South Africa: Guantánamo Bay

Finally, there are the stories of abuse and torture at Guantánamo Bay. When I first heard about this story, I was staying with a family in Pretoria that has hosted me since 1990. We were watching the news one evening, and the images appeared—long shots through the gates and bars. There were hooded, handcuffed prisoners taken from outdoor cement cells/cages to the interrogation centers. And there were reports of starvation, lack of medical treatment, lack of legal access, and potential acts of abuse and torture. The entire family looked to me in silence, waiting. I felt the weight of my citizenship again fall upon my shoulders.

According to the news, it was now publicly acknowledged that the United States was engaging in false imprisonment, starvation, extreme sleep deprivation, and other internationally condemned legal and medical practices. I was eager for e-mail from the States to see how the press was reporting on this. The responses I received from friends and family back in the United States were confusing: "pictures from Guantanamo Bay—there are pictures of prisoners?" and "media reports of abuse—there are reports of abuse?" Things were being presented quite differently on the other side of the ocean.

2003–2004: Apartheid USA

I made sense of it when I returned. My first day back in the United States in late July, I turned on ABC. There it was. The bright faced, well-groomed news reporter that began with the line "The US military is pleased to report that the majority of prisoners at Guantánamo Bay have provided useful leads and intelligence in the war on terror." That was it.

How deeply strange; how strangely familiar. In 1990, I could not wait to get back to the United States so that I could experience our aggressively free press. Now, in 2003, I had seen pictures and heard reports in the South African media of abuse and torture that would take until May 2004 to make regular and widespread U.S. headlines. This pattern of abuse and torture was not new; only the pictures and videotaping were.

One of my oldest friends in South Africa, an Afrikaner who worked at great personal risk opposing apartheid, voiced concern over the U.S. media one night in July:

> You know, I was very confused when I visited the US in the months leading up to the US invasion of Iraq. The media reports were so clearly biased in the US, and there was almost no coverage of dissent and no coverage of the contradictory evidence being presented in the European press and African media. I remember the days when we held up the US press as the paragon of freedom and democracy—as ardent representatives of objective news. Where were they now? How were they missing the story?

How were they missing the story? More importantly, why were they missing the story?

In the 1990s, during the democratic transition, the South African media had taken enormous pride in modeling themselves after U.S. media outlets. There were, for example, frequent and regular exchanges of students and journalists from South Africa and the United States. Creating a free press from the roots of a state-censored media was no easy task. The result is that there are now a plethora of media sources governed by various political viewpoints in South Africa.

Because of this current diversity, and because of a history of state-controlled media, citizens on the ground in South Africa are deeply thoughtful about the press and about its relationship to power. For example, high school students in Mamelodi, a township outside Pretoria, grilled me about U.S. politics. I am always amazed at how much South African students know about domestic U.S. politics— which on average is significantly more than the vast majority of U.S. students know about their own country. Perhaps that lack of knowledge or interest is the luxury of living inside the empire; on the outside, it is impossible not to know. Students posed informed and pointed questions: about how the U.S. public felt about the UN, about kickbacks to members of the U.S. administration for oil contracts, about Dick Cheney's investments and holdings, and especially about the U.S. press. South Africa has CNN International as one of its international news sources, and also the BBC. These students asked me if CNN was a propaganda tool of the Bush administration. They expressed disbelief when I told them the majority of my students in the United States felt that CNN was too critical of the Bush administration because "liberals" had captured CNN. I tried to explain the impact of FOX News and how it had shifted the center to the right and that CNN seemed liberal. These students were not alone in this assessment. There were similar conversations in wider academic and professional circles; many in South Africa were now suspicious of CNN's coverage. I can only imagine what they would think of FOX News. Several activist friends told me that there were strong sentiments in having Al Jazeera replace CNN, because it is *politically less biased* than CNN.

But, back in the United States, these conversations were not widespread, and I began to have the bizarre sense that South Africa and the United States had switched places. What was perhaps most familiar, in a horrifying sense, was that the day that the CBS story on the abuse of prisoners in Iraq was aired in the spring of 2004, I was simultaneously teaching the end of the South African unit in my Introduction to

Comparative Politics course. In class we were having conversations about how South Africa, a society so deeply divided with a history of such violence, continues to move toward democracy and reconciliation. The leaders in South Africa intentionally made the decision to have an open, public accounting of the horrors of apartheid through the now internationally recognized Truth and Reconciliation Commission (TRC). The TRC traded amnesty for truth about political crimes. Its goal was an irrefutable, documented, and comprehensive understanding of the terror of apartheid. This was in contrast to the Nuremberg Trials, where truths may have been lost in legal attempts to secure freedom for war criminals, or in contrast to other national truth commissions, where the hearings were held behind closed doors. While the TRC is not without flaws, it provided documentation of torture, murder, and abuse from the mouths of perpetrators themselves.

On the very morning of the day that the CBS story on the prison abuse in Iraq broke, I had shown clips from the TRC hearing to my students. This is always a difficult moment in my teaching. Students find it hard to see torturers explaining and demonstrating their methods, as well as to observe victims confronting their torturers. No matter how carefully I prepare the students for these stories, there are always a handful of them who are brought to tears. The outrage is universal in the class, and there is usually a strong sense among the students that the TRC did not do enough—that the abusers should be punished, fined, or imprisoned. There are usually a zealous few who want to turn the tables and subject the perpetrators to the same abuses they perpetrated. I try to explain that South Africans selected this direction because perhaps in their situation reconciliation and truth may be more powerful than retribution. Because the majority of my students are usually in favor of capital punishment and often even vigilante justice, this discussion frequently moves in unexpected and tricky directions.

After seeing and hearing the TRC reports, these same students then went home to see the CBS *60 Minutes II* reports of abuse, humiliation, sexual violence, and violations of our own laws. I wondered if they had similar feelings of outrage, shock, and disbelief—or if they found ways to explain, dismiss, or rationalize the actions of the abusers. Of course, this was months after these reports were being discussed internationally. Ultimately it was the pictures and videos that became the story—not the abuse itself. It is difficult to accuse *60 Minutes II* for being insensitive to the U.S. soldiers or antiadministration when they themselves held the story for two weeks at the request of the Defense Department:

> Two weeks ago, *60 Minutes II* received an appeal from the Defense Department, and eventually from the Chairman of the Joint Chiefs of Staff, Gen. Richard Myers, to delay this broadcast—given the danger and tension on the ground in Iraq.
>
> *60 Minutes II* decided to honor that request, while pressing for the Defense Department to add its perspective to the incidents at Abu Ghraib prison. This week, with the photos beginning to circulate elsewhere, and with other journalists about to publish their versions of the story, the Defense Department agreed to cooperate in our report.[38]

The congressional hearings about the pictures and videos of the prison abuse occurred during finals week at my university—and I realized that my students would have to try and make sense of the juxtaposition of the TRC clips and Abu Ghraib shots on their own.

How different the congressional hearings were from the TRC. The focus of the discussions was on the pictures and their release—rarely on the actions. All of this was in violation of our own laws and protocols, and it was apparently not just in the prisons—with additional reports of these activities being found perpetrated in towns and villages in Iraq. How different must have been my students' response to this violation of public trust than their response to the abuses of the apartheid regime. Since many of those students remain staunch supporters of the Bush administration, I imagine it continued to be easier to throw stones across an ocean at another country's abuses than to recognize our own culpability in abuse and torture. Or have we come full circle?

Full Circle

Full circle would mean that the United States has used the actions of 9/11 to construct a narrative in which U.S. power may be deployed unilaterally internationally and indiscriminately domestically. It would mean that the press is either hesitant or blocked from fair and balanced coverage. It would mean that civil liberties are in jeopardy. Full circle would mean that the United States is becoming isolated from world politics while being seen as a pariah state deserving of international sanctions and shunning. It would mean that torture, abuse, and violence would become normalized.

Rather than using the moment of 9/11 to reexamine U.S. foreign policy and to ask why nations like the United States are targets when other democracies are not, the administration, with congressional approval, imposed the Patriot Act. Through intense U.S. pressure, the Security Council's Resolution 1373 gave the CTC, the Security Council, and indirectly the United States significant oversight and influence in the domestic legislative affairs of putatively sovereign nations. We have internationalized our version of domestic control over civilian speech and movement, often to nations with widely recognized deplorable human rights abuses. In many instances, terrorist activity includes democratic dissent and protest, and now we may be seen to legitimize the claim that civil rights and civil liberties ought to be restricted in the name of security.

Bush's first trip as president to Africa highlighted a U.S. agenda for securing additional oil resources and ensuring compliance with the war on terror. Rather than visiting countries similarly victimized by terrorist attacks on U.S. targets, the administration decided to visit states that were supportive of the war in Iraq, that are oil rich, or that are deeply influential in shaping the political and economic agenda for the continent as a whole. The visit interrupted the business of African leaders trying to shape a new vision of Africa, one that emphasizes African solutions to African problems. The United States continues to disregard the push toward African unity within the African Union and Nepad (the New Economic Programme for African Development). Instead, the United States insists on working state by state, thus ensuring that economic assistance comes in exchange for U.S. strategic needs. Imperialism seems to be revitalized.

The United States is now at a pivotal moment in its history. We can as a nation decide to strengthen the foundation of democracy, civil rights, and civil liberties domestically and support similar actions internationally. If the goal is to end terrorist acts, such a foundation is perhaps the only way to ensure an end to violence and tyranny. Or, we could close our borders, look for enemies within our universities and libraries and civic organizations, pursue military action prior to diplomacy, rush "intelligence," dictate domestic policy for sovereign nations, replace a free press with one that is carefully monitored or one that normalizes militarism, create a media that self-censors images of prison abuse and of the destruction of war, redefine patriotism to mean a blind acceptance of authority rather than a love of country, and ridicule those asking questions or raising their voices in dissent.

If we choose the former path, perhaps we might ask Nelson Mandela and Desmond Tutu for guidance. If we choose the latter, we can look to the architects of apartheid—P. W. Botha and Henrik Verwoerd.

Notes

1. Audre Lorde *Apartheid U.S.A.* with *Our Common Enemy, Our Common Cause: Freedom Organizing in the Eighties* by Merle Woo. Freedom Organizing Series, no. 2. New York: Kitchen Table, Women of Color Press, 1986.
2. John Battersby, "Pahad leaves today on a mission to mediate between Iraq and the UN," *Cape Times,* February 7, 2003, http://www.capetimes.co.za/index.php?fSectionId=271&fArticleId=46151.
3. http://news.bbc.co.uk/1/hi/world/africa/2761417.stm.
4. http://www.guardian.co.uk/Iraq/Story/0,2763,888442,00.html.
5. http://news.bbc.co.uk/1/hi/world/africa/2710181.stm.
6. "Mandela lashes out at Bush," *Mail and Guardian,* January 30, 2003, http://www.mg.co.za/articledirect.aspx?articleid=15082&area=%2fbreaking_news%2fbreaking_news__national%2f
7. The Ugandan model came under question in September 2004 following studies by an NGO working in Uganda, the National Guidance and Empowerment Network. See http://news.bbc.co.uk/1/hi/world/africa/ 3677570.stm for further details.
8. "The master of empty promises," *Mail and Guardian,* July 4, 2003, http://www.mg.co.za/articledirect.aspx?articleid=23663&area=%2finsight%2finsight__national%2f
9. "Kenya says Bush snub an intimidation attempt," *Mail and Guardian,* July 11, 2003, http://www.mg.co.za/articledirect.aspx?articleid=24273&area=%2finsight%2finsight__africa%2f
10. Ibid.
11. Darlene Superville, "Bush visits South Africa amid rising anti-U.S. sentiment," Associated Press (Pretoria, South Africa), July 9, 2003.
12. Tsabeng Nthite, "Pretoria braces for Bush invasion," Star, July 4, 2003, http://www.iol.co.za/index.php?sf=68&click_id=13&art_id=vn20030704013210778C680803&set_id=1.
13. But even with this security, the U.S. secret servicemissed a stowaway on the press plane. The problem was not with South African security, but U.S. secret service. "Sapa-AFP reports that in South Africa, a police spokesperson indicated that the security lapse was on the US side. He said South Africa provided 'good and adequate' security for Bush's visit." "Stowaway hitches a lift on Bush press plane," *Saturday Star,* July 11, 2003, http://www.iol.co.za/index.php?set_id=1&click_id=68&art_id=ct20030711232649923S3 00948.
14. Jamaica Kincaid, *A Small Place* (New York: Farrar, Straus and Giroux, 1988).
15. This story was related to me by one of my U.S. friends who had been studying in South Africa.

16. The prison camp that held political prisoners like Nelson Mandela during apartheid.

17. You can also find reference to this story here: Bryan Rostron, "A day out with Indres, and his memories of torture," *New Statesman,* January 19, 2004, http://www.newstatesman.com/site.php3?newTemplate=NSArticle_World&n ewDisplayURN=200401190018.

18. "Anti-Bush Protests Said Under Way in Pretoria, Cape Town," *Financial Times,* July 9, 2003; "Hundreds of anti-Bush protesters said gathering at Pretoria Park," BBC Monitoring International Reports.Wednesday, July 9, 2003. Also see "Anti-Bush protesters march to Parliament" and S. Africa: Anti-Bush protesters to hand memorandum to US Mission," on SAPA news agency website, Johannesburg, carried by the BBC Monitoring International Reports. And seeSahm Venter, "About 1,000 demonstrators march to protest Bush visit," Associated Press (Pretoria, South Africa), July 9, 2003.

19. R. W. Johnson, "Bush flies into South Africa's den of defiance," *Sunday Times* (London), July 6, 2003.

20. Hopewell Radebe, "Protests fizzle out amid tight security," *Business Day* (Johannesburg), July 10, 2003.

21. Joseph K'Amolo, "The other side of Bush's five nation tour of Africa," All Africa News Agency, African Church Information Service, July 21, 2003.

22. Ibid. Also "Group of intellectuals to protest President Bush visit in Dakar," July 7, 2003, Global News Wire (NTIS, U.S. Dept of Commerce, World News Connection).

23. "Uganda People's Congress demonstration would cause little harm," *Monitor,* July 14, 2003.

24. See "Nigeria: Bush should condemn police brutality," Human Rights Watch, July 10, 2003, http://www.hrw.org/press/2003/07/nigeria071003.htm.

25. "Rights body asks bush to condemn police brutality," UN Integrated Regional Information Networks, July 11, 2003.

26. "An act of overkill," *Mail and Guardian,* June 27, 2003, http://www.mg. co.za/articledirect.aspx?articleid=23099&area=%2finsight%2finsight__ editorials%2f

27. Ibid.

28. Ibid.

29. Anti-Terrorism Bill, introduced to the National Assembly by the Minister of Safety and Security, B12-2003.

30. Darlene Superville, "Bush visits South Africa amid rising anti-U.S. sentiment," Associated Press (Pretoria, South Africa), July 9, 2003.

31. "Bush trip to Africa, July 2003," Human Rights Watch, http://www.hrw.org/ backgrounder/africa/bush-africa2k3.pdf.

32. Anthony Stoppard, "Terrorism and oil likely to dominate Bush visit," Inter Press Service/Global Information Network, July 1, 2003.

33. "Bush in Nigeria," *Vanguard,* July 12, 2003.

34. Adekeye Adebajo, "Africa and America in an age of terror," *Journal of Asian and African Studies,* 38, no. 2–3 (2003): 181.

35. South African Human Rights Commission, "An appraisal of the South African Anti-terrorism Bill from a human rights perspective," 2003, http://www.pmg.org.za/.
36. Eric Schmitt, "Threats and Responses: Expanding U.S. presence; Pentagon seeking new access pacts for Africa bases," *New York Times,* sec. A; p. 1.
37. Ahmed Mohamed, "U.S. sends anti-terror team to West Africa," Associated Press, January 12, 2004.
38. "Abuse of Iraqi POWs by GIs probed," *60 Minutes II.* April 29, 2004, http://www.cbsnews.com/stories/2004/04/27/60II/main614063.shtml.

Bibliography

Adebajo, Adekeye. 2003. Africa and America in an age of terror. *Journal of Asian and African Studies* 38: 175–192.

Ajayi-Soyinka, Omofolabo. 2003. The fashion of democracy: September 11 and Africa. *Signs* 29, no.2: 603–607.

Anti-terrorism Bill, introduced to the National Assembly by the Minister of Safety and Security, B12–2003.

Battersby, John. 2003. Pahad leaves today on a mission to mediate between Iraq and the UN. *Cape Times,* February 7. http://www.capetimes.co.za/index.php?fSectionId=271&fArticleId=46151.

Global News Wire. 2003. Group of intellectuals to protest President Bush visit in Dakar. NTIS, U.S. Department of Commerce, World News Connection, July 7.

Human Rights Watch. 2003. Bush trip to Africa, July. http://www.hrw.org/backgrounder/africa/bush-africa2k3.pdf.

Human Rights Watch. 2003. Nigeria: Bush should condemn police brutality. July. http://www.hrw.org/press/2003/07/nigeria071003.htm.

Johnson, R. W. 2003. Bush flies into South Africa's den of defiance. *Sunday Times* (London), July 6.

K'Amolo, Joseph. 2003. The other side of Bush's five nation tour of Africa. All Africa News Agency, African Church Information Service, July 21.

Kincaid, Jamaica. 1988. *A small place.* New York: Farrar, Straus and Giroux.

Lorde, Audre. 1985. Apartheid U.S.A., *Ikon,* 45–51.

60 Minutes II. 2004. Abuse of Iraqi POWs by GIs probed. April 29. http://www.cbsnews.com/stories/2004/04/27/60II/main614063.shtml.

Mohamed, Ahmed. 2004. U.S. sends anti-terror team to West Africa. Associated Press, January 12.

Monitor. 2003. Uganda people's congress demonstration would cause little harm. July 14.

Nthite, Tsabeng. 2003. Pretoria braces for Bush invasion. *Star,* July 4. http://www.iol.co.za/index.php?sf=68&click_id=13&art_id=vn20030704013210778C680803&set_id=1.

Radebe, Hopewell. 2003. Protests fizzle out amid tight security. *Business Day* (Johannesburg), July 10

Rostron, Bryan. 2004. A day out with Indres, and his memories of torture. *New Statesman,* January 19. http://www.newstatesman.com/site.php3?newTemplate =NSArticle_World&newDisplayURN=200401190018.

Schmitt, Eric. 2003. Threats and responses: expanding U.S. presence; Pentagon seeking new access pacts for Africa bases. *New York Times,* July 5, A1.

South African Human Rights Commission. 2003. An appraisal of the South African anti-terrorism bill from a human rights perspective. http://www.pmg. org.za/.

Stoppard, Anthony. 2003. Terrorism and oil likely to dominate Bush visit. InterPress Service, Global Information Network, July 1.

Superville, Darlene. 2003. Bush visits South Africa amid rising anti-U.S. sentiment. Associated Press, July 9.

United Nations Integrated Regional Information Networks. 2003. Rights body asks Bush to condemn police brutality. July 11.

Vanguard. 2003. Bush in Nigeria. July 12.

Chapter 8

Valiant, Vicious, or Virtuous? Representation, and the Problem of Women Warriors

Robin L. Riley

In 2004, the U.S. Defense Department released a report prepared by a task force appointed to investigate complaints of sexual abuse by U.S. military men on U.S. military women stationed in the war zone. The task force was appointed in response to 112 complaints of sexual assaults on U.S. servicewomen by U.S. servicemen in the Middle East over an 18-month period (Clemtson 2004:1; Weiser 2004:1). As of this writing, over 40 U.S. military women have died in Iraq and more than 230 have earned Purple Hearts for being wounded in battle (Sisk 2004:43). In 2005, PFC Lynndie England faced court-martial for her role in the Abu Ghraib prison scandal. Also in 2005, the most visible military hero/ine to emerge from the war on Iraq, Jessica Lynch, acquired a new career as a motivational speaker and has since begun work toward a degree at the University of West Virginia.

The enormous media attention being lavished on women like Jessica Lynch and Lynndie England reflects the enhanced visibility of women participating in the war on Iraq. Such attention prompts feminists to ask questions about how gender and race are at work in this war. In this chapter, I examine newspaper and other popular media accounts of the capture and "rescue" of Jessica Lynch, the capture and release of Shoshana Johnson, and the capture and death of Lori Piestewa. The representations of these three women in mainstream media reveal how race, class, gender, and sexuality are used to construct, recuperate, and reinscribe ideas about femininity, the military, and war. From March 2003 until October 2005, I collected news stories about the three women from major newspapers, news services, news magazines, and local papers from the places where the three women were stationed or from their hometowns. By October 2005, I had amassed 187 articles about Jessica Lynch, 32 about Shoshana

Johnson, and 17 about Lori Piestewa.[1] I also examined transcripts from television news shows on ABC, NBC, CNN, and CBS as well as some from news magazine programs.

Over the last four war-filled years, U.S. women have been used in multiple ways both to reinscribe traditional understandings of femininity and to expand them. The actual practice of femininity is shifting, from traditional practices toward a fuller idea of the capabilities of women, but that shifting is obscured by an emphasis on traditional constructions of white femininity. In this way, gender is still seen as a guarantee of the role women will play in wartime.

In order to preserve male-defined notions of "security," the supremacy of militarized masculinity and the prevailing gender order—contemporary sexism, applied to war stories and manifested in them—must be particularly resilient. In the "war on terror," the inroads made by women have been acknowledged, but simultaneously, women's achievements have been undermined. The convolutions and configurations of gender necessary to legitimate war have sexism, racism, classism, and homophobia as their foundation and use them as a means to create divisions among women. These constructions of gender use women, mostly women of color, but also lesbians and working-class and poor women, to justify imperialism by creating or reinscribing age-old divisions among people, between states, and within ethnicities.

Contemporary configurations of sexism are most apparent in media representations in the West, in which certain women act as tokens or icons meant to stand in for all women of a certain identity, position, or profession. In this configuration, Jessica Lynch represents all U.S. women soldiers, Condoleeza Rice[2] represents all women of color, and Dr. Germ and Mrs. Anthrax (the only two Iraqi women ever named in the U.S. press, who were blamed for the production of the never-found weapons of mass destruction) represent all Iraqi women. The bonds of the body—that is, shared sisterhood and female "weakness"—are exploited as reason to go to war. Simultaneously, shared understandings about the proper practice of femininity are utilized to divide U.S. white women and Iraqi women,[3] and as I will show, to divide white women and women of color in the U.S. military.

In the new configurations of femininity, women assume multiple, sometimes conflicting roles. Iraqi and Afghan women are victims not of the United States of course, but of the Taliban and of Saddam Hussein. U.S. mothers—long believed to be good only for providing sons and nurturance during wartime and already required to send their sons, and now daughters, to war—now take on the additional role of protectors: either as members of the U.S. military or National Guard, or through their efforts to better defend their soldier children when they send food, sunscreen, and body armor to the Gulf (Loeb 2003:A01). U.S. military women, trained to be equals to male soldiers, still require "rescuing" by U.S. male troops even as many are raped by their male colleagues (Schmidt 2003:A01; Weiser 2004; Clemetson 2004:1). Women's participation in the "war on terror" is thus fraught with contradiction and requires more discursive and conceptual work on the part of the military planners, public relations officials, and civilian journalists who create the war stories. They have to figure out how to tell the war story in such a way that they can recruit certain women for the military, keep other women at home producing sons and supporting the war, make women feel the war is being fought for them while keeping them outside of any real voice in decision-making, and finally discourage women from resisting or protesting the war.

From the time of her capture by the Iraqis to her "rescue" and subsequent return to the United States, the attempted deification of white, blonde, Jessica Lynch occurred at the same time as the combat death of Native American Lori Piestewa, which the press hardly noted, as well as the imprisonment of African American Shoshana Johnson. Within these accounts of women's participation in the war on Iraq, one can observe contradictions between the actual contemporary practice of femininity and traditional conceptions of femininity. Even though one white woman soldier is venerated for her service to country, the not-so-subtle message contained in the narrative of her "rescue," and the contention over whether or not she was raped by an orientalized enemy serve as warnings for other white women to stay home, where they belong in wartime. War, the story seems to tell us, is about the protection of white, heterosexual women; soldiering is the business of racialized, defemininized women and militarized, heterosexual men. These accounts simultaneously reify white heterosexual femininity as the ideal to which all women must aspire and devalue and erase the role played by women of color.

Jessica

Almost everyone in the United States has heard or read some version of the story of the capture of Jessica Lynch.[4] On March 23, 2003, a convoy from the 507th Ordnance Maintenance Company got lost in Nasiriyah, Iraq, and came under fire from Iraqis (North 2003). During the firefight, there was an accident involving the truck in which Shoshana Johnson was a passenger and the Humvee in which Jessica Lynch was traveling, and Jessica was badly injured. Subsequently, Jessica, Shoshana, Lori, and several other soldiers were taken prisoner by the Iraqis. Initially, the popular press accounts of this event omitted information about the accident and concentrated instead on depicting Jessica as the smaller, blonder version of the highly masculinized U.S. fighting ideal, Rambo.[5] A *Washington Post* headline on April 3, 2003, read, "She was fighting to the Death." The story reported that according to military officials, Jessica had received "multiple gunshot wounds" and was stabbed by the Iraqis. The story said that as "she did not want to be taken alive," she fought fiercely and "ran out of ammunition" (Schmidt 2003:A01). The erroneous *Washington Post* story—based on information obtained from a military source—probably provided the impetus for similar stories that appeared in other newspapers like the *NY Daily News* (Becker 2003:7) and the *New York Times* (Shankar 2003:B10; Jehl 2003:A3);[6] on radio; and on television networks like CNN, CBS, and NBC. The media created a new war hero/ine based on this initial misinformation.

While there is almost always some myth involved in the creation of heroes, in this case, the heroic narrative is infused with cultural ideals about race and the practice of gender. These cultural ideals, themselves based in mythology, are difficult to maintain in peace time, but adding in the twists of war, geography, and an orientalized enemy renders them unwieldy Consequently, in order to hold onto ideas about male supremacy and feminine weakness and white supremacy and orientalized Arabs, along with notions about what constitutes appropriate kinds of work for men and women, enormous conceptual, rhetorical, and representational work is required. All social institutions must be engaged in order for these ideals to be upheld. The media alone could not have created the myth of Jessica Lynch as warrior. Journalists were assisted by the Pentagon, whose military officials provided the stories of Jessica's fierce self-defense (Burke 2004:225). The media were also assisted by the willingness of family and friends of the new hero/ine(s), who allowed their words to be used to uphold certain ideas about patriotism, security, and gender that are both militarized and normative. When Jessica's mother, Deadra Lynch, was informed by Katie Couric on the *Today Show* that Jessica had apparently emptied her weapon in defending herself, she replied: "I'm not surprised, she's a fighter. That's—that's our Jessie. She's a fighter, and I think that that's exactly what sh—I would expected her—out of her." Even though

Mrs. Lynch was certainly startled by the sudden media spotlight and had to be fearful for Jessica's safety, the stumbling way in which she responds to this question might indicate that these constructions of her daughter are unfamiliar, or at least that the situation of being heroic her daughter finds herself in is quite unexpected. Not wanting to disappoint the interviewer or the public, she likely responded in a manner that, was expected of her.

For a moment it seemed that the unlikely hero of the war on Iraq would turn out to be a small, blonde woman from rural, impoverished West Virginia who had fiercely fought off Iraqi men. The notion of young women as fierce warriors, however, is also one that a nation that went to war in the name of security—to protect women—could not endure. Militarized masculinity is founded on the idea that women like the diminutive, blonde, Jessica Lynch require protecting. If women like her can participate in combat in exactly the same way as a male soldier would, the carefully wrought differences between masculinity and femininity on which militarized masculinity relies become meaningless. Thus, in order for the story to be fully realized, in a very un-Rambo-like fashion, Jessica Lynch herself required "rescuing" by male soldiers. News organizations throughout the Western world put forth the story that U.S. forces had engaged in a daring, videotaped rescue of Jessica Lynch in which troops stormed the hospital where she was being held and returned her to safety. This narrative of U.S. military might and valor while taking care of its own soldiers appealed to an American public that was not only eager for good news from Iraq (Jones 2003:18; Price 2003:3C; Burke 2004:226) but that perhaps also needed the rescue tale in order to counter the destabilizing effects on ideas about the proper practice of femininity that stories of Lynch's heroine-ism had wrought. After all, according to militarized conceptions of how women act in wartime, Jessica was not the proper gender for war heroics and thus could not be the lone hero to emerge from this war.

It wasn't long before the BBC revealed that this glamorous tale of militarized masculine prowess had been staged. One of the Iraqi doctors who worked at the hospital at the time of the rescue related that only medical personnel were present when U.S. troops arrived via helicopter with guns blazing:

> It was like a Hollywood film. They cried "go, go, go," with guns and blanks without bullets, blanks and the sound of explosions. They made a show for the American attack on the hospital—action movies like Sylvester Stallone or Jackie Chan.
>
> (Kampfner 2003)

It was also revealed that prior to this "rescue," once the Iraqi troops had left the hospital, an effort had been made to turn Jessica over to U.S. forces in order to protect her and the other patients from the threat of U.S. attack. This effort was unsuccessful, however, as U.S. forces actually fired on the ambulance as it approached a checkpoint with Jessica inside. The Iraqis retreated and brought her back to the hospital (McIntyre 2003). The Pentagon reacted angrily to this counternarrative and vehemently denied having fired blanks. The rescue tale was never effectively debunked, however, and it seems that the "rescue" was at least partly staged for propaganda purposes. So this staged event that was intended to recuperate Jessica Lynch as properly feminine, to restore the masculinized credentials of the rescuers, to reestablish the racialized gender regime, and to showcase militarized masculine supremacy, ended up further calling it into question.

Once the truer story began to emerge, that is that the "rescue" was staged, that Jessica's injuries were sustained in the accident, and that she had actually never fired a shot (because her had weapon malfunctioned) (Sawyer 2003), the narrative of Jessica Lynch as brave warrior single-handedly attempting to defeat the Iraqi army began to be offset with news stories in which she began to be more closely identified with the ideals of white femininity, with the simplicity of American rural life, and with that which needs protecting. From the time of the first reports, the imperative of white femininity was in tension with the depiction of this young woman as a fierce warrior. Within two weeks, Jessica went from being depicted as a New Age Boudicca to being a 2003 version of Laura Ingalls Wilder in *Little House on the Prairie*. Her cousin, Lorene Cumbridge, described her as "every mother's dream of a teenage daughter . . . She's just a West Virginia country girl. Warm hearted, outgoing" (Steelhammer 2003:1A). On *Dateline NBC* (April 9 2003), reporter Dennis Miller described her as "a kind, spirited, itty-bitty country girl." In these interviews, people who knew her were asked to comment, and if anyone said anything other than what fit the image described above, we didn't hear about it: "She was a sweetheart," said Ron Vincent, whose daughter Jessica used to babysit (Blanchfield 2003:A18). No one says that she was hard to get along with, or that she was mean or moody or promiscuous or transgendered, all characteristics (associated with women of color) that would eliminate her from contention as America's Iraqi-killing "sweetheart."

The Lynch family and community members didn't call the heroic narrative into question. Nevertheless, some members of the media exhibited the tensions inherent in grasping the idea of a woman soldier—warrior or not—in a culture in which it is not quite seemly for women to enter the military, much less fight in a war. Of course, this notion of proper feminine behavior is informed by socioeconomic stereotypes of class and race. The military increasingly relies on women's labor, but it is mostly working-class women, poor women, and women of color who do this work.

Another NBC reporter, Bob Faw, talked about Jessica as "the 19 year old, described as a West Virginia country girl who wore combat boots under her prom dress." His metaphor uncovers the contradiction apparent in having this "sweet little country girl" volunteering for war. Numerous reporters described Jessica in words that differentiated her from other young women who were less suited for, or interested in, war. She was frequently described as "plucky" or "gutsy" (Jones 2003:A01). Never used to describe male military participation, these words hint that she has engaged in "unlady-like" behavior. One writer tried to name the contradictions involved in "sweet little country girl(s)" becoming war heroes:

> If Jessica did, as the Pentagon would have it, trade bullets with Saddam's Fedayeen fighters, there can rarely have been a less likely—or more reluctant heroine . . . She had a tomboyish streak, enjoying softball and chasing around in the woods. However, as a young girl she was happiest with her Barbie dolls. In her teens she was every inch the local catch, turning heads at weekend dances. She had a winning personality too, and was crowned Miss Congeniality at the county fair when she was 17. Her ambition was to become a teacher. Hardly the stuff of a would-be female Rambo.
>
> (Jones 2003: 18)

Is this author guarding against the long-held suspicions of women in the military as lesbians when he is careful to point out that the "tomboy" part of Jessica was only a "streak" and not the majority of her character? Would all of Jessica's desirability as a female war hero, that is, her "pluckiness," whiteness, blondeness, and small stature, be erased if people suspected that she was a lesbian? Another writer tries to name the differences between Jessica and other young military women:

> This diminutive 20 year old supply clerk . . . Her smile, her sincerity and her seeming vulnerability contrast with the battlefield horror she was exposed to, creating a figure to which compassion and gratitude easily attach.
>
> (*Columbus Dispatch* 2003)

What set her apart from other military women and men, this author and others suggest, are "her smile, vulnerability," and "sincerity." This author may be on to something here. While certainly other female members of the military serving honorably in Iraq have engaging smiles, Jessica's smile upon her homecoming was in stark contrast to the look of terror and pain on her face that we had come to know. Of course, her terror was appealing as well, as women's terror in wartime is more familiar, more reassuring that women have stayed in their proper places. Yet the author's reference to "vulnerability" prompts questions about what actually does set Jessica apart from Lori Piestewa or Shoshana Johnson. If Jessica had "fought to the death" and had actually been killed as Lori Piestewa was, would she still have been the focus of such a media storm? If she had been shot or stabbed as Shoshana Johnson was, would she have received nearly as much attention? It seems that recovery from enemy-inflicted bullet wounds, as Shoshana Johnson can attest, is quite uninteresting to the Western media.

Other members of the media, bowing to the culture's insistence that women maintain their status of needing male protection, associate Jessica with childhood. One author described her as "waif-like" (Eagan 2003:018). In a report about her homecoming speech, another reporter noted that she was "speaking with an almost child-like inflection as she sat in the wheelchair" (Blanchfield 2003:A18). Infantilizing the female soldier reassures us as well, as it maintains male supremacy by combining women and children as one entity. Infantilization diminishes women's agency and omits women from considerations in decisions about war, except as property that requires protection. In a piece written in the *Ladies Home Journal,* the author goes further in reinforcing Jessica's youth:

> She's gracious, if guarded here in her cheery bedroom adorned with teddy bears and Beanie Babies. She's petite; just 5 feet 3 inches and 100 pounds with perfect little porcelain-doll features. She often seems far younger than her 20 years. Her voice is high and sweet with a soft country lilt. Even her blond hair is baby fine.
>
> (Barnett 2004:49)

Again, the author's emphasis on Jessica's small stature and "porcelain-doll features," distances her from adulthood, and the mention of beanie babies and teddy bears banishes the image of her holding an M16.

Once Jessica started speaking for herself, she began to object to being depicted as a hero/ine and to being utilized as a propaganda tool or recruiting image. She too contributed to this presentation of herself as a "little girl" by giggling and blushing when asked about her relationship with her then fiancé, Ruben Contreras. In contrast, though, she showed unexpected courage—at least to the eyes of military officials— when she debunked the military's account of how her capture occurred during an interview with Diane Sawyer. She stated, "I did not shoot, not a round, nothing . . . I went down praying, to my knees, and that's the last I remember."

Prior to the Sawyer interview, the media was fraught with contradictory images of Jessica, both rhetorical and actual, but they were almost uniformly united in an attempt to idolize her:

> First she was the country girl from Appalachia, a gutsy teenager who wanted to be a kindergarten teacher and joined the Army for educational opportunities unavailable to kids of modest means, only to end up missing in action. Then, with her nighttime rescue from an Iraqi hospital, she provided a ray of hope at a time when Americans were bludgeoned with bad news from the front.
>
> (Athans 2003:1A)

> For now, as never before, America needs its heroes. And Private First Class Jessica Lynch, a pretty little American girl from a pretty little American town, who may—or may not— have taken on Saddam's finest single handedly, perfectly fits the bill.
>
> (Jones 2003: 19)

Once she was able to talk back, however, Jessica resisted such glorification. In the Sawyer interview, she indicated that she had made a judgment about how the heroic narrative was told: "They used me as a way to symbolize all this stuff, it's wrong" (Sawyer 2003; Barker 2003:A15).

The media were able to use her because she so seemed to fit the bill: she was photogenic (read white), heterosexual (complete with the fiancé to prove it), and from rural West Virgina (one of the most impoverished counties in the country—poverty is good for recruiting). Moreover, she adhered to the proper practices of femininity since she enlisted only to get money for college to become a kindergarten teacher, not out of a desire to shoot somebody. The problem with Jessica was that she was not as malleable as all the above factors would seem to suggest. She eventually refused to allow herself to be used by the military and the administration and she became the fly in the ointment of her anointing as *the* Iraq war hero. The press attention began to wane a bit after she began to object to the administration's use of her.

The media's initial attention seems understandable. After all, fiction or not, it was a compelling story, and she is adorable. One reporter quoting a man from Jessica's hometown writes:

> "Every war needs a hero," reflected James Roberts, 77, the third generation owner of the 117 year-old general store here. "Rickenbacker . . . Kennedy . . . she's the hero in this war. The facts don't particularly matter.
>
> (Whoriskey 2003:A01)

Still, several other women distinguished themselves militarily in the war on Iraq. On that same day, Shoshana Johnson and Lori Piestewa faced the same dangers as Jessica and reacted with just as much determination, only to be virtually ignored by the U.S. media.

Shoshana

Shoshana Johnson is a 30-year-old, Panamanian American woman, and a member of the 507th Maintenance Company. She has a three-year-old daughter (Hockstader 2003:A03). On the same day, in the same incident in which Jessica Lynch was taken prisoner by the Iraqis, Shoshana Johnson too was captured. Although the media paid little attention to Shoshana's capture by the Iraqis,[7] unlike Jessica, she actually engaged Iraqi soldiers in battle (Douglas 2003:A16; Kane 2003:01B; Davidson 2004:72). She was held in captivity for 22 days (Falsani 2003:21), 11 more days than Jessica Lynch (Hockstader 2003: A03; Falsani, 2003: 21). Shoshana was in fact shot by the Iraqis, although press accounts differ as to actually where her injuries were located. While the consensus seems to be that she was shot in the ankles (Douglas 2003:A16; Kane 2003:01B), others have reported that she was "shot in both legs" (Hockstader 2003:A03), or that she had a "shattered left ankle and torn Achilles tendon in her right leg" (Falsani 2003:21).

The few stories about Shoshana Johnson that did appear in the Western press are very revealing of the position of women of color in U.S. culture. First, almost every press account about her or Lori Piestewa (a Native American woman) mentioned at the outset that they were single mothers.[8] It seems as if it was unthinkable to the creators of those stories that women of color would not be single mothers. The media had to keep telling us that these two women were single mothers as if to confirm their own preconceptions about women of color. This same obsession with marital status is not apparent in the stories about Jessica Lynch, as she is never identified as single, nor is her childlessness mentioned until her homecoming, when she is pictured holding hands with her then fiancé, Ruben Contreras. So while it is assumed that white, blonde Jessica is pure and virginal,[9] the public, lest it forgets, requires reminding that Lori and Shoshana, as women of color, are not (Roberts 1997).

Second, with the exception of stories that appeared in publications produced for African American audiences, such as *Ebony* and *Essence*, the media-produced stories about Shoshana tell us very little about her, other than that she has a child. Women of color are represented not as individuals in U.S. media but rather as one homogenized group of "strong" women who can endure terrible circumstances in order to provide security for the United States (Davis 1981). One exception to this is a story that appeared shortly after Shoshana's capture, in which her father, a veteran of the U.S. military himself, is quoted in response to a question about how he thinks Shoshana will endure captivity:

> He believes Shana is mentally and emotionally resilient. She grew up around Army bases all over the country, attended a half-dozen schools before graduating from high school in El Paso and loves cooking enchiladas for her family. He is certain she is taking comfort from prayer; before she left home for the Middle East, she made sure she had her rosary beads, after initially leaving them behind on her dresser. Shana, born in her father's native Panama, is the eldest of Claude Johnson's three daughters, an easygoing person who got along well in school and almost never argued with her parents.
> (Hockstader 2003:A36)

Shoshana is represented here as amiable, family oriented, religious, and obedient, hardly the image that is evoked when a woman is simply identified as a single mother. The single-mother identification, however, was the one most frequently picked up by those members of the media who mentioned Shoshana at all. She and Lori Piestewa were both mentioned most often not in long stories about their hometowns with testimonies from family members and neighbors about their characters. Rather, they were mostly mentioned as contrasting addenda to stories about Jessica Lynch.

Shoshana was most frequently described as "fearful" during captivity and then "depressed, scarred, haunted by the trauma of her captivity and at times unable to sleep, Johnson walks with a limp and has difficulty standing for long periods" (Hockstader 2003:A03). From this description, one still gets no sense of who Shoshana is except that she has been badly injured, both physically and psychically by her experiences in the war. Perhaps because her terrified image had appeared on television while she was being held—

> "Who are you?" barks her interrogator.
> "Shoshana," replies the trembling woman.
> "Where are you from?" he demands.
> "Texas," she says weakly.
>
> (Russell 2003:7B)

—Shoshana seems to have no difficulty describing her fear:

> Yesterday, on her 21st day as an Iraqi prisoner of war, U.S. army Specialist Shoshana Johnson thought she and six other U.S. prisoners of war would be killed because their guards were afraid of the ever-approaching American attacks. "We were a hot potato," said Johnson, 30, an army cook with six-inch braids. The POWs were moved through six holding places in the last six days alone, she said. "It was getting to the point where I believed they were going to kill us."
>
> (Tamayo 2003:A3)

Of course, it is her fear that the press wants to emphasize, not her ability to endure being held as a prisoner of war for 22 days. If they were to focus on her strength, it might topple white, blonde Jessica from her position as media darling of the war.

Scant attention has been paid to Shoshana since those very early days, and we do not have a full explanation of what happened to her during the firefight or any more details of her imprisonment. Crystal Brent Zook presents a possible explanation for the difference between the media attention to Jessica's story versus that of Shoshana and Lori:

> We like our symbols simple: a young, virgin-like girl rescued by dashing, brave men twice her size. This image allows us not to question too closely the notion of "strength," especially as it applies to women of color.

(Brent Zook 2003:04J)

The simplicity of Jessica as a symbol is only part of the story of the disparity between the treatment of Jessica and Shoshana shown by both the military and the media. The military, as an institution, participated in the unfair treatment. Jessica was discharged from the army with an 80 percent disability pension, whereas Shoshana was offered a 30 percent disability pension, a difference of between $600 and $700 per month (Hockstader 2003:A03). Here, along with the media, the military is enacting institutionalized racism. Even in a time of war, with a military increasingly reliant on women and people of color to fill the ranks, inequitable racialized practices prevail. Two young women are injured in the same battle on the same day and are taken prisoner of war as a result of that same incident. The white woman's captivity warrants the manufacture of a spectacular "rescue," whereas the African American woman limps home with little acclamation. A white woman is financially compensated by the military much more than is a woman of color.[10] Surely racism is playing a part here, not only in media representations but also in military policies and decision making.

Of course, Jessica also had a book and made-for-television movie deal. There were no stories in the national press about any offers having been made to Shoshana and her family. Only her hometown paper, the *El Paso Times*, raised the possibility that Shoshana might be able to capitalize on her experiences in Iraq. Immediately prior to her homecoming, according to the *El Paso Times*:

> The 30-year-old cook from Fort Bliss' 507th Maintenance Company and her family have been romanced by magazines, news programs and talk shows from all over the country. Black Entertainment Television, Newsweek, Katie Couric of NBC's "Today Show," Stone Phillips of NBC's "Dateline," CBS, Ebony magazine, Telemundo and Oprah Winfrey have tried to arrange interviews with the single mother of a 2-year-old, said family spokeswoman Elsie Morgan.
>
> (Kareem 2003:1)

The "romance" was short-lived, although Shoshana did appear on Oprah as part of a special report on POWs on April 4, 2004. She has also appeared on Emeril Lagasse's cooking show (McFadden 2003:E1), and she was invited by Larry King to respond to the Abu Ghraib prison photos. She had interviews in *Ebony* and *Essence,* as well as in *People Magazine,* but she got nothing like the media saturation that Jessica Lynch received nor a million-dollar book deal. According to the El Paso Times August 10, 2006, Shoshana is currently writing a book that is scheduled to be relased in May 2007.

These days, while she continues to make some public appearances, she was invited to push the button to drop the ball on New Year's Eve in Times Square (Perez 2004:A05), she was the black history month speaker at Nassau Community College (McCarthy 2004:A3–4), and she spoke at the "Spirit of Sisterhood: Women's Empowerment Weekend" in San Antonio in October 2004 (Ayala 2004: 3K). These invitations seem to be more connected to her race, her nationality, or her occupation as a cook, rather than to her service to the country.

Lori

Lori Piestewa was the third woman taken prisoner on April 2, 2003. At the time of her capture, she was gravely wounded, and she died shortly after arriving at the hospital. She was the first woman and the first Native American to die in the war on Iraq (Younge 2003:24; Monaghan 2003:7). She had two children.

Lori, following the tradition of three generations of military service in her family, joined the ROTC in high school (Stockman 2003:A29; Reid 2003:A30). Like Shoshana and Jessica, Lori was seeking economic opportunity by joining the military (Younge 2003:24). As she stated in a newspaper interview prior to departure for Iraq, she was also interested in seeing the world beyond her small Hopi community. "I'm excited to go see something new . . . I'm also going to learn a lot" (Reid 2003: A30).

Lori Piestewa's service and death were almost lost in the press frenzy over Jessica Lynch. According to Jessica, the two women were roommates and "best friends." Indeed, it is mostly through Jessica that attention gets focused on Lori. In the welcome celebrations when she returned to Palestine (BBC 2003:1), as well as at the "Glamour Magazine 2003 Women of the Year" celebration, where she and Shoshana Johnson were honored (Wadler 2003:1), it was Jessica, not members of the military or the media, who consistently mentioned Lori.

Contrary to the Jessica Lynch mythology, there was great reluctance to valorize Lori for fighting against the Iraqi soldiers who eventually captured her. As a result, there were frequent, persistent rumors that rather than dying of wounds she acquired in battle, Lori had been executed. Finally, her local congressman, Representative Rick Renzi, spoke out:

"My message to her family is that she was not executed. Lori fought courageously, and her family has been informed of this," said Renzi, a freshman representative, whose district includes Piestewa's home in Tuba City, Ariz., on the Navajo reservation. "I think it's important to understand the fighting spirit of the first Native American woman to die in combat," he said.

(Moore 2003:1)

Perhaps it is precisely because Congressman Renzi invokes Lori's "fighting spirit" that the media seemed uninterested in Lori's story. Maybe because we have constructed women of color as strong, as fighters, we expect nothing less from a Native American woman, from a woman of color. On the other hand, Lori's fierceness in fighting might also call women's need for protection into question. Therefore, paying inordinate attention to her actions in battle could threaten militarized masculinity by exposing the fallacious justification for imperialism articulated by the women in the Bush administration in regard to the necessity of "rescuing" Afghan women from the Taliban and Iraqi women from Saddam Hussein.

As in Shoshana's case, the American public is given no real sense of who Lori was. Some reporters did go to her hometown to write stories in an attempt to give their readers a sense of this young woman. These few reporters related, however, that the family's reluctance to talk with the media had influenced other community members to remain silent as well (Younge 2003:24; Frazier 2003:1A). Thus, only the most depersonalized comments were elicited. "She was a great girl." "We are very proud." "It's so sad" (Younge 2003: 24). The Hopi Youth Center director Deana Burgener said: "She had her heart out there all the time. She gave wherever she went" (Frazier 2003:1A). Upon hearing of her death, her brother made the following statement that appeared in the mainstream media: "Our family is proud of her. She is our hero. We are going to hold that in our hearts. She will not be forgotten. It gives us comfort to know that she is at peace right now" (Monaghan 2003:7). The use of this sacrificial language, the naming of Lori as the disembodied "hero" rather than the "sweet, little country girl" that Jessica Lynch became in the media, robs Lori of her subjectivity and makes her into an object that can be offered up for the empire.

In dismay over how Lori was, or was not, being depicted in media representations, her family finally granted an interview to *Rolling*

Stone magazine that appeared in May 2004. They resisted Congressman Renzi's assertion that Lori was a fighter. They wanted to emphasize, instead, her adherence to the Hopi values of peace and nonviolence (Davidson 2004:68). "We're very satisfied she went the Hopi way," her father said smiling. "She didn't inflict harm on anybody"(72). The Piestewa family also urged other Native American people serving in the military in Iraq to leave their units and come home. This urging, as well as this particular construction of Lori, went unreported by other media. When one television network decided to show a videotape of Lori and Jessica, badly wounded in the hospital, a Piestewa family spokesperson reacted: "This terrorism was not from any foreign group wishing to harm the United States, but from our own people wanting to make a quick buck off the misfortune of two young women" (Shaffer 2004:1). Is the Piestewa family simply attempting to get the U.S. media to question its own practices? Or are they questioning U.S. foreign policy and the very foundations of ideas about "terror" and "terrorists"?

Jessica Lynch's community raised $50,000 in order to renovate her family's home, Lori's community raised $37,000 for a fund for her children's education (Mitchell 2003: 14), and after nomination by Jessica Lynch, Lori's family appeared on the May 22 edition of ABC's *Extreme Makeover: Home Edition* (Fields-Meyer 2005:145). The press accounts do not mention whether any fundraising occurred on Shoshana's behalf. It is not known whether Lori's family got offers to do interviews, participate in book contracts, and so on. The state of Arizona did make an attempt to name a mountain after her, but debate is ongoing over the proposal to name "a mountain formerly known as 'Squaw Peak' 'Piestewa Peak'" (Mitchell 2003:14).

Beloved as Lori Piestewa might have been to Jessica and to her own family, the media has not given her a chance to be loved by the American people. Of course, the media might have decided that her "fighting spirit" would undermine the standards of white femininity. She did decide on the military as a route into the middle class, a route that, aside from putting women in positions that upset the proper practice of femininity, also renders women immediately sexually suspect due to the lingering accusations that women in the military tend toward lesbianism. Lori was doubly dangerous since she already had two children with no father in sight (Younge 2003:24). A culture as determined as ours is not to allow women control over their own bodies is not prepared to embrace a hero/ine who controls her own body so specifically

Sorting It Out

Racism is at work in this story of these three unlikely war heroes. White bodies, particularly when they come with a full package of culturally determined aesthetic pleasures, are seen as more valuable in this white supremacist society (hooks 1992). The danger to Jessica Lynch therefore was more dramatic and more terrifying, and her suggested bravery was all the more surprising. Within this same ideological framework, women of color are believed to be stronger than white women and more able to bear oppressive circumstances; hence, what Shoshana and Lori did seemed unremarkable (Davis 1981). The press corps did not value Lori's death or Shoshana's imprisonment as much as Jessica's capture. When women of color act strong, this is to be expected and therefore not as newsworthy. In addition, the specter of white, blonde Jessica Lynch in the hands of Iraqi men had the added benefit of recalling old orientalist narratives about the inherent danger posed to white women by men of color, helping to whip up a frenzy of hatred toward this amorphous "terrorist" enemy. The story of Jessica's "rape" at the hands of her captors also served this purpose, as some press reports were careful to point out that she was "anally raped" (Siemaszko 2003:9; Monaghan 2003:15; Faramarzi 2003:18; Beeston 2003:15). The emphasis on anal rape evokes imperialist ideas about the sexuality of orientalized men who are not believed to be "real" men (read heterosexual) in the Western definition of masculinity. Jessica asserts that she cannot remember any such assault, and Iraqi physicians deny that there was any evidence of a rape when she arrived at the hospital (Beeston 2003:15).

The disparity in attention given to the three women, however, is too complex to be reducible to any one factor. It is not just about supporting empire building or upholding ideas about "national security." It is also about racism and militarized constructions of gender. And, it is pragmatic. Given the military's growing reliance on women to fill the ranks (Enloe 2000:240), the current desperate need for more soldiers to fulfill this administration's imperial missions, and the military's overall growing reliance on women of color (Brent Zook 2003: 04J), Shoshana, at least, might have been put to good use by the military to recruit more young women of color. Perhaps military officials believed that Jessica as hero/ine would be sufficient lure to young women contemplating military enlistment. She seemed to dispel lingering accusations of lesbianism toward women in the military and, despite Larry Flynt's assertions, seemed virginal. Her blonde-haired blue-eyed look is the standard to which all women in this culture, including women of color, are encouraged to aspire (hooks 1992). Blinded by all that country-girl charm, the military and the administration might have believed that she would serve them as a standard to which other young woman might strive. If so, this was a serious mistake. As one columnist points out, people of color are pretty sophisticated consumers of racist popular culture: "Had Johnson looked more like, say, the biracial Halle Berry, she might have had a shot at it. Rather than an American war hero, Lynch is White America's War Hero" (Mitchell 2003:14). Ignoring Shoshana and Lori also might have negatively impacted morale among the women soldiers currently deployed in Iraq. As another columnist noted: "if blond and blue-eyed are the criteria for being 'All-American,' what about all the Americans in Iraq who don't possess any of that?" (Kane 2003:1) Interestingly, the same press/media that made Jessica Lynch such a star, was vociferous in their condemnation of the army's double standard on the pension issue. As such, the media holds the military to a standard of racial equality they don't utilize in their own reporting.

The irony of the military making up a story about Jessica's "rescue" in Iraq, the aftermath of which was then falsely reported by the *New York Times* reporter Jayson Blair in the United States, is never mentioned but it is a necessary part of the work that has to be done to keep the myth of women's helplessness in order. The ideology of "national security" relies on the narrative of helpless women. Within this narrative Jessica Lynch was helpless; she had to be rescued. The story of Jessica's "rescue" had to be manufactured because we have little ability to make sense of women in wartime who step outside historically accepted roles.

Wars have often been fought in the name of "protecting" women without their consent. In his justification of the war on Afghanistan, George W. Bush said of al-Qaeda, "These are people who kill women on airplanes." In Bush's narrative of the war, all three of these women, but especially Jessica, had to be protected. After all, we were doing this for women. If we pay attention, however, to the women's words and deeds—those whose race or socioeconomic status have made them appropriate for use as cannon fodder—we begin to untangle long-held beliefs about women as weak and in need of protection. If we were to focus more appropriately on the actions or Lori and Shoshana, we would call into question notions of "national security."

Too much is at stake in upholding the gender order, it seems, for us to pay attention to the practices of women who step outside the accepted roles of femininity.

Despite the fact that from the military's own point of view, Jessica, Lori, and Shoshana all served the military with distinction, perhaps what these stories tell us is that women are actually unfit for military service. Jessica refused to go along with the government's propaganda efforts, Shoshana was rejected as propaganda material, and Lori's death went mostly unnoticed. If we add in the actions of military women in the Abu Ghraib prisoner abuse scandal, we might be convinced that women should just stay home in wartime.

Still, Jessica Lynch was decorated with a Bronze Star, a Purple Heart, and Prisoner of War medals (Estrade 2003:31; Harnden 2003:03). Lori Piestewa will be one of the few women in the United States after whom a mountain is named. Shoshana Johnson is inspiring young women of color across the country and speaking out about abuses committed by other U.S. servicewomen: "My captors followed the Geneva conventions and I was treated respectfully. I am appalled these soldiers did not do for the enemy what the enemy did for me" (Ballou 2004:008). Then there are Megan Ambuhl, Lynndie England, and Sabrina Harman, to whose actions at Abu Ghraib Shoshana refers, and whose tainted actions also demonstrate that women are not helpless. Perhaps the danger of women's visibility in wartime is greater than first imagined. The presence of women in the military and in war zones is having a profound impact on gender relations. Women's military service is not leading to immediate, true equality as some feminists had envisioned, however our presence and actions, good and bad, must lead to a reexamination of ideas about masculinity and femininity and ultimately remove "women's need for protection" from the list of excuses as to why war has to happen. Were that to occur, women's passive, silent bodies will no longer be territory, excuse, or battlefield upon which men's disputes are enacted.

Notes

Thanks to Naeem Inayatullah, Hannah Britton, Mary Queen, Carol Stabile, and other helpful readers of this piece. Special gratitude to Margaret Himley for reading, for listening, and for caring.

1. The number of articles included in my study is representative of the vast difference in media attention paid to the three women. A Lexis Nexis search

in December 2004 over the last two years revealed over 1,000 articles about Jessica Lynch, 127 about Shoshana Johnson, and 59 about Lori Piestewa.

2. Condoleeza Rice serves as token icon for both the new racism as well as the new sexism. Her position within the Bush administration facilitates several fallacies, among them that high administrative positions are open to all women and people of color.

3. U.S. women of color, other than the token elites, are completely absent in considerations of the proper practice of gender. To the creators of these representations, U.S. women are white.

4. For a good summary of the events of Jessica Lynch's capture and "rescue," see Carol Burke's *Camp All-American, Hanoi Jane and The High and Tight* (Boston: Beacon Press, 2004), 221–227.

5. The *NY Daily news* reported that Lynch had engaged in a "Rambo-worthy fight" (Becker, 7).

6. Disgraced *New York Times* reporter Jayson Blair was assigned to cover the reaction of Jessica's family and friends in her hometown of Palestine West Virginia. It has subsequently been revealed that Blair manufactured many of his stories from other news sources without actually visiting Palestine or interviewing the family. He filed approximately seven stories on Jessica Lynch and her family.

7. So little attention was paid to Shoshana that a photo of her accompanying William Douglas's story in the Montreal Gazette published 8 months later has a caption identifying her that reads; "Shoshana Johnson belonged to the same company as Jessica Lynch, but managed to escape capture."

8. It is inconceivable in Western ideas about motherhood that these women would leave their children in order to soldier.

9. Larry Flynt called Jessica's sexual innocence into question when he claimed to have topless photos of her "frolicking" with male soldiers. There was some question as to whether the photos actually depicted Jessica, they were never published (Rush 2003:LII 1).

10. Public condemnation of the disparity in payments along with Shoshana's appeal ultimately caused the military to reconsider. Shoshana now receives a 50% disability payment (Byrd, 167).

Bibliography

Associated Press. 2003. Ex-POW Johnson is discharged by Army; Lynch captured at same time. *Washington Post*. December 13, A04.

Associated Press. 2003. For Piestewa, honors and a flap; plan to rename peak is disputed. *Washington Post*. April 13, A14.

Athans, Margo. 2003 Jessica Lynch gets hometown welcome. *Baltimore Sun* July 23, 1A.

Ayala, Elaine. 2004. Former POW in public eye. *San Antonio Express-News*. October 10, 3K.

Ballou, Brian. 2004. Female POW: I got better treatment from the Iraqis. *Boston Herald*. May 28, 8.

Barker, Alllison. 2003. Military used me, ex-POW says. *Montreal Gazette*. November 8, A15.

Barnette, Martha. 2004. Jessica's journey. *Ladies Home Journal*. January.

Becker, Maki. 2003. POW Jessica was tortured. *Daily News*. March.3, 7.

Beeston, Richard. 2003. Rape claims nonsense say Lynch doctors. *The Times* (London). November 11, 15.

BBC News. 2003. Emotional return for Lynch. July 22. http://news.bbc.co.uk.

Blanchfield, Mike. 2003. Myth and mystery: the orchestration of yesterday's homecoming of US army private. *Montreal Gazette*. July 23, A18.

Brent Zook, Crystal. 2003. We don't see true picture of women in the military. *Milwaukee Journal Sentinel*. July 6, 04J.

Brown, Charles W. 2004. Where's Jessica? myth, nation, and war in America's heartland. *Social Analysis* 48 Vol I (1): 81–86

Burke, Carol. 2004. *Camp all-American, Hanoi Jane, and the high-and-tight: gender, folklore, and changing military culture*. Boston: Beacon Press.

Byrd, Veronica, and Dan Cohen. 2004. Shoshana Johnson's story: to hell and back. *Essence*. March, 66.

Clemetson, Lynette. 2004. Report calls for accountability and services to deal with sexual assaults in military. *New York Times*. May15, 1.

Davidson, Osha Gray. 2004. A wrong turn in the desert. *Rolling Stone*. May 27, 66.

Davis, Angela Y. 1981. *Women, race, and class*. New York: Random House.

Douglas, William. 2003. Looking into the face of American heroism. *Montreal Gazette*. November 10, A 16.

Eagan, Margery. 2003. Lynch tale stirs desire to believe. *Boston Herald*. November 9, 018.

Editor. 2003. What really happened? *Columbus Dispatch*. July 26.

Enloe, Cynthia. 2000. *Maneuvers: the international politics of militarizing women's lives*. Berkeley: University of California Press.

Ehrenreich, Barbara, and Arlie Russell Hochschild. 2002. *Global woman: nannies, maids, and sex workers in the new economy*. New York: Metropolitan Books.

Estrade, Bernard. 2003. Medals for US hero who wasn't. *Daily Telegraph* (Sydney). July 23, 31.

Falsani, Cathleen. 2003. Jackson seeks recognition for former Iraq war POW. *Chicago Sun-Times*. September 21, 21.

Faramarzi, Scheherezade. 2003. Iraqi doctors dismiss claim that Jessica Lynch was raped in hospital. *Independent on Sunday* (London). November 9, 18.

Faw, Bob. 2003. Operation Iraqi freedom. *The Today Show*. NBC News. March 3.

Fields-Meyer, Thomas, Inez Russell, and Rose Ellen O'Connor. 2005. Jessica Lynch's gift: keeping a pledge to a slain pal. *People Weekly*. May 30, 145.

Frazier, Deborah. 2003. Honoring hero's final wish. *Rocky Mountain News*. April 12, 1A.

Harnden, Toby. 2003. Private Jessica returns and she's still a hero. *Daily Telegraph*. July 23, 3.

Helmore, Edward. 2003. Private Jessica says president is misusing her heroism. *Guardian*.November 9, 2.

Hockstader, Lee. 2003. Families of other POWs share joy but not relief. *Washington Post*. April 3, A36.

Hockstader, Lee. 2003. Ex-POW'S family accuses army of double standard on benefit. *Washington Post*. October 23, A 03.

hooks, bell. 1992. *Black looks: race and representation*. Boston: South End Press.

Howard, John W., and Laura Prividera. Rescuing patriarchy or saving "Jessica Lynch": the rhetorical construction of the American woman soldier. *Women and Language* 27 (2): 89–98.

Jehl, Douglas, and Jayson Blair. 2003 A nation at war: the hometown. *New York Times*. April 3, A3.

Johnson Publishing Company. 2003. SPC Shoshana Johnson: former POW gets hero's welcome. *Ebony*. August, 46.

Jones, David. 2003. So was saving Private Jessica a sham? *Daily Mail*. May 24, 18–19.

Jones, Tamara. 2003. Hope in a hollow for a girl who dreamed. *Washington Post*. March 26, A01.

Kampfner, John. 2003. Saving Private Lynch story flawed. *BBC*. May 15.

Kane, Eugene. 2003. We know all about Jessica, but Shoshana? *Milwaukee Journal Sentinel*. November 11, 01B.

Kareem Nadra. 2003. Spc. Johnson offered scholarships, bakery. *El Paso Times*. April 23, 1.

Kareem, Nadra. 2003. National media vie for Shoshana. *El Paso Times*. April 24.

Kelley, Eileen. 2003. Former POW Lynch to wed Colorado fiance. *Denver Post*. August 17, A1.

Kumar, Deepa. 2004. War propaganda and the (ab)uses of women: media constructions of the Jessica Lynch story. *Feminist Media Studies* November 4 (3): 297–313.

Li, David K., and Bill Sanderson. 2003. Larry Flynt buys purported nude photos of Jessica Lynch. *NYPOST.COM*. November 11.

Lobe, Jim. 2003. Media-US: heroism or hype? *IPS Inter-Press Service*. May 29.

Loeb, Vernon, and Theola Labbe. 2003. Saves lives in Iraq; Pentagon criticized for undersupply of protective vests. *Washington Post*. December 4, A01.

McCarthy, Sheryl. 2004. This former POW takes the stage by storm. *Newsday*. February 5, A34.

McFadden, Kay. 2003. Oh, Shoshana, where's your TV movie? *Seattle Times*. November 17, E1.

McIntyre, Jamie, and Bill Hemmer.2003. BBC says Pentagon embellished Jessica rescue. *CNN Live From the Headlines*. May 18.

Mitchell, Mary. 2003. Three soldiers tales show splits along racial lines. *Chicago Sun-Times*. November 13, 14.

Monaghan, Elaine. 2003. Tribe mourns first US servicewoman to be killed. *The Times*. April 7.

———. 2003. German records back sodomy claim. *The Times* (London). November 11, 15.

Moore, Robert. 2003. "507's Piestewa 'stood and fought' at ambush." *El Paso Times*. April 24, 1.

Murphy, Dennis. 2003. Saving Private Lynch. *Dateline* NBC. April 6.

North, Andrew. 2003. The other side of the Lynch story. *BBC News*. November 11.

Perez, Luis. 2004. Pushing the right buttons. *Newsday.* January 1, A5.

Phillipps, Dave. 2003. Jessica Lynch to wed Army sergeant. *Washington Post.* November 3, C5.

Price, G. Jefferson. 2003. Distractions won't hide truth about war in Iraq. *Baltimore Sun.* July 27, 3C.

Reid, T. R. 2003. In Tuba City, Arizona, pride and sorrow. *Washington Post.* April 6, A30.

Roberts, Dorothy. 1997. *Killing the black body: race, reproduction, and the meaning of liberty.* New York: Random House.

Rush, George. 2003. Jessica's hustled: porn mag to run topless pics of GI. *New York Daily News.* November 11, 3.

Russell, Jan Jarboe. 2003. Women already doing their part for America on front. *San Antonio Express News.* March 27, 7B.

Sawyer, Diane. 2003. Private Jessica Lynch: an American story. *Prime Time Live Special Edition.* ABC News.

Scheer, Robert. 2003. Saving Private Jessica Lynch, take 2. *Startribune.com.* May 23.

Schmidt, Susan, and Vernon Loeb. 2003. She was fighting to the death: details emerging of W. Va soldier's capture and rescue. *Washington Post.* April 3, A1.

Shaffer, Mark. 2004. Piestewa family assails video airing. *AZCENTRAL.com.* January 1.

Shankar, Thom, and John Broder. 2003. A nation at war: liberated: the rescue of Private Lynch. *New York Times.* March 3, B10.

Siemaszko, Corey. 2003. Jessi: "Army used me." *New York Daily News.* November 7, 9.

Sisk, Richard. 2004. The women of war in Iraq, death knows no front line, nor gender. *New York Daily News.* December 14, 43.

Steelhammer, Rick. 2003. POW from West Virginia rescued. *Charlestown Gazette.* April 2.

Stockman, Farah. 2003. Missing in action on Arizona reservation. *Boston Globe.* March 30, A 29.

Tamayo, Juan. 2003. Iraqis lead US troops to POWS; seven rescued. *Montreal Gazette.* April 14, A3.

Tickner, J. Ann. 1992. *Gender in international relations: feminist perspectives on achieving global security.* New York: Columbia University Press.

Wadler, Joyce. 2003. If you don't buy her book, the terrorists win. *New York Times.* November 12. www.nytimes.com.

Weber, David. 2003. Iraq doctors say Lynch didn't suffer sexual assault. *Boston Herald.* November8, 6.

Weiser, Irene. 2004. One hundred twelve women assaulted in Iraq, Afghanistan. *Common Dreams.* May 18. http://www.commondreams.org/cgi-

White, Josh. 2004. Soldier to face military court in N.C. Pfc England's hearing in prisoner case first on US soil. *Washington Post.* May 29, A18

Whoriskey, Peter. 2003. In Lynch country, a puzzled kind of pride. *Washington Post.* July 22, A01.

Wichterich, Christa.2000. *The globalized woman: reports from a future of inequality.* London: Zed Books.

Yardley, Jim. 2003. A nation at war: the prisoner's families." *New York Times.* March 26, 7.

Younge, Gary. 2003. Private Lynch's comrade in arms finds sad place in a nation's history. *Sun Herald.* April 13, 24.

Chapter 9

¹Not Just (Any)*body* Can Be a Patriot: "Homeland" Security as Empire Building

M. Jacqui Alexander

Writing about a decade ago in the context of the organization of the citizenship machinery on the part of Caribbean nationalist state managers, I had examined how neocolonial nationalism had aborted the anticolonial project, reneged on the promise of full citizenship, and opted instead to premise citizenship in partially sexualized terms, criminalizing nonprocreative sexualities and rendering them as threat to nation and national sovereignty. Not just (any)*body* [could] be a citizen any more, I concluded, for some bodies [had] been marked by the state as nonprocreative, in pursuit of sex for pleasure only, a sex that [was] nonproductive of babies, and therefore of no economic gain. In premising citizenship within heterosexuality and in making the heterosexual the proxy for that which was moral, state managers were producing the very contingency that they themselves had promulgated as natural. It is on this contradiction of producing contingency or summoning hegemony in the service of instability and crisis that I wish to focus, in a context that at first appears to be qualitatively different from the neocolonial and at a historical moment that seems quantitatively different from it. My specific focus here is this contemporary moment of empire consolidation. I want to examine the multiple ways in which neoimperial state managers deploy patriotism as a proxy for notions of originary citizenship, the very category they themselves had promulgated as natural. The fact that state relations of rule in apparently different geopolitical sites resemble one another ought to prompt us to question the utility of those analyses that position neoimperialism with modernity, distant and separate from neocolonialism premised in tradition. The patriot in the former functions in the same way as the heterosexual in the later, for not just (any)*body* can be a patriot at a time of empire building.

Some bodies have been marked by the neoimperial state as unpatriotic, with the capacity to destabilize a newly imagined homeland, threatening national sovereignty, and otherwise imperiling the U.S. nation. Of course, these ideological formulations pivot on a set of practices that are violent in their effects, and so this inventory of the requirements of patriotism is a simultaneous inventory of the multiple violences that empire's modernity spawns at this. And this is a necessary inventory, since the U.S. state would want to signal empire not by its name but by an ancient, titanic call to freedom. Situating empire enables us to understand Operation Iraqi Freedom in the words proffered by George Lamming as "the freedom to betray freedom through gratuitous exploitation (1960, 58). In what follows, I lay out the specific ways in which democracy has been eclipsed in order to set the stage for how the new imperialism relies on the dual constitution of a set of internal and external correlates that racialize and sexualize both the internal patriot and the external enemy while at the same time linking the war at home with the war abroad. I use the hegemonic seizure of the homeland on the part of the U.S. state as a way to signal the contentiousness of the idea of "patriotic" homeland and its ideological dissolution in the face of immigrant labor in the imperial fighting force and Indian contestation over land sovereignty. I argue that these different gestures are all organically linked and need to be understood as an ensemble in light of the substantial amount of ideological traffic that occurs among them.[2] I end by pointing to the imperatives that are at stake for radical projects that are deeply committed to crossing boundaries of various kinds.

The New Imperialism: Legislating the Patriot, Sexualizing the Enemy

It is important at the outset to substitute the term *democracy* with the term *neoimperialism,* which I want to understand in two senses: first, as the descriptive term for a form of globalization whose internal character reproduces a set of colonial relations with regard to indigenous and immigrant peoples, people of color, and working-class white communities within the geographic borders of the United States, as well as a set of related external colonial arrangements with, among others, Puerto Rico, HawaiiI, the U.S. Virgin Islands, the Philippines, and Guam; and second, as a way to denote the state's investments in a form of hyperconcentrated capital in local/globalized economies whose operations have unequal gendered and class consequences. These contradictory practices form the basis for an understanding of the contemporary U.S. state that is neither automatically nor self-referentially democratic, although democracy characterizes its self-representational impulse.[3]

Neoimperial also refers to the constitution of a new empire marked by accelerated militarization and war on the part of the United States. Its most recent discursive incarnation codified in three formative documents—the Patriot Act of 2001, its 2002 sequel, and the National Security Act of September 20, 2002—which explicitly and simultaneously link the imperial project to militarization and to nation building. Nation building can be more accurately understood, however, as a form of hypernationalism with a number of constituent parts: the manufacture of an outside enemy to rationalize military intervention and secure control over foreign resources; the internal production of a new citizen patriot; and the creation and maintenance of a permanent war economy, whose internal elements devolve upon the militarization of the police and the resultant criminalization of immigrants, people of color, and working-class communities through the massive expansion of a punishment economy at whose center is the prison industrial complex. Neoimperialism is constituted as well through those state practices that are aimed at constituting a nation that is based in a privatized, originary, nuclear family in ways that couple the nuclear with the heterosexual. While this new phase of imperialism relies on a unilateral exercise of empire in order to consolidate itself, it would be somewhat ineffectual without the network of local masculinities that, as Nefereti Tadiar has shown, serves U.S. interests (and the American dream) through its labor, natural and social resources, its territory, and its symbolic presence (2004: 27).[4]

The confluence of this new moment of empire in which the invasion of Iraq is strategically central, the production of the National Security Strategy, and the two emendations of the Patriot Act signals a major reconstruction within, and a major reconsolidation of, the American state apparatus on a scale that has been unprecedented.[5] In the context of the 1991 Gulf War, the hypermasculine soldier was projected as a symbol of U.S. might. Then, manufacturing the consent of "the American people" was carefully organized around this figure, (more often racialized as white externally so as to be juxtaposed against the dark enemy; sometimes racialized as black internally to signal a dutiful return to family),the white soldier woman, and the "traditional Oriental" woman who needed to be rescued from the enemy. At this moment, however, the state seems so assured by its marketing of the Iraq war that it feels less compelled to invoke "the American people" as ideological foil. It is not so much that the hypermasculine soldier has disappeared. Witness the feminized role of "supporting" the troops that has been assigned to the nation after the manly job of state decision making has occurred. Witness, too, the (necessarily) highly visible, "dangerous" rescue of Jessica Lynch, who had to be young, white, and woman so that white masculinity could undertake its rescue work.[6] It is, rather, that following the attacks on the heart of America's financial capital on September 11, 2001, state action has become more emboldened to promulgate "the war on terrorism" as the major vehicle around which to scaffold the national security state and secure the class interests of its members.

Embedded in that militarized vehicle is the patriot who, like the soldier, is not only hypermasculine, but heteromasculine. And there is an absolute requirement that emerges from the new legal mandate in which he has been produced: this patriot must be silent. He must also be the putative originary citizen who was "here" at the very beginning of the carving of the homeland and therefore entrusted with its guardianship, which he presumably promised never to betray.[7] This white originary citizen is in sharp contradistinction to the dark naturalized citizen, the dark immigrant, or even the dark citizen born of the dark immigrant whose latent "loyalty" is perennially suspect and, therefore, ultimately threatening.[8] It is this dark, inside threat that must be cordoned off, imprisoned, expelled, and matched simultaneously with the extinction of the dark, external threat in order that the borders of the fictive, originary nation may be properly secured. These twin processes enable us to understand the ways in which the war at home is intimately linked to the war abroad. There is no task that can legitimately rival the enormity of this security imperative; no ideological boundary that will not be contravened in this recapitulation of the historical confrontation between "savagery" and "civilization," evidenced in the words of President G. W. Bush, "We will smoke those barbarians out of their caves." Within this matrix lies a collocation that is fundamental to the contemporary political constellation: empire building *is* nation(al) security. Since the latter is an indisputable task in the business of defense against the enemy, then empire building becomes a similarly indispensable undertaking. Twin processes, they are simultaneously racialized and sexualized so that the making of the white heteromasculine patriot has to be undertaken (and therefore understood) along with the demasculinization of the dark enemy. Indeed, if empire building did not require sexuality's garb, it would be altogether unnecessary to demasculinize the enemy. I now turn to examine more carefully the ideological traffic between these companion processes.

At first glance it might appear that the sheer scope of empire building would necessitate the avid collaboration of all "the American people." But on closer examination of the Patriot Acts and their attendant Federal Executive Orders, we see that what is at stake is the production of a citizenpatriot of a very specific sort. As a moment of nation building or hypernationalism instigated by the state—although multinational corporations, independent contractors, and media are powerful allies in this consortium—these Acts delineate and legislate just who this new citizen-patriot is supposed to be, what he must look like, how he ought to behave, the terms of his silent support for a national security state, the limited terms of his speech—all of the prerequisites wherein loyalty to nation is conflated with loyalty to the state and where loyalty to the state can only be maximally fulfilled through defense of the nation. Just who becomes this citizen patriot whom the state feels compelled to legalize so that unpatriotic noncitizens can thus be criminalized? What social fragilities needed repair so that this figure has to be summoned in its service? How is patriotism secured and what are the specific tasks that ostensibly solidify it?

There are two crucial elements in these taxonomies on which our analysis will turn.[9] The first is an expansion of the conduct subject to state investigation under a crime called "domestic terrorism," which is defined as "acts dangerous to human life that are a violation of the criminal laws of the United States or of any State" (ACLU 2002). But it is not simply any act that is "dangerous to human life" that constitutes a crime, because if it were, we could expect acts that are dangerous to human life such as the state mobilization of excessive fear; the state's exhortation to consume as a mechanism to bury grief; the circulation of the false idea that the state owns and therefore can dispense security; the bombing of abortion clinics; escalating hate crimes; racist, homophobic, and domestic violence; retrenchments of the social wage; and the destruction of the environment to count among such acts.[10] It is, rather, specifically those acts that are directed against the state; those that "appear to be intended . . . to influence the policy of a government by intimidation or coercion." We could surmise at this point that anybody with such intent and who committed such acts would be apprehended as a domestic terrorist. We could further conclude that conduct alone—"acts"—would mark the crucial distinction between the terrorist and the nonterrorist.[11]

The second element in the taxonomy would undermine such a conclusion, however, for this is where an important conflation occurs and where the definition of terrorist and nonterrorist shifts. Provision 412 of Patriot Act 1 calls for the "mandatory detention of suspected terrorists," suggesting that not acts alone but someone else's suspicion is the pivot on which the definition rests. But suspicion of whom? And by whom? It is here that the subject shifts suddenly from "domestic terrorist" to "immigrant," for it is in this provision that the attorney general is given broad powers to certify immigrants as "risks." In this move from "act" to "risk," the distinction between terrorist and nonterrorist metamorphoses into the demarcation between citizen and immigrant, and a gross alignment between immigrant and terrorist is drawn. This provision is bolstered by the president's military order, which establishes trials by military tribunal, at the president's discretion, for noncitizens. While the president can order both citizens and noncitizens to be made into "enemy combatants," the denotation of immigrant risk not only fuels detention but directs disproportionate suspicion onto the immigrant. In addition to the attorney general, up to 2 million Americans can secretly provide information to the government about any person whom they consider suspicious, and on whom the state would subsequently establish a file. And in a massive reorganization of the agencies of the state, there are many more who have been authorized to pursue patriotism and suspect the suspicious: the secretary of state, the secretary of defence, the Department of Justice, surveillance agencies such as the FBI and CIA (otherwise known as intelligence), the Bureau of Prisons, the president, bookstore and library personnel, other law enforcement agencies, and the foreign intelligence apparatus, including the Foreign Intelligence Surveillance Court. In the end, it is hardly conduct or "acts" but status—that of immigrant—that shades "domestic terrorism," and that begins to hint, as well, at just who this legalized patriot is supposed to be.

Ultimately, it is the immigrant who is positioned as perennial suspect, risky by virtue of status and bearing the disproportionate brunt of enemy, further criminalized and made to function as nonpatriot in this matrix where status and implied propensity meet—a propensity that is similar to, yet different from, "homosexual propensity" established as part of the Don't Ask Don't Tell policies instituted by the military. While both categorizations depend upon status, the terms of their tacit rehabilitation differ. The queer soldier can be rehabilitated as a patriot only by permanent residency in the closet; for the immigrant, on the other hand, the act of ultimate sacrifice, of dying for a nation at wartime, becomes the mechanism for changing his status from immigrant to citizen.

But the patriot is also designated by what he is not—that is, not immigrant; by what he has been authorized to do, that is, to comply with a legal mandate by actively participating in the task of surveillance, to secretly provide information to the state about suspects, and to disclose to the state information about the reading habits of those whom he has surveilled; and additionally, by what he is being implicitly asked to do— to forfeit consent and to substitute informed participation in civil society with silent loyalty to the state as a consummate patriot.[12] Legalized within the ambit of a militarized state apparatus at a moment of empire building, this patriot is one of the major internal anchors at the nexus of empire building and national security. This patriot-citizen, like the soldier citizen, is a patriot for the consolidation of empire. But this is not the only nexus that this reconfigured map of empire draws.

There is a tacit, or not-so-tacit, ideological division of labor among the different kinds of patriots: state-patriots, who penned the National Security Strategy, securing their class interests through the annexation of land and territory, yet masking their class alignments by arguing the grand narratives of an ancient, titanic call to freedom, civilization, and Christian modernity through war, and positioning free enterprise—which we shall understand as imperialism—as the tradition that requires protection; the "citizen" soldier-patriot, who comprises the imperial fighting force, the class, racial, and national composition of which exposes the contradictions implicit in the racialization of empire; and the citizen-patriot, who, like the state-patriot, stays home, but who exercises patriotism through another of the technologies of globalization—the Internet. But before exploring cyberspace's relationship to the prerequisites of empire's enemy production, let us examine more closely the ideological ground that the "citizen" soldier-patriot is made to inhabit and the contradictory implications of the evocation of that ground as "homeland" in light of the hegemonic seizure of the term and the fact that the state-designated homeland is the very place where shifting genealogies of enemy production have historically taken place.

Whose Homeland Security? "THE ONLY COMPENSATION FOR LAND IS LAND (LaDuke 2002)."

The institutional reification of a seamless homeland and its seizure on the part of the state to make it function *as* a department of state belie a set of frayed discursive practices and social formations that effectively expose the ruses of power (CFP 2003).[13] At the very least, the apparent fixing of the term "homeland" comports, in the words of Anjali Arondekar, with a kind of modern nativism or narratives of "nativeness" that are at odds with an official telos of the United States as a place of asylum and a land of immigrants purveyed both by the state and normative tendencies within disciplinary studies of U.S. politics.[14] Yet at another level, this lexical shift may not be a momentary shift at all but an arbitrary culmination of a set of varied but intersecting genealogies of xenophobia, which cohere around the push to force immigrants out that was under way well before September 11, 2001.[15] Further, in light of the multiple displacements (caused by globalization) that continually bring more and more refugees to the shores of one of the primary instigators of that displacement, the rhetorical insistence on homeland and on homeland security can work to obscure not only the violent histories of the white settler's colonization of the native American homeland, but also the economic reliance on immigrant labor both at home and within the imperial fighting force to secure the social formation labeled the homeland of the United States. The supreme irony of the mobilization of immigrant women's sweatshop labor to churn out millions of U.S. flags, and the detention and deportation of immigrants as a way of containing the threat that immigrants ostensibly pose to the U.S. body politic, underscore how violence is differently mobilized in the interest of securing a homeland that is fundamentally a contingent space.

These troublesome practices have been exposed by the set of claims that Indian tribal nations have historically made to the U.S. state designating their geographic borders as a place of sovereign homeland despite ongoing land seizure. The fact that land and territory have been at the center of native peoples' wars for sovereignty and self-determination sharpens this point and underscores the poignancy of Winona La Duke's position: "The only compensation for land is land" (Adams 2005:197). The white settler state has not only refused to recognize the sovereignty of tribal governments, it has also not recognized tribal governments as having any stake in securing the homeland since they have disappeared from the state's own normative formulation of homeland security. None of the $28 billion assigned to the Department of Homeland Security in 2004 was allotted to tribal governments, a situation which is being strongly contested (Indianz.com 2003).[16]

It is a chilling paradox that the first "American" woman to die in the war against Iraq was Lori Piestewa, who was raised Hopi on a Navajo reservation. She was the first Native American woman ever to die in combat on foreign soil, the soldier whose death had to be erased so that the white, "masculinized" rescue of Jessica Lynch could be seamlessly deployed as *the* only narrative of the events in Nasiriyah. Native Americans continue to serve in the military at higher per capita rates than any other group in the United States, even as the question of participation in the war remains highly contentious, as evidenced in the oppositional statement—"Homeland Security: Fighting Terrorism since 1492"—that reclaims homeland and sovereignty from histories of colonial terrorism and implicitly links, as Winona La Duke maintains, the development of U.S. military might to the underdevelopment of Indian communities (La Duke 2003). Lori Piestewa marks once again the frayed discursive shifts within the state and how the bodies of women of color bear the disproportionate brunt of systematic state violence. In the late 1880s, when the U.S. Cavalry invaded Hopi lands, Piestewa would have been positioned as an enemy. More than a century later she is soldier and patriot on enemy territory elsewhere, neither worthy enough nor feminine enough to become the star American hero (Davidson 2004).

Another contradictory site in this deployment of seamless homeland as the not-so-silent proxy for nativeness is the immigrant composition of the imperial fighting force. Here is where a rupture occurs in the coupling of citizen-soldiering and patriotism. It appears at first glance that immigrant participation in the fighting force is miniscule, constituting a mere 2 or 3 percent of U.S. military personnel, according to official statistics. But it is the disjuncture between this apparently miniscule figure and the decibel level of the state-generated discourse about conferring posthumous citizenship that alerts us to the massive amount of ideological work that is being undertaken on the body of immigrants in order to mask the discourse of immigrant risk and to secure the coupling of citizen and patriot.[17] In the same way in which the decibel level of the welfare queen signaled its generative ideological capacity in light of the miniscule percentage of the national budget allocated to "welfare," (hovering around 1 percent at the height of discursive production), so too this overproduction of the dead immigrant, now posthumous citizen, signals another kind of ideological motor in this hydra-headed "arsenal" of empire. If, as Toni Morrison puts it in her eminently artful "gesture" to those "ancient atoms"—"The Dead of September 11"—"the dead are free, absolute," and if "they cannot be seduced by blitz," as Morrison notes, of what use, we must ask, is this excessive production of the posthumous citizen to the living (2005)?

The Iraqi war is not the first war in which immigrant noncitizens have enlisted, but it is the first war to have promulgated a new set of regulations that accelerate the process of turning immigrant into citizens and of granting posthumous citizenship to those immigrant soldiers who died on the battlefield. Through a special relationship between the Department of Defence and the Department of Homeland Security it is now possible for citizenship to be conferred at the service member's funeral. Accelerating this process required many developments that have been authorized by the president himself, the most pivotal of which was the creation of a new position, the Office of Posthumous Citizenship, at the similarly newly created U.S. Citizenship and Immigration Services, which have both been folded into the Department of Homeland Security. Recruiting strategies have been heightened: some recruiters have crossed the highly policed border into Tijuana; while others admit that the promise of citizenship to immigrant soldiers is a strategic "selling tool."[18] As one avid recruiter admitted: "We use that as a selling tool, join the army and get all the benefits. And then on top of that, if they're looking forward to becoming a citizen it will be expedited and acted on quickly."[19] Between 2000 and 2005 there has been a meteoric rise in this conversion from immigrant-soldier to citizen-soldier, from 518 in 2000 to more than 7,000 in 2005. In addition, since 2002, executive orders by the president have made it possible for enlisted legal residents to petition immediately for citizenship rather than adhere to the earlier three-year waiting period. Finger printing and application fees have now been waived. Upon death, permanent residency status is granted to immediate family members.[20] At times, however, not all parts of the state apparatus can move with requisite speed, and the racialized mechanics of border policing can continue to exist alongside these highly expedient state gestures (as was the case when the Mexican family of a dead immigrant soldier, now citizen, was unable to secure entry into the United States to attend the funeral).

Since the backlog of "civilian" requests for citizenship has increased as a result of the consolidation of immigration and homeland security, and since the five-year waiting period to petition for citizenship has not been attenuated, the idea of dying for nation, not living and working in it, functions as excess, for it is only dying that the office of posthumous citizenship regards as "the ultimate sacrifice." The Army's liaison with U.S. Citizenship and Immigration Services sharpened the ideological traffic between citizen and immigrant even more starkly in this pronouncement, a grand normativizing move that morphs the state into the nation and grants disproportionate agency to families of the deceased: "These people have proven they are willing to die for the United States, they've made the ultimate sacrifice, so it's only right that the country grant them the citizenship they have earned and make sure that their families receive benefits as well."[21] Rightness here has been constituted only recently, however, that is to say, instrumentally. And bodies of color continue to track the lexical, that is to say, ideological, fissures in state practice. As the work of Catherine Ramirez has shown, following the internment of Japanese during World War II, Mexican Americans were positioned as the foreign, subversive internal enemy, prone to being unpatriotic by indulging in unseemly dress instead of engaging in the defense of the "democracy that shelter[ed] him (Ramirez 2002:8–9)."[22] Now, six decades later, Mexicans are pursued to enter the military to defend a "democracy" from which no shelter can be found, either in the meatpacking plants of the South, the migrant labor farms of the North, or the desert lands of Arizona.

It would be difficult not to conclude that political expediency shapes and deploys patriotism and citizenship in soldiering particularly in light of the military's need to bolster the fighting force in an all-volunteer army, where declining volunteerism is provoking a confrontation with aversion to the military and to what military state-managers predict as a long military engagement. Volunteerism is hardly volunteerism in the face of the kinds of desperate recruiting strategies that have been deployed, such as posthumous citizenship and the promise of permanent residency for bereaved immigrants. But the frayed seams of homeland are visible, and the level of political contestation is quite substantial, as evidenced in the disclosures about domestic wiretapping and surveillance; the challenges posed to the marketing of the Patriot Act; the emergence of networks that support soldiers who refuse war as opposed to the official call to support the troops at war; queer soldiers who have upstaged the Don't Ask Don't

Tell policy by serving openly as the "military discharge of gays plummets" from 1,227 discharges in 2001 to 653 in 2004; the steady decline of African American recruits from 23.5 percent in 2000 (when the initial increase in immigrant soldiers morphing into citizen soldiers becomes transparent) to less than 14 percent in 2005, representing the loss of a major ideological symbol for the white patriarchal state that counted on the military to instill responsible paternity in black fathers (White 2005).

In light of a major national shift toward a dehistoricized, instrumental form of affirmation action; its reincarnation, as Chandra Talpade Mohanty has argued, in the service of empire; and the racially militarized prerequisites of the Pentagon, expressed in the belief that "a highly qualified, racially diverse officer corps educated and trained to command our nation's racially diverse enlisted ranks is essential to the military's ability to fulfill its principle mission to provide national security," one could only imagine a heightened racial roulette to sustain a permanent war economy and a logic of permanent invasion (Mohanty 2004; Skrentny and Frymer 2004; Takaki 2004; McAlistar 2001). The military is involved in a huge scampering campaign as it uses welfare as the training ground for heterosexuality and a launching site for the military, and as it uses educational institutions to ensure that the armed forces have access to students and student recruitment information. The No Child Left Behind Act of 2001 states: "Each local educational agency receiving assistance under this Act shall provide, on a request made by military recruiters or an institution of higher education, access to secondary school students names, addresses, and telephone listings"; in this way, it ensures a permanent pool for its permanent war.[23] The generational socialization into enemy production would, in this cynical scenario, be complete. But only in this cynical scenario.

Virtual Warfare: The Citizen Patriot, the Enemy, and the Failure of Heterosexuality

Since 9/11, the Internet has been mobilized as a site of virtual warfare where the enemy is excessively reproduced and terrorized. Of course cyberspace has historically functioned as a mainly masculinized domain, but at this moment it is one of the spaces where the companion nexuses of empire building, enemy production, and failed heterosexualization are secured (Kenway 2005). In short, it is the place where the terrorist, the enemy, and the sexual pervert meet, the place where the sexual anxieties of domination and conquest thrive, enacting a form of violent spectacle similar in function to the postcard texts through which Orientalism was produced[24] and the more grotesque photographic representations of lynching that pervaded the American South at the turn of the twentieth century (Allen 2000). It is not that state patriots have relinquished the heterosexualizing imperatives of nation building. Even grief wore a sexualized face. No lesbian, gay, bisexual, or transgendered family was made to signal national grief in the post 9/11 trauma. While the Defence of Marriage Act (DOMA), as well as other same-sex marriage initiatives in California and Massachusetts, risks the challenge from the recent antisodomy legislation in Texas (*New York Times* 2003), the coalition of traditional interests will not die easily, as illustrated in the presidential call for the constitutional ban against gay marriages in terms that bear a sinister resemblance to those on which DOMA was argued. Indeed, President George W. Bush called for this amendment prior to the 2004 elections as a mechanism to reinforce the tradition of defining marriage as the heterosexual union between a male husband and a female wife. The closeted reevaluation of Don't Ask Don't Tell policy as a way to possibly enlist queer soldiering stands as a staunch reminder that there is a long arc between expediency and justice.

This meeting place that collapses the enemy, the terrorist, and the sexual pervert is the very one that secures the loyal heterosexual citizen patriot. Indeed, it is under his vigilant—one might even say vengeful—directives that the ostensible boundaries between enemy and patriot, terrorist and citizen, pervert and morally abiding collide. These very boundaries dovetail simultaneously with policing the oppositional boundaries of Islamic tradition and Christian modernity. The enemy terrorist offered up by the state patriot to the citizen patriot appears in a garb that is far too incomplete, however, to accomplish fully the task of securing empire, which has historically relied upon strategies of racialization and sexualization. As Jasbir Puar and Amit Rai have argued, "The construction of the [enemy] terrorist relies upon sexual perversity" and upon "deeply racist, sexist and homophobic suggestions" that become, at this historical conjuncture, the transformed technologies through which "heteronormative patriotism" is established (2002).[25] At this point I wish to examine how these technologies accompany one another and how they work as a composite ideological field that is interdependent, and that can demasculinize, feminize, sodomize, and racialize as a way of producing a grotesque enemy.

Puar and Rai and Robin L. Riley have analyzed the representational impulses at work in different forms of media, including the Internet and e-mail, following the destruction of the twin towers on September 11, 2001. Their analyses speak to this composite ideological field. Riley has found on a website (Osamayomama.com) thirty-six photographs in which Osama bin Laden's head has been superimposed on the bodies of figures that include a hermaphrodite, cross-dresser, a gay man, a heterosexual dominated by women, and otherwise having sex with animals. On other sites, the figure is routinely depicted as having sex with animals, and, in one case, of hiding in the rectum of a camel, thus reconciling the sexual pervert with the coward. One part of the representational perversity is cathected onto bin Laden, but its other face is rendered through specific gestures of "sodomizing" him. Puar and Rai analyze this imagery in posters that were rapidly dispersed in New York City after the attack, which display a turbaned caricature of bin Laden being anally attacked by the Empire State building. The poster's caption: "'The Empire Strikes Back,' or 'Do you like Skyscrapers, bitch?'" is a combination of misogyny and heterosexism. On another website the reading audience was invited to assist in the torture of bin Laden through various weapons, including sexual torture through sodomy. And yet another website carried alternating portraits of bin Laden and O. J. Simpson, putting, as Riley suggests, "a new face on an old body, the body of the man of color who has long posed threats," so that we identify and recognize "strangers . . . the stranger we know—O. J. and the "Other" stranger. We can recognize bin Laden because we have seen him before."(2002,3)

Websites are constantly being reconfigured—those described above are now nonexistent. But this fertile ground is never allowed to lie fallow, as the imaginative potential for the expansion of the vulgar and the grotesque, almost singularly cathected onto bin Laden, seems truly exponential. In a short film called *Fist of Allah* on http://www.new-grounds.com/portal/view/34435 readers are invited to "Help the Gimp from Pulp Fiction use, violate, and degrade Osama bin Laden, and make him suffer a grisly demise!" In the image Osama bin Laden, with his wrists bound above him, is bending in a pose that evokes the pornographic, and a gimp shoves his fist into bin Laden's rectum. When the gimp removes his hand it is covered ostensibly in fecal matter. Following this display, the word "Again!" appears in bold green font and the participant may rerun the video. After the second time, bin Laden's head appears on a chopping block and the participant is invited to simply behead him

On a site labeled political humor, bin Laden is featured in several compromising positions, but what is striking about this site is that the visual component does not necessarily depend on any kind of gross representation. Unlike the image from the online film, this site pictures bin Laden in a variety of ways while captions are used to emasculate and demean him. For example, in one image at http://www.politicalhumor.about.com/library/images/blosamaguide.htm, Osama bin Laden is said to carry a gun to "compensate for his tiny penis." Though the racist elements are consistent with earlier comparisons of bin Laden and Simpson, there is, in addition, a feminization of bin Laden—he is "wimpy" and "skinny." On another page of the same website bin Laden is said to be "crawling his skinny little pajama towel headed lanky ass into some elusive Afghan cave." The caption accompanying another image says: "His mother dressed him like a girl until he was 12. The robe reminds him of a dress." Bin Laden is represented as a coward, yet seen as savage by those who presumably own and guard modernity. On http://politicalhumor.about.com/library/images/blosamababy.htm, bin Laden's head has been superimposed onto the body of some creature, and he is holding a white man's hand . . . almost puppetlike, the mechanism of salvation.

No war can be waged without the production of an enemy, but the processes of militarization are never entirely externalized. Processes do not arbitrarily halt at geographical borders, and in this instance, the production of an internal enemy carries the same type of sexual prerequisites as those of the external enemy. Indeed, "sexual perversity" is one of the ideological characteristics that the enemy at home and the enemy abroad share. The enemy constructions of blackness and the stranger found on the Internet are palpably reminiscent of the crowds who assisted the celebratory rituals of the lynchings of an apparently earlier era, but they draws simultaneously from a larger state construction of sexual humiliation and torture evidenced in the sexual torture of Abner Louima by New York City police and similar treatment meted out to the prisoners at Abu Ghraib. (Of course, the state construction ought not to be confounded with the actual perpetration of domestic violence in which Simpson was involved.)[26]

These varied heterosexual anxiety narratives—of violence, of injury and shame, and of punishment and retaliation—simultaneously produce the enemy and issue an invitation to the citizen patriot to attend to the propaganda mechanics of war. But there is a disciplining device at work here as well: "If you're not for the war you're a fag," a threat with disproportionate consequences for immigrant and queer people, particularly immigrant or immigrant-looking brown-skinned men (Puar 2002). Those immigrants not treated to the violence of the state patriot through detention meet with violence of the citizen patriot on the streets; while lesbian, gay, bisexual, transgender, and transsexual (LGBTT) people of color in New York City, for instance, are met with the same. Once this sexualized heterosexual anxiety is unleashed, however, the enemy target can multiply. As we saw in the context of the 1991 Gulf War, violence against the "enemy" in the desert traveled into the U.S. soldier camps, where a number of soldier women were "forcibly sodomized (Enloe 1993,197)." Soldier citizens, "model soldiers," who served in the war against Afghanistan, brought the violence and war home during the summer of 2002 and unleashed it on their wives in Fort Bragg, Texas, "the home of the Airborne and Special Operations Forces." They turned the gruesome techniques of the "activate to kill mode" of the war "out there" onto their military wives, battering, raping, and killing them, and in some instances also killing themselves (Orth 2002,222). And all this happened while their civilian, citizen patriots, in the wake of 9/11, instigated domestic violence in the privatized space of home.[27] The practices of violence on this continuum of violence render borders entirely inconsequential.

Policing the National Body: The War Abroad Meets the War at Home (Silliman 2002)

We should not assume that the militarization apparatus is mobilized only at the moment of war. Indeed, its swift mobilization elsewhere is indicative of a prior "local" existence, if you will, a prior episteme that bears close ideological resemblance to the war weaponry deployed "over there" while at the same time assembling an entirely new vocabulary that intercepts yet intersects with the citizen patriot, the noncitizen nonpatriot, or the disloyal suspect immigrant here at home. This more local apparatus, assembled over the last two decades at the level of both the macro state and the micro state, has been directed toward displacing the "war" on poverty with the "war" on crime, thus making imprisonment, as Angela Davis has argued, the "response of first resort to . . . the social problems that burden people who are ensconced in poverty (2003: 52)." In this war, the police are the transplanted soldiers drawing from the training curriculum of the police academy, which has targeted particular neighborhoods disproportionately inhabited by people of color and by immigrants. The curriculum has perfected a microscopic level of policing that is able to intervene more systematically in the daily lives of people through both increased surveillance and increased force attendant with its own system of categorizations: the "disorderly," and "symbolic assailants," those who look like people with the propensity to assail. Of course, these categorizations ultimately reinforce their own rationale for the existence of increased policing. But it is policing of a very particular sort.

Urban policing has taken on altogether different character in the past decade, spurred by what Diane Weber has called "the ominous growth of paramilitarism" (1999:1). The elements of this culture of paramilitarization are constituted through the adoption of a military curriculum as the police curriculum, an increased role for the Pentagon in daily policing, and the use of the technologies of war on urban streets, including SWAT teams and special weapons and tactics units. As Weber reports, nearly 90 percent of the police departments surveyed in cities with populations over 50,000 had paramilitary units, as did 70 percent of the departments surveyed in communities with populations under 50,000 (1999, 3). This paramilitarism has been accompanied by another, related, technology of disciplining called "order maintenance policing," which is euphemistically called "community policing." At its center resides the broken windows theory, the notion that if left unattended misdemeanors such as aggressive panhandling and turnstyle jumping will promulgate more serious crimes. Popular national diffusion of a methodology that has been largely uncontested, but whose findings are highly contestable, has produced some alarming, but not surprising results: for instance, that the majority of the over 140,000 women in the penitentiary system are black, Latina, and poor women incarcerated for petty crimes, and that there was a 50 percent increase in misdemeanor arrests in New York City in the mid-1990s. On a nationwide basis, African Americans—who comprise a disproportionately low percentage of the population, but a disproportionately high percentage of the imperial fighting force—constitute 46 percent of those arrested for vagrancy and 58.7 percent of those arrested for suspicion as "symbolic assailants."[28] Again, here there are powerful ideological symbols at play, as indicated in Bernard Harcourt's apt assessment: "The techniques of punishment create the disorderly person with a full biography of habits, inclinations and desires . . . as an object of suspicion, surveillance, control, relocation, micromanagement and arrest . . . while carefully managing its boundaries" (1998, 293).

Much like the categories discussed above, of "homosexual propensity" and "immigrant propensity," these categories of the "disorderly" and the "symbolic assailant" create their own propensity apparatus, which propels conduct to devolve upon status. The racialized citizen patriot, the noncitizen nonpatriot, the disloyal suspect immigrant, and the suspect citizen are all made to occupy this underworld as the urban internal enemy, violence against whom underwrites the forms of massacre directed against the external enemy.

The link between militarization at home and militarization abroad also finds expression in the export and marketing of punishment technologies. The former commissioner of the New York City Police Department, Bernard Kerik, who served in 2003 as Iraq's interim minister of interior and senior policy advisor to U.S. presidential envoy, Paul Bremer, was entrusted with "the development and reconstruction of Iraq's police force." According to Kerik, thirty-five police stations were established within a five-month period "out of nothing"; the police officers were to be trained according to "the principles of policing in a new society, a free and democratic society." It is significant that apart from focus on the weaponry to be introduced, "handguns, rifles, long guns," the training curriculum that would anchor freedom and policing remains largely unspecified (MSNBC 2003).[29]

From the vantage point of the state patriot, now injured by a relation of the "sodomite/cross-dressers" with whom the Balboa army had presumably dispensed at the onset of Spanish colonization of the Americas, punishment and retaliation must be even more severe (Warner 1993). The enemy has to be made feminine enough to be subordinated, aberrant enough to be grotesque, barbaric enough to require civilization, Islamic enough to require Christianity, and yet potent and destructive enough to legitimize war: hence the invention of weapons of mass destruction. As ideological productions, these weapons of mass destruction need never be found, since the purpose of their production was already served: to reside in the imagination of the citizen patriot (indeed of the world) as the "thing" that had to be destroyed to bring about security, which only the national security state could provide: that is, the United States at the helm of the new world order. These weapons were publicly invented and fully integrated into the National Security Strategy first diffused on September 17, 2002. And even two years later, with the 9/11 commission's findings that such weapons never existed, the weapons continue to live their intent: to serve as a major piece of ideological weaponry in the arsenal of militarized intervention.[30]

In a fundamental sense, the National Security Strategy laid out the template on which the Patriot Acts, full-scale war, the defense of imperialism, and the defense of America would rest. At the outset, however, this far-reaching project of empire was not rendered by that name, but based instead in America's cosmic mandate to mind, in the wording of the text of the strategy itself, the "great struggles of the twentieth century between liberty and totalitarianism [that] ended with a decisive victory for the forces of freedom—and a single sustainable model for national success: freedom, democracy and free enterprise."[31] Further, "the duty of protecting these values against their enemies," the strategy reasoned, was "the common calling of freedom-loving people across the globe and across all ages."[32] These terms by themselves, do not necessarily carve out a special place for America, particularly, in light of a common calling which has such a vast and long genealogy. How does freedom move from being a common mandate to being a uniquely American mandate? And if it is a common mandate, how, or rather why, is it to be entrusted and managed by a singular entity—the United States of North America? The answers to these questions come through the positioning of what the president termed "a distinctly American internationalism" that emanated from its "unparalleled military strength and its great political and economic influence . . . its fundamental commitment to defend the nation against its enemies," and—here comes the twist—to seize this "moment of opportunity to extend the benefits of freedom, democracy, development of free markets and free trade. The special role of the United States is to build on common interests to promote global security." In a word, this unique American mandate is a capitalist mandate that has been thrust upon itself by itself and in the face of popular global opposition to the war and opposition of a majority of nation-states—which at the very least suggests that the interests were not common after all. The self-designated mandate to promote global security becomes all the more transparent in light of current disclosures of fabricated intelligence on the part of the state (which ironically play on the same oxymoronic impulse at work in the conflation of freedom, democracy, free market and free trade) and a series of imperial tactics through which the provision of "development" is administered. Thus the link between national security and empire building presumably becomes secure. According to the president, in the text of the strategy, "To defeat this threat, we must make use of every tool in our arsenal—military power, homeland defenses, law enforcement, intelligence, and vigorous efforts to cut off terrorist financing. The war against terrorists is of global reach, a global enter-prise of uncertain duration. America will help nations that need our assistance in combating terror. And America will hold to account nations that are compromised by terror, including those who harbor terrorists—because the allies of terror are the enemies of civilization." The bombing of Falluja two days after the reinstallation of militarized masculinity in the face of the presidential elections of 2004 is a further attempt to consolidate this globalized definition of terror.

To be an enemy of civilization—which in essence suggests a propensity for barbarism—with the power, as the strategy outlines, "to turn the power of modern technologies" against a country that "enjoys a position of unparalleled military strength and great eco-nomic and political influence," invites conquest and a mode of peren-nial retaliation that is contradictory enough to undermine the very tradition of freedom that is presumably a cosmic responsibility to uphold. Some traditions are, however, more worthy of being upheld than others: for instance, the tradition of capitalism upheld by mod-ern militarized masculinity, which is far superior to an outmoded bar-baric masculinity, a caricature of modernity, and heterosexual masculinity simultaneously—since its only power derives from the power of modern technologies itself. The paradox here is that both masculinities have been built upon military might and different forms of terror, but the struggle for empire can never be positioned as a struggle between equals (Petchesky 2001:15).

A Map Outside the Mandate for Conquest (Morrison 1993, 3)

The extent of violence that has been mobilized to produce the patriot and to secure the state-designated homeland makes of democracy a veritable farce. Indeed, this level of violence makes innocence impos-sible, for the mobilization of all of the cognates of empire means that shelter from violence in the form of a secure homeland can only be granted to very few, and its makeshift character inevitably makes it ephemeral. Empire building is neither an archaic process that is some-how "over there", nor is it constituted solely through the "modern." Colonial relations figure in this matrix, and this explains why social theorists such as Annette Jaimes Guerero and Cathy Cohen conceive of the U.S. state as an advanced capitalist colonial enterprise. Once we bring colonialism into neoimperialism's ambit, then we must also bring tradition into ideological proximity with modernity. Such a move would make of tradition and modernity profitable political currency, not fixed constructs divested of interest, committed to stasis on the one hand and to change on the other. Neocolonialism and those local masculinities on which the new imperialists rely choose selectively from modernity. Indeed anticolonial nationalism was predicated upon modernist claims about statehood and nation building, and while neocolonial formations function within a subordinated relationship to neoimperial states, it is these very imperial relations that compel them to assist in the production of subjectivities that favor fantasies of imperial allegiance above those of sovereignty.

Tradition circulates in the commerce of modernity's war traffic wearing the garb of heterosexuality. And it does so at the nexus of fundamentalism and militarization to uphold ostensibly natural teleologies of propagation and of market capitalism simultaneously, both of which require privatized heterosexuality and, increasingly, privatized homosexuality as well. Neoimperial state managers laud heterosexuality as the bedrock of the ancient civilization from which they sprung. Their investment in an originary claim to the "West" has enabled them to present themselves as the owners of modernity, the guardians of the heterosexual, the bearers of good tradition, and the guardians of democracy, despite some of the most egregious infractions in its name.

On this map, heterosexuality's imperatives are quite large and necessarily differentiated. Among them are the acquisition of land and property, the territorial appropriation of land that is sealed through the territorial marking of whiteness; the consolidation of regimes of citizenship around various statuses that range from heteromasculine soldiering to the nuclear unit of heterosexual family; underwriting the project of nation building in ways that paradoxically render the boundaries of the nation-state as fixed by designating loyal heterosexual patriotism along normative hierarchies of race, gender, and class in ways that guard the boundaries of the nation-state from sexual perversity; guarding the nation-state from certain classes of immigrants who ostensibly undo the nation's interests by relying on public assistance and whose movement across the borders of the nation must therefore be curtailed; and simultaneously rendering those same boundaries as highly permeable for a hypermobile capitalist/corporate managerial class that does not require the nation-state to consolidate a set of global interests, including global citizenship.

But neoimperial masculinity is an injured masculinity, an injury that emanates from a psychic memory of the Crusades (hence, George

W. Bush's early evocation of it at the outset of the war against Iraq), of being now outmaneuvered by a relation of the very savage whom Christian Spanish civilization was supposed to have annihilated centuries ago, but who reappears on a different continent, at a different historical moment, in a different guise (AP 2001; BBC 2001).[33] Its brand of hypernationalism enables the organization of massive violence that inheres in the simultaneous production of spectacularization. Both the violence of spectacularization and the violence of forced heterosexualization can be seen as operating hand in hand and indispensable, therefore, to how this masculinity conducts itself. Given what we have learned from the Combahee River Collective's analysis of the simultaneity of oppression, it would be difficult to establish a hierarchy of violence as a way to distinguish between democratic violence and savage violence, and it would be indeed difficult to sustain an argument in which the experience of democratic violence is somehow more desirable than that of savage violence.

Mapping the various ways in which patriotism and its concomitant practices are manufactured, we see how different populations are summoned to live on its behalf. The propensity apparatus, which the Military Working Group developed to discipline lesbian, gay, and bisexual soldiers (and which later took the form of the Don't Ask Don't Tell polices), derives from a long and varied pedigree: the ideological taxonomies that were affixed to various Native American and African ethnic groups during the process of enslavement, and the racialized and gendered U.S. Exclusion Acts that constructed Asians as a "yellow peril," ideologies that were intended to function as truth about character (Mohanty 1991, 25; Mauge 1996, 118–119). But these are not the only propensities at work, playing on that odd slippage between conduct and status. The judgment of a reasonable heterosexual unit commander can identify the propensity of the lesbian soldier; legalized citizen patriots, "Americans," the Attorney General, and the president can make judgments about immigrant propensity for terrorism; reasonable taxpaying, consuming citizens can make judgments about the propensity for laziness of recipients of public assistance. The point here is that propensities work to marginalize, that is, they exact different forms of terror and violence on the bodies of different groups of people. What this means as well, however, is that there is an opening to build strategic solidarities among these very marginalized constituencies once we refuse to mimic the practices of the state. Indeed, the question of just how *not* to do state work at a moment of empire is one of the most crucial questions we must confront in living a transformative politic.

The neoimperial state's cordoning off of the originary citizen from the immigrant in order to delineate the legal, loyal heterosexual patriot and secure the "homeland" has implications for radical political projects, including political organizing. Histories of xenophobia and the various state mechanisms that keep "immigrants out" find ready settler places at moments of crisis. Because of the collusion between the media and the state, and because the task of figuring out multivalenced political struggle is such a steep challenge—one can oppose the war yet continue to be an avid consumer whom the war defends—only an eagle-eyed vigilance can prevent state constructs from seeping into peace and justice movements. If the very terms upon which we organize are constituted through the ideology of the secure citizen—the very construct that the state deploys to position the loyal patriot—then we will continue to make invisible the widespread detention of immigrants and their criminalization, and mystify the ways in which these detention practices work to secure the mythic secure citizen. As Carole Boyce Davies has argued, citizenship is simply far too fragile (and, I would add, far too fraught and far too subject to state manipulation and co-optation for it to become the primary basis upon which radical political mobilization is carried out (2002).[34]

This analysis has not pivoted state power upon ongoing contestation, political mobilization and social movements from below, or class struggle, although one might posit the predominantly working-class character of the imperial fighting force as a strategy of ruling-class warfare. But we can argue that the different attempts to legalize and ultimately criminalize the patriot, the citizen, or the immigrant are installed as the direct result of a provocation of "failed" heterosexuality, whether in the form of same-sex marriage contextualized through LGBT political mobilization, feminist anti-imperialist movements read as lesbianism, or the heterosexual refusal of marriage. These provocations are profound. And the fact that oppositional movements instigate state judicial violence suggests that we should move away from theorizing resistance as reactive strategy to theorizing power as interwoven with, and living alongside, marginalization. It may not be a power that reverses state action—as these massive global antiwar mobilizations have demonstrated—but the very point of power and marginalization is evidenced in U.S. state attempts to position these global mobilizations as narrowly sectarian and self-interested. The threat of a rival global power that imagines a map outside of a mandate for conquest is quite profound. Conceiving of this power hinges on whether we think of moral agency and freedom as ontological categories with clear political expression, but not necessarily derived, in the first instance, from the political, that is, from the outside, as something that an outside entity more powerful than ourselves can confer.

If this analysis has prompted us to think about the ways in which privilege confers innocence, then it must also mean that we are similarly prompted to think that the practices of imperialism cannot be hidden in an analytic closet. If, from a privileged location in the United States of North America, some of us have been seduced into believing that imperialism was "then and there," this new round of empire consolidation and state restructuring must have brought a violent end to that seduction, for imperialism is simultaneously "then and there," and "here and now." Indeed, the here-and-nowness of it means that we must confront again questions that Winona La Duke, among others, posed about the importance of internal colonization and land struggles to the feminist project (La Duke 1992; Kay-Trask 2003; La Duke 2003): the claims that Puerto Rican feminists made more than three decades ago about U.S. imperial investments in the sterilization of Puerto Rican women; the arguments Hawaiian feminists have made about American imperialism via tourism; Pacific women's mobilization against U.S. military maneuvers that result in violence to the environment and to their bodies in the birth of jelly fetuses—"Why Haven't [we] Known?";[35] Kenyan women who have brought charges of rape against British militiamen stationed in their country (BBC 2005); the East Asia–U.S.–Puerto Rico Women's Network Against Militarism, whose contemporary mobilizations have yielded new insights about the meaning of human security that are based in "a sustainable environment, the fulfillment of people's basic needs, respect for people's fundamental human dignity and cultural identities and protection of people and the natural environment from avoidable harm" (2002):[36] the various ways in which imperialism traffics in the war at "home"; the fact that every decade after World War II has been marked by U.S. intervention in other countries (Roy 2002); and the long-standing Israeli occupation of Palestine, which is consistently being rewritten, even more so with the death of Yasser Arafat.[37] The continued absence of empire in the study of American culture is complicitous with cultures of imperialism (Kaplan 1994). Charlotte Bunch's (2004) observation that U.S. feminist mobilizations have provoked transformations in the social relations of gender at the national cultural level, but have been less successful in transforming state imperial policy, is a strong reminder of the task ahead, and it dovetails with Ella Shohat's assessment that opposition to racism, sexism and homophobia in the U.S. has never guaranteed opposition to U.S. global hegemony (Shohat 2001, 38; Enloe 2004). To ignore the centrality of imperialism is to continue to live a dangerous privilege that only the analytic habit of conflating capitalism and democracy can mistakenly confer.

At this moment of empire consolidation the academy continues to figure prominently in what Johnathan Feldman (1989) identified more than a decade ago as the state's web of militarism and intervention. The dominant iterations of our various disciplines continue a collusion with state practice that we can no longer ignore by virtue of our different institutional locations in women's studies, queer studies, or postcolonial studies, particularly in light of our dual, sometimes triple residence in these analytic homes. Sociology's implication in the punishment industry in ways that provide the rationale for "order maintenance policing" and the increased criminalization of daily life has almost wrenched it away from any plausible social justice claims. Normative political science has strong investments in a neutral, benign, disinterested state, even as the state continues to preside over a racial, gendered, heterosexual order, and continues to position this discipline as well as international relations schools as feeders for the managers of the militarized state. Normative economics remains wedded to explaining immigration according to push-pull factors, never paying attention to how assimilation functions as a form of violence, or how its own formulations prop up the nexus of capitalism's racialized and gendered inequities. Additionally, the deployment of the academy within the policing functions of the state has been actualized most visibly in the regulations of the USA Patriot Act of 2001, according to which international students and scholars and their dependents on F and J visas are required to be registered on SEVIS (Student-Exchange Visitor Information System), which is a web-based data collection and monitoring system designed to link institutions of higher education, the Bureau of Citizenship and Immigration Services (which replaces the INS, or Immigration and Naturalization Service), consulates and embassies abroad, ports of entry, and other U.S. state agencies. And terrorism studies has been enjoying a boom that is more compatible with the rise of cottage industries of a previous era (Puar 2002).

Not paradoxically, the academy has not escaped state surveillance. In the same way in which multicultural studies was positioned as a scapegoat for the frayed economy of the 1980s, postcolonial studies is now being aligned with terrorist efforts that "undermine American foreign policy."[38] How will queer studies, ethnic studies, and women's studies engage the recent state attacks that position postcolonial studies as the breeding ground for anti-Americanism, particularly since radical transnational feminism has also been brought into the state's orbit?[39] There is a great deal of urgency for us to map—that is, reimagine, practice, *and* live—some crucial analytic shifts that will prompt postcolonial studies to engage more strategically with the "here and now," to position immigration, for instance, as an important site for the local reconfiguration of subalternity and the local reconfiguration of race, and to develop a less fraught relationship with a radically formulated ethnic studies by practicing what Donaldson, Donadey, and Silliman call "subversive couplings."[40] As certain strands of queer studies move to take up more central questions of political economy and racial formation, and of transnational feminism and immigrant labor, the analytic vise in the discipline will be sharpened between those who hold on to a representational democratic impulse within U.S. borders and those who wish to engage the former questions. Addressing them can challenge a similar nationalist representational intellectual impulse insinuated within women's studies that renders the transnational and related critical approaches as consumptive or as an epistemic option.

What does a path outside our various disciplinary segregation mean, bearing in mind that part of what is at stake in a radical project is the rewriting and living of a history that is fundamentally at odds with the intentions of the national security state, and a refusal of the prescriptions of the permanent war economy that requires permanent enemies (both epistemic and political) as fuel and a patriot who must forfeit consent with silence? If there were ever a moment that we needed a radical interdisciplinarity, it is now, but we need a kind of interdisciplinarity that fashions simultaneous articulations with radical political movements in ways that bring the necessary complexity to the multiple narratives about how history is made. We cannot escape the fierce contradictions that are posed for queer soldiering, people-of-color soldiering, and working-class soldiering on behalf of empire.

As we recognize that the nation state matters more to some than others, we also need to recognize that the borders of the nation state cannot be positioned as hermetically sealed or epistemically partial. Our knowledge-making projects must therefore move across state-constructed borders to develop frameworks that are simultaneously intersubjective, comparative, relational, yet historically specific and grounded, frameworks that demystify the fictitious boundaries of academy and community. And because fragmentation is both material and metaphysical, both epistemic and ontological, these frameworks would need to be attentive to the underbelly of superiority and the psychic economies of its entrails as part of an explicitly political project. The fiction in the "West" of eliminating threat as a way to eliminate opposition has left a sort of residual psychic memory, the belief that physical removal ensures that what has been expunged will never reappear. And it leaves this memory precisely because it confuses the metaphysic with the material, believing that material removal is, simultaneously, a metaphysical removal. Fortunately no material violence, no matter its scope, can tamper with cosmic imprint. Ultimately we have to confront the matrix of grief and the yearning for belonging that have issued from the morbid seams of late capitalism across multiple geographies in ways that are not partial to 9/11. If we are to "pluck courage," as Toni Morrison exhorts, from the multiple disasters that produced 9/11 and those that continue in its wake; if we are to be "steady and clear"; if we are to avoid deception, including self-deception; if we are to act outside of the strictures of classroom, institution, discipline, and nation, then our gestures of reconciliation to the living must of necessity be perennial, engaged, nonpartial, and ultimately humble, since what is at stake is not the patriot or the homeland but the climate of our collective Soul.

Notes

1. This essay takes its title from my earlier article, "Not Just (Any)Body Can Be a Citizen: The Politics of Law, Sexuality and Postcoloniality in Trinidad and Tobago and the Bahamas," *Feminist Review,* no. 48 (Autumn 1994). An earlier version of this essay appears in *Pedagogies of Crossing, Meditations on Feminism, Sexual Politics, Memory and the Sacred* (Durham, NC: Duke University Press, 2005). I wish to thank Michelle Zamora, Evelyn Asultany, Cherríe Moraga, and graduate students at Stanford University for the public forum they organized in April 2004 where these ideas were first tested; the Gender, Race, and Militarization project at the University of Oregon organized by Sandi Morgen; and participants in the Women's Studies seminar organized by Gina Dent and Angela Davis at UC Santa Cruz in July 2005. I am especially thankful to Anjali Arondekar, Catherine Ramirez, and Nefereti Xina Tadiar for their insightful interventions that prompted me to rethink some of my earlier formulations. I am also grateful to Payal Banerjee, whose formulation of ideological traffic was indispensable to me in bringing

seemingly unconnected discourses into proximity. Plenty of thanks to Tamara Irons, my assistant, for scouring the websites and compiling the final notes; and to Robin L. Riley and Naeem for conceiving of this volume and for their commitment to working dialogically.

2. See Payal Banerjee "Integrated Circuits," Ph.D dissertation, Syracruse University, 2006.
3. See Zillah Eisenstein (2005, 1–21) for a discussion of how oppressive moments get reconstituted as democratic.
4. Tadiar is making this argument for the Philippines and other U.S. colonial possessions, but her project deftly examines how fantasy and dreams figure in the sexual economies and political economic strategies of nationalist and multinational capitalist regimes, particularly those of the Philippines and the Pacific.
5. See Jasbir Puar and Amit Rai (2002) for an insightful discussion of this trend in "Monster, Terrorist, Fag."
6. An altogether different war story is told by Lynch herself. See Bragg, *I am a Soldier Too: The Jessica Lynch Story* See also "Debunking Early Rescue Myths
7. Richard Delgado has examined the ways in which recent legislation evokes the premises of the Dred Scott decision of 1856, which held that black people could not be citizens since they were not "here" from the beginning. See Delgado, "Citizenship," in Perea, *Immigrants Out,* 318–323.
8. The coupling of the Immigration and Naturalization Service with the Department of Homeland Security in the new Bureau of Citizenship and Immigration Services in the post-9/11 period is not, then, an incidental gesture.
9. These following attributions derive from the two USA Patriot Acts.
10. The ongoing bombing of abortion clinics and the state refusal to intervene against this level of systematized misogynist violence has been carefully analyzed in this collection. See Baird-Windle and Bader, *Targets of Hatred.*
11. The ACLU discussion of how Operation Rescue and mobilizations against the militarization of Vieques might well be put together under the heading "domestic terrorists" under abrogations of free speech. But this is not the category I am invoking here, even though it is important to recognize that constitutional rights are being fundamentally jeopardized and the category of citizen is being consistently constrained. See "Interested Person's Memo: Section by Section analysis of Justice Department draft 'Domestic Security Enhancement Act of 2003,'" also known as "Patriot Act II." February 14, 2003. *American Civil Liberties Union.* August 14, 2005. www.aclu.org/SafeandFree/SafeandFree.cfm?ID=11835&c=206
12. The Bill of Rights Defense Committee has conducted a very thorough analysis of the Patriot Act I, the ways in which it changes existing legislation, and the various ways in which it can be misused. See http://www.gjf.org/NBORDC
13. "CFP Homeland Security: Sovereignty, Law, & Figures of Speech—Call for Papers." January 1, 2003. University of North Carolina, Chapel Hill. August 14, 2005. http://cfp.english.upenn.edu/archive/2003-01/0172.html.

14. Thanks to Anjali Arondekar for making these points that urged me to move beyond a whisper of the homeland to these more explicit considerations.
15. See Perea, *Immigrants Out!* for discussion
16. Also see Senator Dan Inouye's bill S68, the Filipino Veterans Benefits Improvement Act.
17. The idea of immigrant risk still exists, however, as certain practical career benefits are not extended to noncitizen service members. Noncitizen members are barred from reenlisting in the Air force after their first four-year term; because commanding officers must be citizens, the noncitizen member may also be held back from promotion; additionally, security clearances required for some are not granted to noncitizens. See "Hardest Way to Become an American." 2005. *Military.com.* June 30, 2005
18. Ibid.
19. Ibid.
20. See "'Non Citizens Told: Enlist for Iraq and Earn Your Green Card' (Catch? Posthumously)."2005.
21. Ibid. 3
22. Ramirez (2002). Ramirez focuses on the Zoot Suit Riots of World War II Los Angeles to analyze the links among patriotism, class, and ethnicity and the slippage between the criminalization of fashion and the criminalization of working-class Mexican-American men—the pachuco. Her main focus, however, is on the pachuca and the complicated ways in which she embodied wartime fears of juvenile delinquency and dangerous sexuality while challenging these very constructs; also see Takaki (2002).
23. See section 9528 of the No Child Left Behind Act, 2002; I also want to thank Catherine Ramirez for suggesting these linkages.
24. See the classic, Alloula, *The Colonial Harem.*
25. See Puar and Rai (2002), especially section, "Heteronormativity and Patriotism."
26. See Hersh (2004). A similar move has been made to make Abu Ghraib the work of a few rotten apples. A distinction needs to be made here between the ideological longevity of the representational impulses at work in the demonization of Simpson and the perpetration of domestic violence or murder. I am not arguing that Simpson did not engage in domestic violence.
27. The entire issue of *Spare Change,* the newspaper of the Homeless Empowerment Project, was devoted to domestic violence, just a month after 9/11. See "Domestic Violence and the World Trade Center," *Spare Change,* Special Issue (October 18–31, 2001).
28. Bernard Harcourt (1998) has done a most compelling and extensive analysis of these technologies and their deployment in different parts of the country, underscoring the specious scientific evidence supporting them. There are of course implications for the organization of this symbolic archive that are manifested in the concrete committing of hate crimes. For the translation from symbol to hate, see Jakobsen (1999). I am also drawing indirectly from my own research on the contradictory ways in which immigrant identities are mobilized, not in the interest of assimilation, as melting-pot theories purport,

but in the interest of violence. The empirical focus is the 1997 police torture of Abner Louima, whose bloodied body bore the mark of the reciprocal antagonisms between the war on crime and a global economy that relies upon the very immigrants who have been criminalized. Louima's status as naturalized citizen had no bearing in media representations of him or some of the violent anti-immigrant and homophobic sentiment that was unleashed. A recent report by the Justice Policy Institute has revealed that during the 1980s and 1990s, state spending on prisons grew at six times the rate of spending on higher education, and that by the close of the millennium, there were nearly a third more African American men in prison and jail than in universities and colleges. Justice Policy Institute, New Report (2003).

29. Bernard Kerik's tenure as commissioner of the New York City Police Department coincides with the police torture of Aber Louima and a marked increase in civilian complaints filed against police brutality. In speaking about the "war at home," I am not utilizing the normative stance in the *New York Times* that understands the war at home as the difficulties the state confronts in marketing its economic agenda. A radical mobilization about the war at home is quite widespread. In addition to those movements already cited within *ColorLines,* in particular the special section "A New Era: Race after 9/11, 'The War at Home,'" *ColorLines,* Spring 2002, there are the following: "From 9.11 to World War 3," *The Independent,* no. 21, September 2002 (entire issue); "Bush's Permanent War," *News and Letters,* March 2002, Editorial; "War Times: The First Casualty of War is Truth," September 2002, no. 5 (entire issue); *People's Weekly World,* Saturday, August 31, 2002, vol. 17, 4o 14; "Our Grief is not a Cry for War," http://www.notinourname.net; "Against War, Colonial Occupation and Imperialism," A.N.S.W.E.R.-Act Now to Stop War and End Racism—Coalition, May 3–4, 2002.

30. National Commission on Terrorist Attacks. 2004. *The 9/11 Commission Report.*

31. The National Security Strategy of the United States of North America, http://www.whitehouse.gov/nsc/nss.html, 1. September 2005

32. All subsequent quotes are taken verbatim from the National Security Strategy.

33. Approximately four days after the attacks on the center of U.S. financial capital, the president stated, "We will rid the world of evil doers . . . This crusade, this war on terrorism is going to take a while." The state alignment of this war with the Crusades was stridently critiqued, resulting in the retraction of the statement. Our interest, however, lies in its psychic production, its nostalgic anxiety for an earlier historical moment and psychic residues it deposits.

34. See also Nobles, *Shades of Citizenship;* Torpey, *The Invention of the Passport.*

35. Women Working for a Nuclear Free and Independent Pacific, *Pacific Women Speak.*

36. This network, started in 1997, links violence against women, children, and communities to U.S. economic and military dominance around the world.

37. See the *New York Times/Week In Review* following the 2004 presidential elections. November 7. 2004

38. The context here is a series of hearings in the U.S. House of Representatives, Committee on Education and the Workforce pertaining to Title VI funding for "International Programs in Higher Education and Questions about Bias." The

bias in question is postcolonial studies and "its efforts to potentially undermine American foreign policy." The companion legislation that has been introduced to curtail Title VI funding is HR 3077. *Committee on Education and Workforce*, December 3, 2003. http://edworkforce.house.gov/hearings/108th/sed/titlevi61903/wl61903.htm, accessed on August 14, 2005. These hearings can be considered part of what Kaplan and Grewal (2002:66–81) call "the backlash narrative."

39. The consequences of this "backlash narrative" can be grave, particularly when immigrants are singled out for their "anti-American" politics. A statement by Stanley Kurtz, research fellow at the Hoover Institution, on June 19, 2003, is cited on NYU's Kevorkian Center website. According to Kurtz, "Everyone that takes a stand sharply criticizes American policy. Ella Shohat criticizes America's 'crimes' of 'oil driven hegemony' and America's murderous sanctions on Iraq."

40. Dirlik, *The Postcolonial Aura*. Postcolonial studies most often imagines the subaltern as residing elsewhere, rarely in conversation with local subalterns or with political movements that provoked decolonization. See also, Wing (1999); Grewal (1994); DuCille (1995); and Donaldson, Donadey, and Silliman (2002).

Bibliography

Adams, David. 2005. Internal military interventions in the United States. *Journal of Peace Research* 32, no. 2 (1995): 197–211.

Allen, James, Hilton Als, Congressman John Lewis, and Leon F. Litwack, eds. 2000. *Without sanctuary.* Hong Kong: Twin Palms Press.

American Civil Liberties Union. 2002. How the USA patriot act redefines "domestic terrorism." December 6. www.aclu.org/Nationalsecurity/NationalSecurity.cfm?ID=11437&c=111 (accessed on August 14, 2005).

AP 2001. Bush pledges crusade against "evil doers." Recordonline.com. September 17 www.recordonline.com/archive/2001/09/17/rdp16.html

Baird-Windle, Patricia and Eleanor J. Bader. 2001 Targets of hatred: anti-abortion terrorism. New York: Palgrave Macmillan.

Banerjee, Payal. 2006. Integrated circuits. Ph.D dissertation, Syracuse University.

BBC News. 2001. America widens crusade on terror. September 16. http://news.bbc.co.uk/1/hi/world/americas/1547561.stm.

BBC Online. 2005. Kenyan women take rape case to the UN. March 30.

Bragg, Rick. 2003. *I am a soldier too: the Jessica Lynch story.* New York: Knopf.

Bunch, Charlotte. 2004. Talking and doing citizenship. Graduate Forum, Center for the Critical Analysis of Contemporary Culture, Rutgers University. April 2.

Davidson, Osha Gray. 2005. A wrong turn in the desert. *The Native Press.com.* May 27. Educate Yourself. 2005. Non citizens told: "Enlist for Iraq and earn your green card" (Catch? Posthumously). *Educate Yourself, The Freedom of Knowledge, The Expression of Thought.* http://educate-yourself.org/cn/posthumouscitizenshipfasttrack13mar05.shtml

Davies, Carole Boyce. 2002. "Half the world:" the transnational black socialist feminist practice of Claudia Jones. Paper delivered at African American

Studies: Transnationalism, Gender and the Changing Black World, Syracuse University, April.

Davis, Angela. 2003. Masked racism: reflections on the prison industrial complex. In *Sing, whisper, shout, pray: feminist visions for a just world*, edited by Alexander, M. Jacqui, Lisa Albrecht, Sharon day, and Mab Segrest Berkeley: Edgework Press.

Donaldson, Laura, Anne Donadey, and Jael Silliman. 2002. "Subversive Couplings." In *Women's studies on its own: a next wave reader in institutional change*. Wiegman, Robin, ed. Duke University Press. 438–456.

DuCille. 1995. Postcolonialism and Afrocentricity: discourse and dat course." In *Black Columbiad: defining moments in African American literature and culture*, edited by Werner Sollors and Maria Diedrich. Cambridge: Harvard University Press.

East Asia-US-Puerto Rico Women's Network Against Militarism. 2002. Final Statement, Seoul, Korea, August 15–19.

Eisenstein, Zillah. 2004 *Against empire: feminism, racism and "the west."* Zed Books, London

Enloe, Cynthia. 1993. *The morning after: sexual politics at the end of the cold war.* Berkeley: University of California Press.

———. 2004. Plenary Address, National Women's Studies Association Meetings. Milwaukee, Wisconsin.

Feldman, Jonathan. 1989. *Universities in the business of repression: the academic-military-industrial complex in Central America.* Boston: South End Press.

Grewal, Inderpal. 1994. The postcolonial, ethnic studies, and the diaspora. *Socialist Review* 24 (4): 45–74.

Hersh, Seymour M. 2004. Torture at Abu Ghraib: American soldiers brutalized Iraqis. How far up does the responsibility go?" *New Yorker,* April 30.

Harcourt, Bernard. 1998. Reflecting on the subject. *Michigan Law Review* 97 (November): 291.

Indianz.com. 2003. Homeland security push leaves tribes behind. May 12. Noble Savage Media, LLC and Ho Chunk, Inc. Accessed on August 11, 2005. http://www.indianz.com/News/show.asp?ID=2003/05/12/homeland

Jakobsen, Janet R. 1999. Tolerating hate? Or hating intolerance? *Sojourner: The Women's Forum* (August): 9–11

Justice Policy Institute, New Report (2003). *State spending on prisons grows at 6 times the rate of higher education; more African American men incarcerated than enrolled in college; African American imprisonment worsened during the "good times."* Washington, D.C.

Kaplan, Amy, and Donald Pease, eds. 1994. *Cultures of United States imperialism.* Durham, NC: Duke University Press.

Kay-Trask, Haunani, 2003. Self determination for Pacific Island women: the case of Hawai'i. In *Sing, whisper, shout, pray! feminist visions for a just world*, edited by Alexander et al. Fort Bragg, CA: Edgework Press.

Kenway Jane. 2005. Backlash in cyberspace and why girls need a modem." *Deakin Centre for Education and Change, Deakin University, Geelong, Australia.* August 14. http://www.ed.psu.edu/englishpds/Articles/Technology/-Backlash%20In%20Cyberspace.htm.

LaDuke, Winona. 2003. The case against the war. *Indian Country Today.* www.indiancountry.com/content.cfm?id=1049471134. Posted April 4.

———. 2003. Nitassinan: the hunter and the peasant. In *Sing, whisper, shout, pray! feminist visions of a just world,* edited by Alexander et al. Fort Bragg: CA: Edgework Press.

La Duke, Winona, and Ward Churchill. 1992. Native North America: the political economy of radioactive colonialism. In *The state of native America: genocide, colonization and resistance,* edited by M. Annette Jaimes. Boston: South End Press.

Lamming, George. 1960. *The pleasures of exile.* London: M. Joseph, 158

Maugé, Conrad E. 1996. *The lost orisha.* Mount Vernon, NY: House of Providence.

Military.com. 2005. Hardest way to become an American. June 30. http://www.military.com/NewsContent/0,13319,FL_american_063005,00.html?ESRC=army-a.nl

McAllister, Melani. 2001. *Epic encounters: culture, media and U.S. interests in the Middle East: 1945-2000.* Berkeley and Los Angeles: University of California Press.

Mohanty, Chandra Talpade. 2004. Affirmative action in the service of empire. Paper delivered at the Modern Language Association.

———. 1991. Third world women and the politics of feminism. Bloomington: Indiana University Press.

Morrison, Toni. 1993. *Playing in the dark: whiteness and the literary imagination.* Vintage, New York 3

———. 2005. To the dead of September 11 (2001). The Literacy Project. August 14. http://www.legacy-project.org/lit/display.html?ID=83

MSNBC News. Hardball with Chris Matthews. 2003. Interview with Bernard Kerik http://www.msnbc.com/news/976580.asp. Friday, October 3.

New York Times. 2003. Justices, 6-3, legalize gay sexual conduct in sweeping reversal of Court's '86 ruling. Friday, June 27, 1, A19.

Orth, Maureen. 2002. Fort Braggs deadly summer. *Vanity Fair,* no. 508 (December): 222–240.

Perea, Juan. 1997. *Immigrants out!: the new nativism and the anti-immigrant impulse in the United States.* New York: New York University Press.

Petchesky, Rosalind 2001. Phantom towers: Feminist perspective on capitalism and fundamentalism. In *Women's Review of Books* 19 (2) 15–29.

Puar, Jasbir K and Amit S. Rai. 2002. Monster, terrorist, fag: the war on terrorism and the production of docile patriots. *Social Text* 20, no.3 (Fall). Duke University Press.

Ramírez, Catherine S. 2002. Crimes of fashion: the Pachuca and Chicana style politics. *Meridians* 2: 1–35.

Riley, Robin L. 2002. 'OsamaYo Mama': The de-masculinization of an enemy. Presented at International Studies Association Meetings. New Orleans, March

Roy, Arundhati. 2002. *Power politics.* Boston: South End Press.

Shohat, Ella. 2001. Introduction. In *Talking visions multicultural feminism in a transnational age.* Boston: MIT Press, 38.

Silliman, Jael, and Annannya Bhattacharjee. 2002. *Policing the national body: race, gender and criminalization in the United States.* Boston: South End Press.

Skrentny, John, and Paul Frymer. 2004. The rise of instrumental affirmative action law and the new significance of race in America. *Connecticut Law Review* 36: 677–723

Tadiar, Nefereti Xina M. 2004. *Fantasy production: sexual economies and other Philippine consequences of the new world order.* Manila: Ateneo de Manila University Press, 27.

Takaki, Ronald, 2002. *Double victory: a multicultural history of America in World War II.* Boston: Little, Brown and Co.

University of North Carolina, Chapel Hill. 2003. CFP homeland security: sovereignty, law, & figures of speech—call for papers. January 1. http://cfp.english.upenn.edu/archive/2003-01/0172.html. August 14, 2005.

Warner, Michael. 1993. *Fear of a queer planet: queer politics and social theory.* University of Minnesota Press.Minneapolis

Weber, Diane Cecilia. 1999. Warrior cops: the ominous growth of paramilitarism in American police departments. *CATO Briefing Papers.* August 26. 1.

Wing, Bob. 1999. Educate to liberate. *ColorLines* 2, no. 2 (Summer).

White, Josh. 2005. Steady drop in black army recruits: data said to reflect views on Iraq war. *Washington Post,* March 10. http://www.washingtonpost.com/wp-dyn/articles/A18461-2005Mar8.html

Afterword: Newly Seeing

Zillah Eisenstein

The unilateral imperial arrogance of the United States in making war in Afghanistan and Iraq is differently new. In his 2004 inaugural address, Bush did not even mention the Iraq war and instead focused all eyes on what he terms the "struggle for freedom and liberty," at home and abroad. "The survival of liberty in our land increasingly depends on the success of liberty in other lands." His democratic message silently codes politics as war. By October 6, 2005, he is more defensive and aggressive. "We will not rest until the war on terror is won." He says that the choices are simple: freedom's triumph or Islamic radicalism and its militant Jihadism/Islamo-fascism. He speaks of the murderous ideology of Islamic radicals and compares it to communism, also an ideology with "cold-blooded contempt for human life."

The politics of homeland security—creating a camp for detainees in Guantanamo, Cuba, using extreme interrogation and "rendition" to facilitate C.I.A. torture of detainees in other countries—is an old story and also newly different. As such, imperialism—the process of occupying and disciplining the mind and body, as well as the nation—is also newly old. And catastrophic moments such as September 11, 2001, and Hurricane Katrina, rather than changing everything, uncover a mirror on ourselves that reveals a sustained historical politics of abandonment, exploitation, and occupation.

How does one attempt to live in a world when the ground beneath us shifts? The shifting implicates those of us who live inside the United States in new-old fashion. As the site we occupy becomes more singular, defensive, and aggressive, we have less information, less freedom, and less ability to see beyond ourselves. This imperial condition is both old—embedded in history—and new—openly defended by the imperial policing nation.

The flows of dialogues that have enriched the United States are more silenced than ever. More is appropriated by the United States; more is distorted; more is made suspect. As a nation we have become less equal, less kind, less intelligent. There is a new need to know more, see more, travel more, to make sure that "we"—progressives committed to racial, sexual, gender, and class equality and social justice—continue to believe in the possibility of resistance and democratic struggle.

I have read here that the billions appropriated for addressing AIDS in Africa is more about enforcing compliance with U.S. military operations and supporting the moral absolutism of the U.S. religious right around the world, than it is about dealing with the health crisis. That Bush says he cares about Africa and then travels to five different countries in five days bringing along his own furniture and food. That the United States depicts Islamic countries, especially Pakistan, as extremist misogynists while the United States practices misogyny and has fewer women in its own Congress. That Afghan and Iraqi women have long histories of activism that have been silenced by U.S. missionary rhetoric, which demonizes the Taliban and Saddam Hussein without recognizing the deployment of new forms of U.S. patriarchal colonialism in the wars waged by the United States. The United States claims the language of women's rights as its own while disregarding the role of Vietnamese women in naming the 1970s U.S. women's liberation movement. That people visit museums with little regard for the plunder of artifacts that they represent; that we visit them as a form of ignorant seeing, as a way of not knowing, or of controlled memory. The multiple origins of any location or site reflect the deep and conflicted histories of imperial wars and conquest. But the power-filled routes of these histories are silenced and buried.

People in the United States hear of apartheid and think of South Africa. Yet, schools in the United States are as segregated today as slavery historically segregated black from white. Our prisons are filled with similar numbers of black men as when U.S. blacks were enslaved. Women of all colors in the United States suffer the sexual hierarchies of racial and class privilege in extreme fashion. Too many are too poor, too burdened, too lonely, too tired.

Imperial minds are closed and oppositional. They are not searching for new ways of knowing, new ways of living, or new ways of imagining the impossible. The authors here ask us to keep thinking and opening ourselves to the unknown, to recommit to being uncomfortable and tense with our ignorance. We must stand against empire and for the flows of dialogues and the resistances that emerge in this process. Fear must be rejected as reactionary. We must interrogate ourselves and one another to dislocate the limits of our knowing. And we must find the new sexes, genders, races, classes, and cultures that define the new possibilities for recognizing an ever-changing humanity.

At this point of our newly imperializing and imperial nation there is little choice. The United States is moving toward a police state. Some would say that policing has always been present in our history, that it is a part of our origin and our acquisitions as a nation; and that it lives on today, in our ghettos, in our prisons, in our schools, and in our wars. But now the wars are also inside the United States, so that more people are suspect and suspected than ever before.

Move against, and through, and with, to new beginnings, before we cannot. There is still time and possibility but it is not clear that this will remain as fascistic democracy takes firmer hold.

Contributors

M. Jacqui Alexander is Professor of Women's Studies and Gender Studies at the University of Toronto. She is the author of *Pedagogies of Crossing: Meditations of Feminism, Sexual Politics, Memory and the Sacred* (Duke University Press 2006) and coeditor of *Sing, Whisper, Shout, Pray! Feminist Visions for a Just World* (Edgework 2001) and *Feminist Genealogies, Colonial Legacies, Democratic Futures* (Routledge 1997).

Elisabeth Armstrong is Assistant Professor of Women's Studies at Smith College. She is the author of *The Retreat from Organization: US Feminism Reconceptualized* (SUNY Press, 2002). She is at work on a book about the All-India Democratic Women's Association (AIDWA), an eight-million-member organization.

Shampa Biswas is Associate Professor of Politics at Whitman College. Her research interests include issues of nationalism, globalization, global development, postcolonial theory, and South Asian politics. She has published articles on religious nationalisms, South Asian nuclearization, race in international relations, and the nation-state in the context of globalization.

Hannah Britton is Assistant Professor of Women's Studies and Political Science at the University of Kansas. She is the author of *Women in the South African Parliament: From Resistance to Governance* (University of Illinois Press, 2005). She recently completed a coedited collection with Dr. Gretchen Bauer, *Women in African Parliaments* (Lynne Rienner, 2006).

Monisha Das Gupta teaches in Women's Studies and Ethnic Studies at the University of Hawaii at Manoa. She has been involved with South Asian feminist and labor organizations in Boston and New York. In Hawaii, she works within the local antimilitarization movement. She is the author of *Unruly Immigrants: Rights, Activism, and Transnational South Asian Politics in the United States* (Duke University Press, 2006).

Cynthia Enloe is Research Professor of International Development and Women's Studies at Clark University. Among her most recent books are *The Curious Feminist: Searching for Women in a New Age of Empire,* (University of California Press, 2004), *Maneuvers: The International Politics of Militarizing Women's Lives* (University of California Press, 2000), and *Bananas, Beaches and Bases* (University of California Press, new edition, 2000).

Zillah Eisenstein teaches in the Department of Politics at Ithaca College. Her most recent books track the intersections of polyversal feminisms, neoliberal globalization, racialized patriarchy, war-rape, AIDS, and so on. A few of her most recent books are: *Against Empire, Feminisms, Racism and the West* (2004), which has been simultaneously published in England (Zed Press), India (Kali Press), Australia and New Zealand (Spinifex Press); *ManMade Breast Cancers* (Cornell University Press, 2001); *Global Obscenities* (NYU Press, 1998); and *Hatreds, Racialized and Sexual Conflicts in the 21st Century,* (Routledge, 1996).

Naeem Inayatuallah is Associate Professor of Politics at Ithaca College. He is author with David Blaney of *International Relations and the Problem of Difference* (Routledge, 2004). He is working on a book titled *Savage Economy: Capitalism, Poverty and International Political Economy.*

Ayesha Khan is Senior Researcher with the Collective for Social Science Research in Karachi, Pakistan (www.researchcollective.org). Her work has covered a range of issues, including conflict and security, Afghan refugees, health, and policy analysis. She has studied at Yale University and the School of Oriental and African Studies at the University of London.

Himadeep Muppidi is Assistant Professor, Department of Political Science, Vassar College. He is the author of *The Politics of the Global* (University of Minnesota Press, 2004).

Vijay Prashad is Professor of International Studies at Trinity College. His latest book is *Darker Nations: The Rise and Fall of the Third World* (The New Press and Leftword Books, 2006).

Robin L. Riley is Assistant Professor of Women's Studies at Syracuse University. She has published articles about gender and defense workers, gender and antiwar protest, and is working on a new project about how U.S. college students form their ideas about the war in Iraq.

Index

(Please note that page numbers in *Italics* indicate an end note.)